HEZBOLLAH

HEZBOLLAH

A HISTORY OF THE "PARTY OF GOD"

Dominique Avon and Anaïs-Trissa Khatchadourian

Translated by Jane Marie Todd

HARVARD UNIVERSITY PRESS
Cambridge, Massachusetts & London, England
2012

Library of Congress Cataloging-in-Publication Data

Avon, Dominique.
  [Hezbollah. English]
  Hezbollah : a history of the "party of god" / Dominique Avon and Anaïs-Trissa Khatchadourian ; translated by Jane Marie Todd.
    p. cm.
  Includes bibliographical references and index.
  ISBN 978-0-674-06651-9 (alk. paper)
  1. Hizballah (Lebanon)—History. 2. Shiites—Lebanon—Politics and government. 3. Islam and politics—Lebanon. 4. Geopolitics—Middle East. 5. Lebanon—Politics and government—1975–1990. 6. Lebanon—Politics and government—1990– I. Khatchadourian, Anaïs-Trissa. II. Todd, Jane Marie, 1957– III. Title.
  JQ1828.A98H6219513 2012
  324.25692'084—dc23   2012007747

To Magali

To Ali

CONTENTS

FIGURES AND TABLES

ILLUSTRATIONS

TABLE

ACKNOWLEDGMENTS

This book would not have come into being without the help of many in France, Lebanon, and Iran. For various reasons, they cannot all be named. We wish, however, to express our profound gratitude to Nahed, Sayde, Mona, Sabine, Amin, Catherine, Georges, Jean-François, Abdellatif, Jean-Jacques, Adnan, Antoine and Paulette, Ivan, Bachir and Houda, Nabil, and the members of A's family.

INTRODUCTION

Our working conditions in writing this book—nations at war, keen international tensions, and two opposing Lebanese spheres of influence—have not been the most serene, and we have little control over the context within which it will be received. Then there is an even more difficult matter. The Hezbollah is a politico-religious entity whose frame of reference will be somewhat foreign to those unfamiliar with Arabic and Persian culture, which is profoundly Islamic. Readers are therefore invited to grapple with that reality. They would do well to heed the French intellectual Michel Foucault. Responding to those who interpreted every revolutionary movement in terms of the French Revolution of 1789 or the Russian Revolution of 1917, and who were baffled by what was happening in Tehran in 1979, he wrote, "I felt at the time that the recent events did not mean that the most backward groups were stepping away from an overly brutal modernization, but rather that an entire culture and an entire people were rejecting a form of modernization that was in itself archaic."[1] And although Foucault elsewhere denounced "the bloody government of a fundamentalist

1. Michel Foucault, "Lo scià ha cento anni di ritardo," *Corriere della Sera* 103, no. 230 (October 1978): 1.

clergy,"[2] his remark, combined with other reflections, marked a profound shift. Orientalism had received a slap in the face from Edward Said. The substance of Said's book—useful but vulnerable to criticism—has often been reduced to an axiom: contemporary knowledge is not neutral, it is "Western," an instrument of cultural domination that perpetuates the exploitation of "Orientals," who have already been subjected to military, political, and economic domination. Yet historians intent on placing their views within a particular space and time, on not indulging in essentialism, have found it difficult to come to terms with the dual ideological component of the Hezbollah—Shiism and Third Worldism—arising from the Khomeinist revolution and the extreme violence of the Lebanon War.

Some authors are still intimidated by the heirs of Frantz Fanon and by those of Ali Sharīʿatī, one of the complex inspirations for the Iranian revolution. They hesitate to take on issues whose underpinnings are sometimes viewed as alien to their readers' concerns and conduct. That situation gives free rein to diatribes on the one hand, pleas for the defense on the other. Fortunately, some remarkable studies, often governed by sociology and political science, have avoided falling victim to the antinomy between culturalism and universalism. The epistemological position defended in this book rests on a dual postulate, which marks the limit to the claim of neutrality that we posit from the outset: time has a value, and the "religious object"—we will seek to grant it its proper place—can, like any other object, be considered within time. Our discipline recognizes no authority but science. We want to be free to write that French and U.S. diplomats have adopted proconsular behaviors by, for example, exerting pressure for the appointment of one Lebanese minister or another or even for a president of Lebanon; that, for the most part, successive Israeli governments have based their regional policy on the axiom "a state of war without war"; and that pressure

2. Michel Foucault, "Inutile de se soulever?" *Le Monde,* May 11–12, 1979.

groups exist at ministries of foreign affairs. Similarly, we want to be free to write that the cause of the Palestinian refugees has been and still is being instrumentalized, particularly by opinion makers in the Arab and Muslim world, and that some Shiites have never believed that "God's government on earth" was established in Tehran in 1979. As researchers, we refuse to be recruited by one camp against another. We acknowledge, however, that the conditions for producing our study are favorable in one part of the world and not in another. We assume responsibility for the resulting distortions.

The subject is no easier to grasp than it ever was. The "cancer" imagery that the Hezbollah and Iran use to refer to Israel has been turned against them. Furthermore, since 1997 the "Party of God" has been on the U.S. Department of State's list of foreign terrorist organizations. From Washington's standpoint, it has a strong case: the attack on the U.S. embassy in Beirut (1983) and on the Marines barracks of the Multinational Force; the taking of hostages, from the president of the American University of Beirut to journalists and the CIA bureau chief (1982–1991); the hijacking of TWA Flight 847 between Athens and Rome (1985); the assassination of a U.S. officer belonging to the United Nations Interim Force in Lebanon (UNIFIL) by a group linked to the Hezbollah (1988); and attacks on the property and persons of Jewish citizens in Argentina (1992 and 1994). Israel also applies the epithet "terrorist" to the Hezbollah to justify its own policy, noting that, since the early 1990s, this enemy has supported various Palestinian groups, particularly Hamas. The term became central after the attacks of September 11, 2001. Under pressure from the American Israel Public Affairs Committee, the United States included the Hezbollah within the group of enemies in the "War on Terror." The Hezbollah has in turn accused the United States of being the "sponsor of international terrorism," "responsible for the deaths of the largest number of innocents in the world and the principal vendor of weapons and instruments of bloody torture." Terrorism, an amorphous concept, is used to denounce the acts and person of the "enemy" every time the violence perpetrated takes primarily civilian lives. The political and legal usefulness of the category is disputable, and its relativity has been demonstrated. For example, the term ceased to be applied to the Palestinian Liberation Organization (PLO) after the Oslo Accords of 1993. The word has lost a good share of its analytical validity. Because it hampers considered reflection, we shall not use it in this book.

The "Open Letter" from the Hezbollah is a founding text, the only official document in nearly twenty-five years. It was delivered publicly in February 1985, a month after the announcement that Israel would withdraw its troops to a so-called security zone in Lebanon. Augustus Richard Norton published the letter and translated it into English,[3] and a partial French translation appeared in *Les Cahiers de l'Orient*.[4] Another section later became available online, thanks to Feki Masri.[5] Freely accessible on an Arabic website (www.hassannasrallah.info) two years ago, it has since disappeared, along with the site itself. We produced our translation in the summer of 2007. It was our wish to place the letter within the context in which it was uttered and to determine how the terms of that doctrine have survived for a generation, weathering profound changes. The interest of the doctrine lies in the timelessness of its key elements. Since its publication, no other document has invalidated its three pillars: first, a polarized view of the world that pits "oppressors" against "oppressed," leading to a path that is neither capitalist nor socialist; second, a

---

3. Augustus Richard Norton, *Amal and the Shi'a: Struggle for the Soul of Lebanon* (Austin: University of Texas Press, 1987), pp. 167–187. [A new English translation has been prepared for this book on the basis of the authors' French version.—trans.]

4. "Le 'Manifeste' du Hezbollah," *Les Cahiers de l'Orient* 2 (1986): 253–259.

5. http://jcdurbant.wordpress.com/2008/12/11/charte-du-hezbollah-1% e2%80%99amerique-est-la-source-de-tous-nos-maux-america-is-the -source-of all-evil/.

partiality for an Islamic form of government, which alone can guarantee justice through the application of the Sharia, based on the authority of the clerics surrounding the Iranian jurist-theologian *(walī al-faqīh);* and third, the pursuit of jihad, with the aim of liberating the "Muslim territories," which entails armed struggle to destroy the state of Israel, the rejection of any form of compromise that would lead to an acknowledgment of the "Zionist entity," and opposition to the aims of Israel's allies, the United States in the first place. The new charter of the Hezbollah, published on November 30, 2009, places the emphasis on the first and third of these issues. The second, though not abandoned, moves to the background and has been modified in two ways: the authority of the (Iranian) jurist-theologian is evoked only once and sotto voce, as it were; and there is an acknowledgment that the citizen is "a value in himself," borrowed directly from General Michel Aoun's Free Patriotic Movement (FPM).

The rhetorical subtlety and flexibility of the members of the "Party of God," notable in certain televised broadcasts and other interviews—where one or another of them declares the 1985 program obsolete—should not lead us to overlook the unchanging features of the Hezbollah's ideology. These are confirmed in every one of the speeches by Secretary General Hassan Nasrallah,*[6] in the book by Naʿīm Qāsim,* and in the monograph, translated from the Persian into Arabic, by Masʿud Assad Allahī.[7] The project to establish an Islamic society has been set aside, however, because the civil war has dissipated and because the party was intent from the outset on not using violent means to achieve it. At the cost of sharp internal tensions, compromise has become necessary. It is based on two elements: first, a pragmatic recognition of the religious plurality of Lebanese society; and second, a

6. Names followed by an asterisk appear in the "Portraits" section at the end of this volume.

7. Masʿud Assad Allahī, *Al-islāmīyūn fī muijtama taʿaddudī: Hezbollah fī Lubnān namūzajan* (Beirut: al-Dār al-ʿarabīya lil-ulūm, 2004).

theoretical slippage from the discourse of "revolution" to the discourse of "Resistance" (Islamic, patriotic, Arab . . .). The continuities appear in the internal documents of the party that we were able to procure, especially in the manuals intended for future party members:[8] "Given that the Hezbollah is an Islamic jihadist movement arising from the circumstance of the Zionist occupation of Lebanon, and which crystallized through jihad and Resistance to the enemy, in accordance with the prescriptions and orders of the late Imam Khomeini* and the Imam Guide Khamenei* . . . we define our goals as follows: to construct the human being and society . . . , to combat the enemy, . . . to incite the awakening of the *ummah* . . . to confront the domination of the forces of arrogance . . . , to defend the interests of the disinherited . . . to introduce a vanguard experiment."[9] To our knowledge, these sources have never been put to use.

To obtain additional information, we approached a number of leaders of the "Party of God" in Lebanon and Iran (a country where the Hezbollah enjoys official "diplomatic" representation). All these initiatives, well received at first, ultimately foundered. Were these leaders afraid that they would be unable to control all aspects of a monitored communication? Their concern is not unfounded. We have compared the original Arabic version of Naʿīm Qāsim's book to the French translation, *Hezbollah, la voie, l'expérience, l'avenir,* and found that references specific to Shiism are sometimes minimized in the French version (among other things, Alī's name is omitted);[10] the religious dimension of concepts is toned down (*ummah* is usually translated as "nation," which, though etymologically accurate, does not allow French-

8. The first two years of courses are based on these manuals. According to our sources, the third-year courses are based exclusively on selected texts.

9. *Al maʿārif al-islāmiyya* (first level) (Beirut: Jamʿiyyat al-maʿārif al-islāmiyya al-thaqāfiyya, n.d.), p. 394.

10. [Alī: the cousin and son-in-law of Muhammad, considered by the Twelver Shiites to be the first imam and the Prophet's rightful successor.—trans.]

speaking readers to grasp the notion of *ummah* in the Islamic sense;[11] and *mu'min*, "Muslim believer," is sometimes translated as "follower," which leaves an ambiguity about the nature of the "Resistance"). Moreover, some events are truncated (for example, the role of Rafic Hariri* in the "massacre of September 13, 1993"), and passages have been omitted, including a paragraph about jihad being the "gateway to life" and particulars about the *wilayāt al-faqīh*.[12] In times of war, words are weapons. Occupying the high ground in a combat zone is precarious, but it is necessary to stand fast. The group we are studying is at war with an "enemy": choosing not to take sides can be viewed as a pledge to one or the other. Nevertheless, there is a great distance between words ("break the arm," "cut out the tongue," or "cut off the hand" of those who get in the way) and actions. And these words and actions are not the monopoly of any one camp.

11. [*Ummah* refers to the Islamic community generally, without respect for national boundaries.—trans.]

12. For the examples cited, see Na'īm Qāsim, *Hizballah, al-minhaj, al-tajriba, al-mustaqbal*, 4th ed. (Beirut: Dār al-Hādī, 2008), pp. 52, 73, and 166; and *Hezbollah, la voie, l'expérience, l'avenir* (Beirut: Al Bouraq, 2008), pp. 56, 75, and 154.

THE "PARTY OF GOD"

AN ITINERARY (1982–2009)

I

A Militia of Professional Revolutionaries
for the Disinherited Fringe

The Hezbollah came into being in the midst of the Lebanon Civil War (1975–1990). Lebanese society is more fractured than most, divided by religion, standard of living, and region (the very urbanized coast, the mountain villages and cities, the Bekaa Plain). Over the centuries, the various groups have continually appealed to foreign powers to gain an advantage over their internal adversaries. A given group will characterize one power as a "conqueror," another as a "liberation force," while the opposing camp will reverse the terms. There has been progress toward developing a single history textbook for all Lebanese, but in 2010 the realization of a unified curriculum was still a work in progress. Long known as the "Switzerland of the Middle East," Lebanon emerged as a liberal, inegalitarian, and paternalistic society. The IRFED Report (1960)[1] revealed that 4 percent of the population possessed a third of the country's wealth, whereas half the Lebanese citizenry held less than a fifth of it.[2]

---

1. IRFED: The Institut international de recherche et de formation, éducation et développement (International Institute of Research and Training, Education, and Development), in which the French Dominican Louis-Joseph Lebret played an important role.
2. "Étude préliminaire sur les besoins et les possibilités de développement au Liban," compiled by the IRFED mission in Lebanon, 1959–1960. Six volumes of studies by that mission, as well as many documents written

Despite President Fuab Chehab's attempts to establish a state conforming closely to the Jacobin model, the traditional elites' mode of self-reproduction has operated at full capacity, whatever the community. As Ghassan Salamé has shown, at the turn of the 1970s nearly one member of parliament in two had family ties to a former MP, and confessionalism[3] was regaining strength under the presidency of Suleiman Frangieh. In addition, Lebanon's financial power is related in part to the absence of the religious restrictions in place among its neighbors in the region. And finally, the country's cultural influence lies in a freedom of expression unparalleled in the Arabic-speaking world and in a university system whose foundations date back to the last third of the nineteenth century.

Three major events allow us to trace the interplay among the national, regional, and international levels. In 1920, the French mandatory power carved out the territory of Greater Lebanon, extending the borders beyond those desired by some of its Maronite allies. This did not hurt the Maronites, however, since they constituted the largest share of the Christian population, which was in the majority at the time. It took a generation for the Sunnis to begin to accept the idea of an independent Lebanon in an Arab environment: such was the intent of the unwritten national pact of 1943 and of the proclamation of independence, which in 1946 led to the reluctant withdrawal of the last French soldiers. That fragile balance, resting on a scaffolding of religious communities favored by the mandatory power, collapsed in 1948 with the proclamation of the state of Israel, which undertook a war—ongoing to this day—against most of its neighbors, including Lebanon. That country welcomed more than 150,000 Palestinian refugees onto its soil. Some had left volun-

---

in 1960–1964, are held in the Maurice Gemayel archives at the Holy Spirit University in Kaslik.

3. [Confessionalism: a system of government based on the representation of "confessions," that is, religions or faiths (Sunnism, Shiism, Christianity).—trans.]

tarily, hoping for a quick victory by the Arab armies, while others were forcibly expelled. The annexation of Cisjordan by the kingdom of Transjordan, and Egypt's administration of the Gaza Strip, prevented the establishment of an embryonic Palestinian state. Twenty years later, following the so-called Six-Day War (June 1967), Israel occupied Cisjordan and the Gaza Strip, a major trauma for the Arabic-speaking populations, who reproached Lebanese leaders for not getting involved. The Yom Kippur War (1973) was only a balm on a still-smarting wound when the history of the Hezbollah began.

LEBANESE IDENTITY, ARAB IDENTITY, ISLAMIC IDENTITY

The tension between a Lebanese identity and an Arab identity, which does not altogether coincide with that between Christianity and Islam, was complicated by the tension between the historical Occident and Orient and, within the context of the cold war, between the Western and Eastern blocs. For example, U.S. troops landed in Lebanon in 1958 with the aim of preventing an incipient civil war from erupting between Maronites on one side and Druze and Sunnis on the other, which is to say between those Lebanese committed to national independence and those wishing to join the United Arab Republic (Egypt-Syria) supported by the Soviet Union. In the early 1970s as well, two groups faced off: a majority-Christian nationalist Right that believed the "Palestinian question" was not its affair, and a majority-Muslim Arabist Left that made that issue its rallying cry. The Iranian Shiite revolution in 1978–1979 changed the situation completely. Contemporary with the Camp David Accords between Israel and Egypt, it traced a course that did not belong to any one bloc, producing a shift to the religious domain of the debate on Lebanese versus Arab identity. The "liberation" of Jerusalem now became a religious duty to be performed in the name of Islam.

Lebanon's two neighbors exert a disruptive effect, which the Israelis call the "open game strategy." The Armistice Agreement of 1949 governs Lebanese-Israeli relations. The two states do not recognize each other, and Israeli leaders publicly express their wish to extend the northern border of their country to the Litani River. Israel conducts attacks to weaken the military potential of the Palestine Liberation Organization (PLO), and assassinations target militant intellectuals supporting the Palestinian cause. The number of operations of both kinds increased tenfold in 1968–1969, when the Fatah, under the leadership of Yasser Arafat,* took control of the PLO. Over the years, Tel Aviv's plan has not become any clearer. What political configuration of Lebanon best suits the interests of Israel? Even in 2008, there was no dearth of Israeli analysts to explain that the best solution would be a Lebanon integrated into a strong Syria, a state with which Israel could negotiate a lasting peace. Leaders in Damascus, for their part, have confined themselves to a de facto recognition of Lebanon. They neither accepted the proclamation of independence nor defended the creation of a Palestinian state covering the southern Bilād al-Shām. Their aim, whether they admit it or not, was to establish a "Greater Syria," a project the British and French colonial powers aborted when they dismantled the Ottoman Empire between 1918 and 1923. The Syrians, moreover, fear a liberal contagion emanating from Beirut.

A "Greater Lebanon" was proclaimed and recognized, and that nation became a founding member of the League of Arab States. Damascus therefore had to be satisfied with implementing a monitoring policy, playing on the divisions between the factions. In the Lebanese view of things, it has always been difficult to grant equal weight to their two neighbors, even when they were carrying out analogous acts. Ground troops from both countries have been present on Lebanese soil for a quarter of a century, Syria's since 1976 and Israel's since 1978. They have clashed only once, in June 1982, during a violent conflict in the region between Jezzine, Beirut, and Southern Matn. Otherwise, each side has warily kept watch over its respective zone. The Golan Heights,

Syrian territory occupied by the Israeli army since 1967, is a front that has never come into play. In 1984, on the eve of a discussion that was to take place in Lausanne, Switzerland, to mend the fabric of the Lebanese nation, President Amine Gemayel* officially abandoned two expressions: "triple occupation," referring to the Palestinians, the Israelis, and the Syrians; and "symmetrical withdrawal," a policy desired by the Reagan administration, which had endeavored to induce Lebanon to join Egypt on the path of peace with Israel.

The Lebanese government's guiding principle reflects the state of power relations among the different religious communities. We must take care not to succumb to the widespread myth of persecution; nevertheless, the Shiite Lebanese, more than others, possess a combination of disadvantages that has resulted in what has been called a *tā'ifa tabaqa* (class community). The Ottoman authorities neglected and often oppressed that Muslim fringe, and the wealthy feudal families ruled over an impoverished population. The territory of Jabal 'Amil in the southern part of the country is not continuous with the Bekaa Plain and the *dāhiya* (the southern suburbs of Beirut), the three zones where the majority of the Shiites live. The collective consciousness of the Shiites came into being later than that of the other groups. According to Ahmad Beydoun's analysis, it was the result of a new generation of clerics: Imam Mūsa al-Sadr,* Ayatollah Mohammad Hussein Fadlallah,* and Ayatollah Mohammad Mahdī al-Dīn.* Mūsa al-Sadr took three decisive initiatives. First, he created the Supreme Islamic Shiite Council (SISC) of Lebanon in 1967, whose members are elected to appoint the muftis and to manage the *waqf*s (pious foundations), which became distinct from those of the Sunnis at that time. Second, he mobilized the working classes, leading the government to create the Council of the South. And third, he launched the Harakat al-mahrūmīn (Movement of the Disinherited) in 1974, the first Shiite political organization, along with its armed branch, Amal (*Afwāj al-muqāwama al-lubnāniyya,* the battalions of Lebanese resistance). All three clerics embraced the *marja'iyya*[4] of Abū al-Qāsim al-Khū'ī,* established in Najaf, Iraq. To it they paid the *khums,* that is, a fifth of annual revenues, and the *zakāt* so that the *marja'iyya* could distribute these funds among its various *wakīls* (local representatives).

Despite differences of opinion and personal rivalries, the dynamic engagement of these three men shunted aside the traditional Shiite notabilities and led to a tenfold increase in the number of clerics at the start of the 1970s (more than four hundred, according to Eitan Azani). Actions occurred at two interconnected levels. On one hand, Sadr, Fadlallah, and Shams al-Dīn proposed to reform the national pact, the "Lebanese formula" of 1943, pinning their hopes on an acknowledgment of true *huqūq al-insān* (human rights) and the establishment of a *dawlat al-insān* (humane state). On the other, they undertook to unite the Palestinians and the Shiites, those "disinherited from their land and [those] disinherited on their land," into a single community of interests. These are the terms of Sadr himself, who defended on principle military intervention within the framework of the state. Each of these three clerics called for jihad, but in different contexts and in terms of different modalities. Fadlallah published *Al-islām wa mantiq al-quwwa (Islam and the Logic of Force)* after being driven from the neighborhood of Nabaa, along with all the other Shiites, by Pierre Gemayel's Lebanese Phalanges in 1976. Shams al-Dīn and Sadr invited their followers to defend "their homeland from the enemy."

Mūsa al-Sadr was a pragmatist. He relied on Iranian specialists such as Mostafā Chamrān,* met with Christian leaders, and agreed to work with nonreligious or multifaith organizations such as Monsignor Grégoire Haddad's Social Movement. Invited to Libya by Muammar Gaddafi, he mysteriously disappeared in

4. A *marja'* is a cleric considered to be a spiritual "source of imitation," who is in charge of managing and redistributing material goods within the Shiite community.

that country during the summer of 1978. His activities, like those of his colleagues, were directed against the leftist secular parties recruiting from Shiite training grounds: the Communist Party, the Communist Action Organization, and the Lebanese branch of the Baath Party. The Shiite militants, determined to fight Israel, thus became involved in three groups: Yasser Arafat's Fatah, which appeared to be the most heavily armed; Amal, whose fighters were in fact trained by the Fatah; and al-Da'wa Party, a "school for [revolutionary] cadres" supported by Mohammad Bāqir al-Sadr* in Iraq, whose Lebanese branch decided to infiltrate Amal to make it more revolutionary. That core of groups gave rise to the Hezbollah, which punctuated its discourse with select references from the clerics cited, and above all from those of Ayatollah Khomeini, whose fatwas were published in *al-'Ahd,* the party's weekly newspaper.

THE DESTABILIZATION OF LEBANON

The war that erupted in 1957 pitted Palestinian forces linked to Arafat's PLO against Gemayel's Lebanese Phalanges. In a secret accord—signed in Cairo in November 1969 under pressure from Egypt and Syria and complemented by the Melkart Protocol (May 1973)—Arafat obtained the right to prepare to do battle with Israel in coordination with the Lebanese army, which was charged with guaranteeing state sovereignty. The Jordanian army's elimination of the Palestinian fedayeen in September 1970 (Black September) gave rise to a mass influx of Palestinians into Lebanon. There they found support from the forces of the Lebanese Left, represented by Kamal Jumblatt, leader of the Druze community and of the National Lebanese Movement. In the name of Arabism, that camp aimed to put an end to Israel's existence. In the name of pluralism, it intended to eradicate the domination of Maronite community leaders within state institutions. In the other camp, under the slogan "Lebanon First," the Phalanges claimed to be defending the principle of an independent state within the Arab world, one open to Europe and North America.

We need to introduce nuances into that schematic picture, however. In some places, Christian clans such as those of Gemayel, Camille Chamoun, Michel Eddé, and Suleiman Frangieh fanned rivalries. In others, the Palestinians on the left disagreed with the Lebanese about the objectives and timetable. They were soon outdistanced by specifically sectarian *(confessionelles)*[5] demands. Bloody battles spread throughout the Lebanese branches of the Baath and al-Da'wa parties, and Islamized groups such as the Student Brigade left the Fatah because of its Western, secular, or Marxist frames of reference. Within Amal, two opposing tendencies created turmoil: one wished to be faithful to Mūsa al-Sadr's reformism within the state framework, whereas the other believed that the Khomeinist revolution, the Egypt-Israel peace accord, and the Israeli invasion had set in place radical conditions for action.

In 1976, Syrian president Hafez al-Assad,* who maintained close contact with the Frangieh clan, provided assistance to Christian groups against the PLO. Under the name "Palestine Liberation Army," in fact, Syrian soldiers had been present in Lebanon since 1973. When the war broke out, Damascus was in a position of strength for formulating and implementing cease-fires and for elaborating the Constitutional Document, which was made public in February 1976. It increased the power of the Sunni prime minister[6] and made Lebanon an Arab country and no longer simply a country "with an Arab face." Lebanese institutions were in a state of complete decay, especially the small national army of fifteen thousand men, which shattered into half a dozen "armies," each in the service of a cause. After Frangieh's presidential term expired, a Damascus candidate, Elias Sarkis, was elected in May 1976. At the end of the month, Assad shifted

5. [I have generally translated *confession* as "religion" or "faith," *confessionnel* as "religious." Here, however, the term refers specifically to the fractious relations between the religious communities.—trans.]

6. [Power in Lebanon is shared between a Christian president and a Muslim prime minister.—trans.]

his allegiance. Worried about the autonomy acquired by his Palestinian allies, who were moving closer to Arafat's Fatah, and convinced that he would be exonerated by the Europeans—frightened by the sight of a weakening Christian camp—he ordered his army to advance into Lebanon. Only Iraq declared its opposition to that occupation. The Arab League allowed Syria to give a legal veneer to that enterprise by including its soldiers in an "Arab Peacekeeping Force," which quickly became an "Arab Force of Dissuasion" (AFD). Composed primarily of Syrian soldiers, the AFD had nearly blanketed the country by summer 1977, but without managing to disarm the opposing forces. The key figure of the Lebanese Left, Kamal Jumblatt, was assassinated in March.

It was then that a second Syrian about-face occurred, linked to the rejection of its supervisory role by part of the Lebanese army and, above all, by the militia of the Lebanese Forces headed by Bachir Gemayel.* Egypt was anxious; Israel supported the Lebanese Forces; and the United States supported Damascus, even though Syria was the privileged ally of the USSR in that region. Violent clashes occurred during that Hundred Days' War, until the Beiteddine Conference in October 1977. The restoration of peace, approved by UN Resolution 436, was short lived. In mid-March 1978, in reprisal for a commando action by the Fatah that killed dozens near Tel Aviv, Israel launched Operation Litani. The invasion of Southern Lebanon was marked by widespread destruction, about a thousand deaths, and the mass exodus of a portion of the population, but also by encouragements directed at another part of the population, which no longer supported the "Fatahland" regime. The unqualified assertion that Jabal 'Amil and Palestine had a "shared destiny" did not withstand the test of the Palestinian forces' brutality and the increasingly frequent skirmishes between the fedayeen and the Shiites of Amal, a situation that would be acknowledged and deplored by the members of the Hezbollah. UN Security Council Resolution 425 condemned the invasion, demanding the unconditional withdrawal of the Israeli troops and establishing a United Nations Interim Force in Lebanon (UNIFIL). But the Israeli army, known as Tsahal, was able to rely on a small Army of Free Lebanon under the leadership of Major Saad Haddad. It was composed of a few hundred dissident officers and soldiers, Maronites as well as Shiites, joined by three hundred Phalangists, the base of the South Lebanon Army (SLA). A year later, Commander Haddad proclaimed the independence of the zone he controlled.

Military cooperation between the Israelis and the Lebanese Forces increased with the non-Syrian forces' withdrawal from the AFD, which then redeployed its troops on the Bekaa Plain, and the reconstitution of a real Lebanese army. Bachir Gemayel resorted to coercing his militia to "unify the Christian guns" and to impose his authority as potential leader of his community. In December 1980, in the city of Zahlé, an inter-Christian conflict gave rise to a new clash between the Lebanese Forces and the AFD. Gemayel petitioned the UN Security Council and, under international pressure, obtained a temporary withdrawal of the Syrians. In April 1981, Syrian troops—by then, no one was fooled by the cloak of the AFD—besieged the city but did not prevail. One text, known as the "Lebanese document," was submitted to the Quadripartite Committee (Syria, Saudi Arabia, Kuwait, and the secretary general of the Arab League) as well as to the Lebanese authorities. It focused on three points: breaking off relations between the Lebanese Forces and Israel; applying the Cairo agreement of 1969; and effecting the gradual withdrawal of the Syrian army. Meetings led to no agreement, and Philip Habib, special presidential envoy of the United States since 1981, managed to obtain only a fragile cease-fire. Israel felt directly threatened during the Battle of Zahlé. Its air fleet attacked the Syrians, and its officers prepared a new plan, baptized "Operation Peace for Galilee."

The Israelis conducted a mass invasion of Lebanese territory beginning on June 6, 1982. The attempted assassination of Shlomo

Argov, Israeli ambassador to London, by members of a fringe Palestinian group headed by Sabri al-Banna, alias Abu Nidal, served as the trigger for the implementation of a plan that, according to Zeev Schiff and Ehud Yaari, entailed the integration of Cisjordan and Gaza into a greater Israel that would impose peace on its vulnerable northern neighbor. Tsahal bombed Beirut and the suburbs of Sidon and toppled the UNIFIL. It ignored UN Security Council Resolution 509 (June 5) demanding its immediate and unconditional withdrawal. At Bachir Gemayel's request, a National Salvation Committee was established. It included three militia chiefs (Gemayel himself; Walid Jumblatt,* who quickly stepped down; and Nabih Berri,* representing Amal), plus President Sarkis, Prime Minister Chafic Wazzan, and Minister of Foreign Affairs Fouad Boutros, as well as Nasri Maalouf, the Greek Catholic MP for the capital. West Beirut was besieged, bombed a second time, and then occupied. After intense fighting, the Syrians were pushed back twenty kilometers. Among the Lebanese, Arafat's proclamation to have Beirut become an "Arab Stalingrad" fell largely on deaf ears. Ronald Reagan, representing the United States, and François Mitterrand, in the name of France, then proposed a diplomatic solution: the departure under international supervision of the combatants led by Arafat, then an Israeli withdrawal. In early August, the PLO gave its agreement to the Habib plan, simultaneously stipulating that a French contingent and a multinational force (MNF) would be sent in and that the fedayeen would be evacuated to Arab countries that agreed to accept them.

A tripartite naval force—from the United States, France, and Italy—dropped anchor outside the port of the Lebanese capital, where occupying Israeli troops, international troops, the Lebanese armies, and the militias were all thrown together. Evacuation operations proceeded between August 21 and September 3. On August 23, Bachir Gemayel was elected president of Lebanon, prevailing over the National Movement, which united most of the forces on the left and considered Gemayel Israel's patsy.

Nevertheless, among the MPs, five of nineteen Sunnis, twelve of eighteen Shiites, and two of five Druze became convinced of the viability of his candidacy, backed by a government program whose main lines had been drawn in late 1981. Three weeks later, on September 14, 1982, after the international force had withdrawn, Gemayel was assassinated. That triggered the massacre of Palestinians in the Sabra and Shatila refugee camps in three waves, according to Alain Ménargues: first at the hands of special Israeli units, whose troops reoccupied West Beirut; then by groups in the SLA; and finally by men from the Jihaz al-Amn, a Lebanese Forces fringe group led by Elie Hobeika.*

The international outcry was almost immediate. At the request of the Lebanese government, the United States, France, and Italy again provided contingents, this time with the mission of protecting the civilian population by supporting the Lebanese army, which was charged with disarming the militias. Amine Gemayel was elected president of Lebanon on September 21. To counter the occupation of Israeli troops, which abandoned the capital (including the port and airport) at the end of the month, the Lebanese National Resistance Front was constituted from the Communist Party, the Communist Action Organization in Lebanon, and the Arab Socialist Action Party. Their common ground was the condemnation of all discrimination on tribal or religious grounds. In September, a U.S. warship bombed positions held by that front, which was suspected of threatening the Lebanese army. That act of war was interpreted as a breach of neutrality. Specifically Shiite movements, organized under the names "Young Believers," "Believers," or "Islamic Committees," provided scattered support for the anti-Israeli mobilization. Then came the signing of the Manifesto of the Nine, which represented three movements on equal footing: the Ulema of the Bekaa, Islamic Amal, and Islamic Committees under the control of the dissolved Lebanese branch of al-Da'wa Party. These groups soon received training from the Iranian Revolutionary Guard Corps (Pasdaran), whose first base, in Baalbek, was called Ochak al-

Shahāda (Lovers of Martyrdom). They fought for nearly three years without a centralized command, then—at an unidentified moment—decided to organize and to proclaim the birth of the Hezbollah. The party's internal history, available only to militants, alludes to the obscure circumstances surrounding its origins, linking them to the war Iran had conducted against Iraq since 1980 and leaving lingering doubts about the person responsible for Mūsa al-Sadr's disappearance:

> [The years] 1978 to 1982 [were characterized] by the rise of political Islam, in keeping with the path of the Iranian Islamic revolution . . . especially after the Iranian war victories, which shifted the power relations and allowed the Iranian revolution to advance to the stage of concrete influence outside the circle of war. . . . The Zionist military force increased in scope and undertook to penetrate Lebanon, in the form of support for the Christian war forces. The enemy played an active role in the civil war, then invaded the border region and established what it called the security zone. This was accompanied by the kidnapping of Imam *Sayyid* Mūsa al-Sadr.[7]

PAN-SHIISM

The Arab promoters of the upsurge of revolutionary Shiism presented it as a return to the point of origin after a Persian detour. In the sixteenth century, ulema from Jabal 'Amil and Bahrain helped establish Shiism in Iran at the request of the Safavid dynasty. In the 1950s, the revival was marked by the advent of Mūsa al-Sadr, who settled in Lebanon at the request of a family member, 'Abd al-Hussein Sharaf al-Dīn. Sadr's disappearance in Libya on August 31, 1978, threw the Lebanese Shiites into confusion, but the Iranian revolution and subsequent overthrow of the shah in January 1979 quickly resolved it. Ayatollah Khomeini proclaimed the Islamic Republic on April 1. That regime, dedicated to serving as the universal model for revolution, was

---

7. *Al ma'ārif al-islāmiyya* (first level) (Beirut: Jam'iyyat al-ma'ārif al-islāmiyya al-thaqāfiyya, n.d.), p. 381.

hailed in Beirut and other Lebanese cities where committees of support existed. The first foreign political leader welcomed to Tehran—in February—was none other than Yasser Arafat, who was handed the keys to the Israeli embassy. Khomeini had clearly made the struggle against Israel and its principal ally, the United States, sponsors of the Egypt-Israel Peace Treaty, his top priority. Fakhr Ruhāni,* the new Iranian ambassador to Beirut, was convinced that the revolution, unless exported, was doomed to failure. Having established an analogy between the Lebanese situation and that of Iran under the shah, he viewed Lebanon as a platform for disseminating subversive ideas. Young Shiite clerics received attractive financial offers to attend seminaries in Qom, which replaced those of Najaf and Karbala, where Saddam Hussein had been conducting a policy of persecution since 1978.

Two sources of tension ran through the Lebanese Shiite community. The first had to do with how the Iranian Islamic Republic was to be viewed as a frame of reference; the second, with the type of relation to be maintained with the Palestinian fedayeen. According to Saoud al-Mawla, an al-Daʿwa Party congress was held in Iran in 1981. The Lebanese delegation, which included Subhī al-Tufalyī* and Naʿīm Qāsim, accepted Khomeini's *wilayāt al-faqīh;* others rejected it, producing a split in the party. A year earlier, Hussein al-Husseini, who became the secretary general of Amal after its founder's disappearance, had ceded his place to Nabih Berri after disagreements with Hafez al-Assad regarding the PLO. The son of a trader doing business in West Africa, Berri, a lawyer, had few contacts in clerical circles. He agreed to the principle of U.S. mediation by Philip Habib and to the departure of PLO combatants from Beirut, and he participated in the National Salvation Committee. His gestures signified not only a tacit recognition of Israel but also a rejection of all-out war against the occupation of Southern Lebanon. That choice was the pretext for the aforementioned fracture within Amal: Hussein al-Husseini broke away from Berri, as did other cadres, including Hussein Mūsawī, who founded Islamic Amal with members from the former al-Daʻwa Party. Syria did not look favorably on the development of a Palestinian-Shiite alliance over which it would have little control, since the alliance would be under Tehran's influence. As a result, Assad, even as he oversaw the consolidation of the Hezbollah's founding elements—with Iran as its binding agent—decided to strengthen his ties with Amal.

In June 1982, Iran sent the "forces of Muhammad, prophet of God," a commando headed by Ahmad Motevasselian, to the Syrian-Lebanese border. Damascus did not permit the elite troops to penetrate into Lebanon, and they were repatriated to Iran. But in November, after the summer uprisings, fifteen hundred Pasdaran established themselves on the Bekaa under the supervision of the Syrian army to train battalions against Israel. Mohsen Rafiqdoost, leader of the Iranian Revolutionary Guards, was there, and, according to Augustus Richard Norton, he participated in training new fighters for the PLO. The chief organizer was Ali Akbar Mohtashamipur,* at the time Iranian ambassador to Damascus, who maintained relations with al-Tufaylī. The Hezbollah, he would write in 2006 (*Charq*, August 3), is "the spiritual child of Imam Khomeini and the Islamic Revolution." "Each class comprised three hundred combatants, who in turn served as trainers. . . . The Hezbollah thus trained, directly or indirectly, more than one hundred thousand volunteer forces." The Syrians authorized the establishment of a military training center in the village of al-Zabadani. Its headquarters were located in the Sheikh Abdallah Barracks. In early 1983, the various Shiite factions coordinated their actions to create the Council of Lebanon. According to a hypothesis reported by Sabrina Mervin, this was the origin of the Hezbollah. The council adopted the structural model of the Pasdaran (militia, social support, cultural activities, economic power), and combatants trained in Iran, which also used other relay organizations: al-Haraka al-islāmiyya (the Islamic Movement); Harakat al-tawhīd al-islāmiyya (the Islamic Unity Party), assembled around Sunni sheikh Saʻīd Chaʻbān in Tripoli; and Tajammuʻ al-ʻulamāʼ al-muslimīn (the

Gathering of Shiite and Sunni Ulema Who Agree to Follow Imam Khomeini).

The Hezbollah resolutely situated itself within the dual Khomeinist perspective of revolutionary struggle and the fight against Israel. It embraced marginality, rejecting any compromise with the established Lebanese system. Its top priority was jihad against the occupier, as indicated by the War Information Unit, which benefited from the advice of Kamal Kharazi, director of the Iranian press agency at the time. But Iranian involvement came at a price. On July 4, 1983, four members of the Iranian embassy staff in Lebanon, returning from Syria, got into a security vehicle belonging to the Lebanese state. They were seen for the last time at the Barbara checkpoint, held by the Lebanese Forces, in a sector controlled by Elie Hobeika. The names of the disappeared were Mohsen Mousavi, chargé d'affaires for the Iranian embassy in Beirut, which was under threat from the Israeli advance; Ahmad Motevasselian, military attaché and head of the commando sent in during the month of June; Taghi Rastegar Moghadam, technician for the embassy; and Kazem Akhavan, a journalist for the Islamic Republic press agency. Two days later, armed men kidnapped Patriarch Elias al-Zoghbi and two other members of the clergy, intending to exchange them for the Iranian nationals. On July 19, David Dodge, acting president of the American University of Beirut, was also abducted. Questioned about the fate of the Iranians, Bachir Gemayel is reported to have said that they were sent north, where their vehicle was discovered. Ambassador Fakhr Ruhāni supposedly threatened to send in the Pasdaran if nothing was done to ascertain their fate. The Lebanese Forces then published a communiqué declaring that the Iranian delegation had returned to Tripoli. Since then, directly or through the voice of the Hezbollah, the Tehran authorities have proclaimed that its nationals are being held prisoner in Israel. But, according to an Israeli report, these men were killed by the Lebanese Forces. That was confirmed by Robert Hatem, known as "Cobra," former bodyguard to Hobeika, who added that three hundred

Lebanese Shiites met the same fate in the headquarters in La Quarantaine.

South of the Litani River, Israel favored and imposed the establishment of collaborative institutions: religious militias, a Southern Union—which unified the village leagues—and a National Guard. Opponents were held in detention centers and camps, the largest of them al-Ansar camp. On November 11, 1982, Ahmad Qassir perpetrated the first of a dozen Hezbollah actions called "martyrdom operations" against the headquarters of the Israeli military governor in Tyre. The Hezbollah did not claim responsibility for three years, so as not to endanger the residents of the village, occupied by Israeli troops. The first popular uprising was incited by the presence of Israeli soldiers, who disrupted the Ashura procession in Nabatieh in autumn 1983. The angry crowd began throwing stones; the occupiers responded with gunfire, killing several people. In reaction, the SISC promulgated a fatwa calling for civil disobedience and forbidding all contact with the Israelis. Targeted attacks against Tsahal followed.

At the same time, attacks were perpetrated against interests and persons linked to what was sometimes erroneously called "NATO forces." On April 18, 1983, a suicide bomber rammed his explosive-stuffed vehicle into the U.S. embassy, killing sixty-three (a previous suicide attack, against the Iraqi embassy, occurred in December 1981). MNF soldiers were targets several times, the bloodiest attack coming on October 23, 1983, in which 239 Americans and 58 French citizens died. In the saga of the Hezbollah militants written by the party's leaders, these occurrences, like the attack on the French embassy in Kuwait, are mentioned only in passing or not at all. The authors feign ignorance of the reprisal against bases on the Bekaa Plain, carried out by French airpower on November 17 (Operation Brochet). Khomeini, for his part, praised the bravery of a "limited number of Muslims" who sacrificed their lives to impel the MNF and all the "little satans" to leave Lebanon definitively in early

1984 and to put an end to their oversight.[8] In sermons widely disseminated on cassette tape (they have been studied by Olivier Carré), Mohammad Hussein Fadlallah justified these attacks as the response of the weak, "taking into account the situation of extreme oppression." He was himself the target of an attack, from which he emerged unscathed, but which caused eighty-three civilian deaths. U.S. agencies are suspected of involvement in that assassination attempt.

The complex question of the 110 Western hostages, which arose in 1982 and reached its conclusion in 1991, belongs to a context in which the capture of individuals, of Lebanese or other nationalities, occurred on material and ideological, local and regional grounds. The Islamic Jihad, the Movement of the Disinherited on Earth, and the Revolutionary Justice Organization have claimed responsibility for the kidnapping of European and American nationals, and the language they use is consistent with the Khomeinist vulgate. The designated ringleaders are Sheikh Zoheir Kenj and especially, Imad Mughniyah,* now celebrated as one of the martyr-heroes of the Hezbollah and of Tehran, where a street is named after him. One of the detention sites for the French hostages was in a building complex that, until 2006, would be the political and operational headquarters of the Hezbollah. Emissaries met a number of times with Rafiqdoost in Beirut and Mohtashamipur in Damascus. The hostages were pawns in negotiations with several different aims: to buy weapons at less disadvantageous conditions than those proposed indirectly in Tehran, within the context of the Iran-Iraq War; to put pressure on Israel to provide information about the fate of the four kidnapped Iranian diplomats; and to secure the release of Shiite prisoners. Two issues complicated the situation of the French hostages. The first had to do with the Eurodif nuclear program, which had been blocked since the 1979 revolution,

8. Until 1986, France maintained a mediation force in Lebanon called the "Casques blancs" (White Helmets).

even though the shah of Iran had committed a billion dollars for its realization. The second was linked to the presence of opponents of Iran in France: Shapour Bakhtiar, the shah's last prime minister; and Massoud Rajavi, one of the leaders of the People's Mujahideen, who was finally expelled in 1986.

During that period, a dozen U.S. citizens were taken hostage, and William Francis Buckley, paramilitary operations officer in the Special Activities Division of the CIA in Lebanon, was executed. Terry Waite, assistant for Anglican communion affairs to the bishop of Canterbury and an envoy of the Church of England, was abducted in 1987. French citizens[9] were kidnapped at various times between March 1985 and May 1988. Michel Seurat, a researcher, died after being denied proper treatment for health problems. In June 1985, TWA Flight 847 from Athens to Rome was hijacked over Beirut. A U.S. Navy diver on board was murdered, but the other hostages were released following mediation by Nabih Berri, who obtained in exchange the release of Shiite prisoners held in Israel. The Iran-Contra scandal, which erupted after the revelation of illegal U.S. arms sales to Iran, dealt a serious blow to the credibility of the Western powers' policies. The sale of French arms to Iran at a time when Paris was officially and intensively supporting Iraq became known only later, as did the rivalry between the majority party and the opposition in France, which in 1986 and 1988 led to an escalation in the kidnappers' demands and a delay in releasing hostages held in Lebanon. They were liberated in the midst of the French presidential campaign, following the return to Iran of Vahid Gorji, suspected of being the organizer of the wave of attacks in Paris in September 1986 (11 dead, 150 wounded). That release also came after an agreement to liberate Anis Naccache, imprisoned with his accomplices since 1980 for an assassination attempt on

9. In addition to Michel Seurat, these were: Marcel Carton, Marcel Fontaine, Philippe Rochot, Aurel Cornéa, Jean-Louis Normandin, Georges Hansen, Jean-Paul Kaufmann, and Roger Auque.

Shapour Bakhtiar, and following the settlement of the Eurodif litigation.

The Hezbollah leaders denied any involvement in these attacks and also in the assassination of eight Lebanese hostages of the Jewish faith and in the hijacking of a Kuwaiti airplane (1988) to obtain the release of Shiite prisoners. These prisoners were the producers or the victims of a tense religious climate, because of Kuwait's involvement with Iraq in the fight against Iran. The Hezbollah's rhetoric portrays these events as part of a defensive strategy, which is lawful from a religious standpoint because it comes in opposition to a "foreign occupation" engineered by the United States and France. The Hezbollah leaders condemned President Amine Gemayel for two sins: having signed a treaty with Israel and having told the army to bomb neighborhoods where Muslims lived. The "ignominious accord of May 17, [1983]," was sponsored by the United States, even though, according to John Boykin, Philip Habib harbored no illusions. Paris, still attached to the Franco-Egyptian plan proposed in July 1982, ignored it. The May 17 accord was supposed to establish peace between Israel and Lebanon, with borders characterized as secure, after lopsided and difficult negotiations that gave Tel Aviv de facto control over the southern part of Lebanon. The agreement could not be binding, because, at the last moment, Israel made it conditional on the withdrawal of the Syrians and PLO forces, which had not participated in the negotiations. It was ratified by the Lebanese parliament but was not promulgated by Gemayel, who officially renounced it on March 5, 1984.

A month earlier, on February 6, Amal and the Progressive Socialist Party (PSP) had taken control of West Beirut with the aid of the army's Sixth Brigade, which was primarily Shiite. Berri accused Gemayel of giving his allegiance to Israel and its ally the United States. Jumblatt, who had just won the battle against the Lebanese Forces in Chouf, causing a mass exodus of Christians, proclaimed that, given the option between an "Alawite" Syria and a "Maronite" Lebanon dominated by the Phalangists, he chose Syria. The Harat Hreik neighborhood was emptied of its hundreds of Christian families, just as those of Nabaa and Sin al-Fil had been emptied of their Shiite families. The embryonic Hezbollah took advantage of that offensive to establish bases for sanctuary in the southern suburbs of the capital where, as in West Beirut, Gemayel lost all control.

But the "Party of God" soon denounced the leftist opposition, accusing it of compromising itself in an order in which corruption, prevarication, favoritism, and a confusion of public and private interests prevailed. It defended the principle of a new path, departing from both capitalism and communism, systems that were rejected because of the imperialist ambitions associated with them and the inability of their leaders to champion the cause of the "disinherited." From Baalbek, under the authority of Subhī al-Tufaylī, the Hezbollah proclaimed the Islamic Republic of Lebanon. A year later, the spokesman for the movement, Ibrahim Amine al-Sayyid, opting for the path of persuasion, defended the project: "If our people are allowed to choose freely the form of their political system in Lebanon, they cannot fail to wager on Islam. . . . We call for the founding of an Islamic regime based on the free and direct choice of the people, not on the imposition of force as some imagine." The Hezbollah's "Open Letter," from which this excerpt is taken, followed by a few weeks the Israeli government's announcement of a withdrawal behind a "security zone" in Lebanese territory, ten kilometers wide and seventy-nine kilometers long, designed to "protect" the villages in northern Israel and to divert water resources. The SLA stood firm, with the support of Tsahal, which continued to disregard the international resolutions.

Following Shams al-Dīn's fatwa, which in March 1985 called for defensive jihad so long as Israel occupied Lebanese territory, Amal ultimately rejected the idea of a formal accord with the Israelis, even while opposing the military action of the Hezbollah because of the risks of reprisal against the civilian populations, a portion of which had already been expelled. The Lebanese Forces,

cut loose by the Israelis in spring 1985, decided in favor of a rapprochement with the Syrians. Elie Hobeika closed the bureau
representing the Lebanese Forces in Jerusalem, developed contacts with Damascus, and reconciled with the Frangiehs. He went
to the Syrian capital in September as part of a tripartite committee
representing the three militias (Shiite, Druze, and Christian) to
negotiate and then sign an accord with Assad. Berri, who had
been invited to the Reconciliation Conference in Lausanne in
March of the previous year, agreed to join Rashid Karami's national unity government. He became the ardent supporter of the
tripartite accord signed in Damascus in December 1985, but
he ran into two obstacles. The first concerned the Shiites: the
Hezbollah rejected the accord and enthusiastically welcomed
the arrival in their ranks of Mustafa Dirani, who had left Amal.
The second came from the Maronites: in mid-January, Samir
Geagea*—an associate of President Gemayel, who got his personal guard involved—successfully launched a military operation
against Hobeika and his loyalists. He assumed the leadership of
the Lebanese Forces and undertook to build the infrastructure for
a proto-state in the Christian regions of Lebanon, all the while
holding off the Syrians.

That tactical reorientation explains in part why the military
jihad against Israel was not accompanied by an open confrontation between the Hezbollah and those it called "collaborators,"
the Phalanges and the Lebanese Forces. Another reason is that
Syria had reduced the Hezbollah's margin for maneuvering, and
the Hezbollah openly demonstrated its support for the PLO beginning in 1984. But Arafat, under threat from the Syrians and
their Palestinian allies in Tripoli, had to flee Lebanon in 1983
under the protection of the French navy; he was then transported
to Tunisia. A third explanation is that the money was coming
not only from Iran and the diaspora but also from drugs: hash-
ish and poppies were cultivated north of the Bekaa, in Hermel,
where the government's influence was particularly weak. That
production flowed especially through the port of Jounieh, which

was in the hands of the Lebanese Forces. Money is nonpartisan, disregarding even religious cleavages.

A FLOOD OF *FITNAS*

The Iran-Iraq War (1980–1988), the bloodiest in the region since the early 1920s, brought Damascus and Tehran closer together. To the Arab world, Assad justified his position by explaining it might allow him to play the role of mediator during future negotiations. At a deeper level, the Iraqi and Syrian Baathists were enemy brothers, and the leadership of the Arab world was at stake. But the Iranian-Syrian allies had different agendas, and the visits to Tehran by Syrian minister of foreign affairs Farouk al-Sharaa,* especially during periods of tensions between Syria and its allies in Lebanon, were evidence of a complex strategy. The Syrians could not ignore Arab attempts to resolve the Lebanon War: those of King Fahd of Saudi Arabia, King Hassan II of Morocco, and Algerian president Chadli Bendjedid. In fact, the aim of their plan was not to favor the spread of the Iranian revolution but rather to maintain a balance of powers that would allow the Syrians to continue to play the role of permanent arbiter. That explains a certain reticence on their part when hostages were taken and a consummate skill at maintaining rivalries within all the communities, which, at one time or another, were torn asunder. In addition to the inter-Christian conflicts marked by the opposition between Geagea and Hobeika, then between Geagea and Aoun,* in which President Gemayel himself became involved, there were inter-Palestinian, inter-Sunni, Sunni-Syrian, Shiite-Syrian, and inter-Shiite conflicts.

The PSP and Amal fought a losing battle against the "Nasserians." The PSP also battled (Sunni) al-Mourabitoun, in a conflict that subsided only with the intervention of the Grand Mufti of Lebanon, Hassan Khaled. The Tawhīd group, before being dismantled, fought against the Syrian occupation of Tripoli. Amal, with the support of Syria, conducted a three-year war (1985–1988) against the Palestinian combatants to prevent the PLO from installing itself again in Beirut. That "camp war" led to the destruction, full or partial, of Sabra (100 percent), Shatila (85 percent), and Bourj al-Barajneh (50 percent), and it gave rise to a new wave of departures from the ranks of Nabih Berri's party. Some militants joined the Hezbollah, which prided itself on its neutrality in these battles. Yet Norton indicates that the Hezbollah on the one hand provided substantial aid to the fedayeen and, on the other, "proved to be especially intolerant of the Communist Party." "Dozens, if not hundreds, of party members were killed in a brutal, bloody campaign of suppression and assassination in 1984 and 1985."[10] At the request of Lebanon's prime minister, Selim al-Hoss, who sought a means to attenuate the exactions among militias, Damascus deployed eight thousand soldiers in West Beirut. In 1986, incidents erupted several times with combatants from the "Party of God." On February 24, 1987, the Syrians occupied the Fathallah Barracks in the Basta neighborhood: twenty-seven members of the Hezbollah were executed on the spot, without provoking any response on the part of the movement. According to Jubin M. Goodarzi, the funeral of the Fathallah "martyrs" attracted more than ten thousand people, some of them shouting "Death to Syria." But in *al-'Ahd,* the Hezbollah leaders—cognizant of power relations—urged militants and sympathizers not to succumb to anger.

The inter-Shiite divisions appeared in early 1986, during the Fourth Conference on Islamic Thought in Tehran (January 30). Major meetings were held between the Lebanese and Iranian clerics. Together they elaborated a constitution proposal for an Islamic Republic in Lebanon. Modeled on the Iranian constitution, it would have guaranteed the Shiite clerics greater authority while offering local autonomy to the regions dominated by other minorities. The preamble read as follows: "Islam is a religion of justice and mercy for all men. Under its protection, the sons of

10. Augustus Richard Norton, *Hezbollah,* 5th ed. (Princeton, N.J.: Princeton University Press, 2009), p. 37.

all communities and heavenly religions live in complete freedom and enjoy justice, security, and tranquility. Since the Muslims constitute the majority of the Lebanese people, the creation of an Islamic Republic in Lebanon will be in the interest of all Lebanese."[11] The vice chair of the SISC, Mohammad Mahdī Shams al-Dīn, who was close to the two Sadrs and linked to Amal, received as a delegation the leadership of the Lajnat wilāyat al-faqīh (Commission for the Oversight of the Jurisconsult). But once he returned to Lebanon, he criticized the clerical training institutions, which taught political ideology and the handling of weapons more than knowledge of religious science and a personal spiritual life. He targeted the Hezbollah in particular through two *hazwas,* al-Imām al-Muntazar and al-Rasūl al-Akram, the latter of which was founded by Iranians and their Lebanese partners in 1983–1984. In opposition to the literal reading of Husayn's "martyrdom" at the Battle of Karbala in 680,[12] Shams al-Dīn attempted to promote a normative and ethical sense of the term. In conjunction with the Grand Mufti of Lebanon, Hassan Khaled, he spearheaded activities promoting interfaith dialogue. At the same time, according to Theodor Hanf as cited by H. E. Chehabi, Amal dissociated itself from the 1986 Iran-Lebanon plan defending a parliamentary democracy that would increase the Shiites' political influence.

The two militias' rivalry for leadership of the Shiite community had continued to spread since the initial fracture, linked to the rejection of all-out war against Israel, that is, to the acceptance of Resolution 425 (which recognized Israel's right to ensure its security and therefore its right to exist). The Hezbollah

11. Among the signatories of that text were Mohammad Mahdī Shams al-Dīn, Mohammad Hussein Fadlallah, Mohammad Ali Assaf, Sadek Mūsawī, Hussein Mūsawī, and Ali Mūsawī ("La Constitution islamique," *Les Cahiers de l'Orient* 2 [1986]: 248).

12. [Husayn: grandson of the Prophet Muhammad, considered the third imam by the Shiites. The Ashura celebration commemorates his death at the hands of Yazīd, the second Umayyad caliph.—trans.]

also accused Berri of having tried to play the role of mediator in the hostage situations. The conflict was fratricidal in the literal sense: there was no dearth of divided families, like that of Hassan Nasrallah himself, whose brother remained loyal to Amal. In August 1987, Daoud Suleiman Daoud, leader of Amal in the South, threatened anyone who questioned his authority and banned the distribution of Hezbollah publications. In February 1988, Lieutenant Colonel William R. Higgins, a member of UNIFUL, was abducted after leaving an interview with one of the Amal leaders in Southern Lebanon and was later assassinated. Considering that act a provocation by the Hezbollah, with which the kidnappers maintained ties, Amal launched reprisals. The Hezbollah, in a position of weakness, began a strategic withdrawal from the South. It then imposed its authority on the Beirut suburbs. A cease-fire agreement was signed in May 1988, and another in February 1989, but neither held for very long, and this allowed the Hezbollah to implant itself once more in the South. The violence was so extreme that the new president of the Iranian Republic, Ali Akbar Hashemi Rafsanjani, condemned both sides. Berri accused the Hezbollah of resorting to Nazi tactics; the nickname "executioner of the Shiites" was in turn foisted on him. It took several quadripartite meetings—among Berri; al-Tufaylī; Syrian foreign minister Farouk al-Sharaa; and Ali Akbar Velāyatī,* Iranian minister of foreign affairs—before an accord could be signed in November 1990. It focused on three points: the release of prisoners, the return of the thousands of displaced persons, and a halt to propaganda. The number of victims is unknown. Despite the support of Shams al-Dīn and of Qabalān, who in March 1989 promulgated a fatwa banning the Shiites from joining the Hezbollah, Amal emerged weakened from its dual confrontation with the fedayeen and the members of the Hezbollah. Three of Amal's leaders had been assassinated, including Daoud. Conversely, within the socially emergent classes of the Shiite community, the Hezbollah enjoyed a reputation for strength and integrity far superior to that of its rival.

A resolution to that multifarious war was outlined in the Taif Agreement, signed on October 22, 1989, by a large portion of the Lebanese MPs who had served since 1972. Saudi Arabia took the initiative, imposing the agreement on Syria with the approval of the United States. The cease-fire between Iran and Iraq (August 6, 1988) and the weakened state of the USSR led Damascus and Washington to a rapprochement. The Arab identity of Lebanon was ratified; a clause recognized "Syria's special interest" in the country; and the Maronites lost their institutional preeminence, with part of the duties of the (Maronite) president of the Lebanese Republic now allocated to the (Sunni) prime minister. In addition, the number of MPs was revised to establish absolute parity between Christians and Muslims. The agreement in its entirety was presented as a restoration of the religious balance in view of demographic shifts. The strongman of the accord was the Saudi-Lebanese Rafic Hariri. The parliamentary session of November 5, 1989, adopted the text as Lebanon's constitution and proceeded to elect René Moawad* president of the country. But he was assassinated on November 22 in an attack in which, according to William B. Harris (who is rather isolated on this point), the Hezbollah was involved. Moawad's successor was a loyal ally of the Syrians: Elias al-Hrawi.* Through Nasrallah, the Hezbollah voiced its opposition to the agreement, which came about only because Arab negotiators had kept the Iranians away, and which stipulated a truce with Israel. Twenty years later, the leaders of the "Party of God" would attenuate the extent of that rejection, reducing it to reservations about political confessionalism.

The Taif Agreement was not applied immediately. According to its detractors, it was simply a dressing up of the "old order." General Aoun, head of the Lebanese army, to whom Amine Gemayel had entrusted the government at the end of his term on September 23, 1988, rejected the accord. As a result, two authorities faced off in autumn 1989: one incarnated by Aoun, who held the presidential palace of Baabda and controlled the Lebanese

army with vast and enthusiastic popular support; the other by
al-Hrawi and his prime minister, Selim al-Hoss, who headed a
government formed in West Beirut. To display his impartiality,
Aoun—who received financial and military aid from Saddam
Hussein—waged war against Samir Geagea's Lebanese Forces.
Suspicions arose about a collusion existing between him and the
Hezbollah, voiced by the political leaders of Amal, who presented
the situation as a confrontation between "moderates" and "ex-
tremists." That situation went on for a year. General Aoun was
forced into exile on October 13, 1990, when the United States
gave Syria the green light to occupy Beirut. At that time, the
United States' priority was to bring the largest possible number
of Arab allies into the coalition against Iraq, which had occupied
Kuwait on August 2, 1990. Standing with Saudi Arabia, the oil-
producing monarchies, and Egypt, therefore, was Syria. The
price to be paid was Lebanon, which was pacified under Syrian
control. At the same time, Iraq—the Arab, Sunni, and "secular"
bastion against revolutionary Iran—was forced to withdraw. All
the militias officially agreed to proceed with disarmament before
the end of April 1991, and their members were invited to join
government institutions. In actuality, they handed over some
heavy weapons, sold others (in the case of the Lebanese Forces, to
the Croats especially), and kept still others concealed. The Palestinian groups were not affected by the Taif Agreement. The Hezbollah, though considered Lebanese, opted out for two reasons:
first, its leaders (al-Tufaylī and Mūsawī*) refused to place their
fighters under the orders of a Christian officer; and second (this
would soon become the sole argument), they wanted to incarnate the "Resistance" against the Israeli occupier.

A State within the State, the Vietcong in the Heart of Singapore

The end of the war made it possible to resume public administration operations and the reconstruction of Lebanon. The country had been bled dry: according to the estimate most often given, 150,000 had died (5 percent of the population), and tens of thousands of families had fled the country. The *Pax syriana* was ratified by the Treaty of Brotherhood, Cooperation, and Coordination (May 1991), which placed all questions of security and defense under the control of Damascus and established most-favored nation status for Syria in economic matters. That armed peace led to the marginalization or exile of some of the key actors from the previous period, particularly Christians. Samir Geagea, arrested in April 1994, was the only militia leader to be convicted of a crime. The Syrian takeover of Lebanon was forceful, tacitly accepted by the United States and, to a lesser extent, by France. Two presidents of the Lebanese Republic, Elias al-Hrawi (1990–1998) and Emile Lahoud (1998–2007), displayed flawless collaboration with Syria, as did the speaker of parliament, Nabih Berri. The headquarters of the Syrian army was in Anjar, on the Bekaa Plain, but the cities of Beirut, Batroun, and Tripoli were all under military control. Abdel Halim Khaddam, the Syrian vice president, held the rank of *missi dominici,* with General Ghazi Kanaan as his enforcer. In all their speeches, Lebanese officers pronounced the requisite clichés, lauding cooperation with Syria. The road to Damascus was taken more or less as a matter of course by most of the political actors, and, at the local level, some mayors received their orders by fax from Syria.

Iran maintained close relations with the Hezbollah, but these relations shifted slightly. Khomeini's death in 1989 was preceded by the expulsion of his heir apparent, Sheikh Montazari—who was critical of the *wilāyat al-faqīh*—in favor of a troika composed of Ahmad Khomeini, son of the "supreme guide"; Ali Khamenei, the future successor of the first *walī al-faqīh*; and Hashemi Rafsanjani,* who was elected president of Iran in 1989 and again in 1993. The Iranian presidential candidate and then president Mohammad Khatami (1997 and 2001), who had family ties to the Sadrs, went to Lebanon in 1996 and again in 2003, and he received Rafic Hariri on three official visits. In July 1997, when al-Tufaylī launched his "revolution of the hungry," the newly elected Khatami defended the Hezbollah and recalled to Iran some diplomats living in Beirut who had expressed their support for the insurrection. A short time later, in October 1997, Hassan Nasrallah was welcomed in Tehran and received confirmation of Iran's support.

The Hezbollah thus enjoyed dual protection, from Syria and from Iran, and acknowledged the benefits provided after the "seventeen-year war." The group displayed anxiety on only two occasions: in 1991, during the Madrid Conference; and in the second half of 1995, given the imminent peace agreement between Damascus and Tel Aviv. The only official reservations about the Hezbollah's supporters came sporadically from the prime ministry, where Rafic Hariri, a Sunni, was largely in charge. His refusal to meet with Mohammad Kazem al-Khonsari, Iran's deputy foreign minister, at the height of the 1996 crisis, is one illustration among others. Religion became a more prominent aspect of the political landscape because of the collapse of the secular-leaning "leftist" parties that accompanied the disappearance of the USSR and because of Marxism's loss of status as an alternative to liberalism. Did this mean there would be an opportunity to found the envisioned Islamic regime? That did not seem to be the case. The Hezbollah leaders were informed of a survey conducted by a researcher at the American University of Beirut in the early 1990s: less than a quarter of Shiites wanted such a state established in Lebanon.

AN OPPOSITION PARTY IN QUEST OF NORMALIZATION

The early 1990s brought changes within the Hezbollah. Its central agency, the Consultative Council *(majlis al-shūra),* was reduced from nine to seven members. Debates were keen on whether to join the political life of the criticized Taif system or rather to oppose it at the risk of being marginalized. Shortly before the end of the war, a public polemic arose between al-Tufalyī and Fadlallah, who dismissed any notion of overthrowing the Lebanese regime. For the most part, the Hezbollah rallied behind Fadlallah's position, which had itself evolved, and in May 1991 named ʿAbbās Mūsawī to the post of secretary general previously occupied by al-Tufaylī. The opinion of the *walī al-faqīh* Ali Khamenei was solicited, to see if it was permissible to participate in the legislative elections. The fatwa (May 1992) was affirmative, meaning that the establishment of an "Islamic order" in Lebanon was no longer viewed as an imminent political objective but only as a horizon. The theme of "revolution" receded to the background: on the Hezbollah's emblem, the expression "Islamic revolution in Lebanon" was replaced by "Islamic resistance in Lebanon." After succeeding Mūsawī, who had been assassinated by the Israelis, in February 1992, Hassan Nasrallah adopted that line. This episode shows that obedience to the *walī al-faqīh* remained complete "for political matters and everything belonging to the general conduct of public affairs," even after Khamenei was appointed by the Iranian Assembly of Experts. In face of criticism, the Hezbollah minimized the importance of "national or regional membership" in that agency, and its leaders explained to the militants in training that the *walī* was not "specific to the [Iranian] Islamic republic, as [some naysayers] might think": "The one whom the council of experts designates as the most competent becomes the *walī* for all the Muslims in the world, based on the uniqueness of the *wilāya,* of which we have already spoken, even though the Iranian Constitution did not speak of it and the experts did not mention it in their report, because of known political considerations that prevent them from declaring it."[1]

The Hezbollah's allegiance to the *walī al-faqīh* was nonetheless the source of tensions within Shiite Lebanese religious circles. The *maʿhad* of Mohammad Yazbak* in Baalbek, and the Maʿhad rasūl al-akram (Institute of the Noble Prophet) created in Beirut in 1983–1984, were also *hawzas* (religious institutes) attended by most of the clerics who embraced the party. These institutions possessed women's branches bearing the name "al-Zahrāʾ *hawza.*" Khomeinist thought was taught there and in two other establishments in Southern Lebanon. These *hawzas* stood apart from their most prestigious competitor, Mohammad Hussein Fadlallah's Maʿhad al-sharʿī al-islāmī (Islamic Legal Institute). The fundamental difference between them concerned the attribution of the function of *marjaʿ al-taqlīd* (source of imitation) after Ayatollah al-Khūʾī's death in 1992 and that of his successor, Ayatollah Mohammad Reza Golpayegani, in 1993. Jamal Sankari reports that, from that moment on, Fadlallah chose to consult the Iraqi ayatollah Ali Sistānī,* and his disciples conferred the title of *marjaʿ* on that leader (1995). Fadlallah then became the target of a campaign orchestrated by the Hezbollah. Its leaders had chosen Ali Khamenei, who combined the duties of *marjaʿ* and of *walī al-faqīh.* Hassan Nasrallah and Mohammad Yazbak were designated as *wakīls,* responsible for representing Khamenei and for collecting money in his name. A fracture between the two sides was avoided as a result of a powerful common denominator: the

1. *Wilāyat al-faqīh fī assr al-ghayba,* 2nd ed. (Beirut: Jamʿiyyat al-maʿārif al-islāmaiyya al-thaqāfiyya, 2000), p. 57.

struggle to be waged against Israel until "all of historical Palestine" was recovered.

As for Mohammad Mahdī Shams al-Dīn, the other historical figure of Lebanese Shiism, he was marginalized. His quietist orientation, his invitations to preachers not to become involved in politics, and his determination to recognize secular forces alongside the "Muslim parties" in order to reach compromises no longer reflected Khomeinist doctrine. He turned away from the choices made in the 1980s, especially the previously defended principle of "proportional democracy"—which favored the community that was strongest demographically—pronouncing himself in favor of the spirit of the 1943 pact. As vice chair of the SISC, he did not manage to federate the twenty-something schools that trained Lebanese Shiite clerics, whose leaders embraced a strong tradition of autonomy. In 1994, he organized a congress on the theme "Islam and the Muslims in a Changing World," at which he sought to promote an association on equal footing between Muslims and Christians. He died of cancer in 2001, but not before formulating a "testament" that his son would use to oppose the Hezbollah, reminding the group that the Shiites of Lebanon ought to have no "project other than that of the state." His successor to the vice chairmanship of the SISC was Sheikh ʿAbd al-Amir Qabalān, the loyal ally of Amal.

The frame of reference embraced by the Hezbollah was that of a *mujtamaʿ al-muqāwama* (society of resistance), the one likely to garner the most widespread approval. Out of a clear concern for effectiveness, some of its cadres studied in Europe and the United States before going to work for the 150 institutions (schools, hospitals, free clinics, presses, publishing houses) that were gradually associated with the party. At the regional level, the Hezbollah wanted to smooth out differences between Sunnis and Shiites. It sought the broadest sympathy and support possible, portraying "victory" against the "Zionist enemy" as something belonging to all Lebanese, Arabs, and Muslims. At the national level, it organized meetings with the members of other communities under

the auspices of *infitāh* (openness). It adopted the line of practical
and rhetorical flexibility, but without any written concessions as
to doctrine. Al-Tufaylī began to distance himself from the party
in 1991, breaking away completely in July 1997. Within the context of an agricultural crisis aggravated by the free circulation
of cheaper products from Syria, he denounced the betrayal of
the original ideals, which had favored the oppressed, and in the
remote region of Hermel he proclaimed the "revolution of the
hungry." The Hezbollah was paying the price for a certain political normalization. It broke all ties with its former leader the day
before the Lebanese army crushed a demonstration in Baalbek,
which had taken the form of a local insurrection. But defeat only
increased the reprimands coming from al-Tufaylī, who accused
the "Party of God" of being an instrument in the hands of the
Syrians and a servant of Israel, with Nasrallah in the role of
Iranian agent.

Implicitly, the Hezbollah leaders introduced a distinction between an ideal situation (an Islamic state) and the concrete situation (a partly secularized, multifaith state), which coincided
with a problematic that all religious faiths since the nineteenth
century have faced. Under the circumstances, since the use of
force was rejected, it became possible temporarily to integrate
a parliament into a communitarianist system. Judith Harik even
mentions a formalized agreement between the Hezbollah and
the government. The gains appear to have been greater than the
losses, particularly since the parliament brought with it official
recognition and could become a "political forum," in the expression of Naʿīm Qāsim. In 1993, Qāsim again declared it "possible
to persuade non-Muslims to accept the political concept of an
Islamic state." The first legislative elections took place in 1992.
Offers of oversight by international observers came to nothing,
and the Syrians controlled the polls. That induced part of the
Christian opposition to boycott the election. The Syrian takeover in no way constituted an obstacle for the Hezbollah, whose
platform emphasized national themes: "resistance" to the "en-

emy," abrogation of the confessionalist system, defense of political freedom and freedom of the press, and the correction of social and regional inequities. Anxious to unite the Lebanese, the Arabs, and the Muslims, its leaders were prepared to make major concessions in any area not affecting the principal objective and to establish the alliances necessary to win, with the (theoretical) exception of those who had, or had had, ties to Israel. They wasted no time in becoming part of an operation in which everything was negotiable, posts as well as licenses and contracts.

Distribution of the Twenty-Seven Shiite Seats in the Lebanese Parliament

	Hezbollah	Amal	Others
1992	8	9	10
1996	7	8	12
2000	9	6	12
2005	11	11	5
2009	11	11	5

The Lebanese parliament has 128 seats. Since the 1992 election, its speaker had always been Nabih Berri. After each round of voting, the Hezbollah could count on the support of only three or four allied legislators (generally a Maronite and two Sunnis). At the urging of Syria, which wanted to maintain a balance between the Hezbollah and Amal, the two groups formed a partial electoral alliance in 1996 (on the Bekaa Plain and in Southern Lebanon), which benefited Berri's organization in the first place and Nasrallah's in the second. A change in the electoral law, coming just before the 1996 elections, explains in part the relative weakening of the Hezbollah, whose military strategy had been called into question after the Israeli bombings of 1993 and 1996. Slogans nevertheless lauded the warriors' heroism: "They resist with their blood, resist with your vote." The municipal elections of 1998 were the occasion for an aborted effort by Berri and Hariri to block the Hezbollah. The leader of Amal expressed outrage at the Hezbollah's political exploitation of its military successes but failed to convince. The call for political parties to abstain, so as to allow technocrats dedicated to the common good to be elected, was not heeded. Clans and conspiracies operated at full tilt. The Hezbollah managed to eliminate Amal in the *dāhiya* (southern suburbs of Beirut), carrying Shiite-majority municipalities in Mount Lebanon and obtaining an overwhelming majority in Nabatieh. But it was defeated in Tyre, which remained a loyal constituency of Nabih Berri, and especially in Baalbek—a city affected by Subhī al-Tufaylī's failed uprising—where the Hezbollah also met with strong opposition from the Sunnis and Christians. In 2000, the legislative elections followed close upon the Israeli withdrawal from Southern Lebanon, and the "Party of God" reaped the benefits of that liberation by relying on a reconstituted alliance with Amal. Nevertheless, it did not manage to topple the candidates of the traditional elites and of the outliers, the Communist Party and the Syrian Social Nationalist Party, whose diminished ranks included a large proportion of Shiites.

Ideological and tactical concerns dictated the opposition's choice. In November 1992, Rafic Hariri became prime minister. From the Hezbollah's standpoint, his societal ideal, to make Lebanon the "Singapore of the Near East" by reasserting certain state prerogatives, was radically different from that of the "Resistance." Criticism focused less on the technical aspect of the measures (monetary stability, economic recovery through consumption, services, or industry) than on the overall vision. For the Hezbollah, choosing economic recovery meant accepting, in one way or another, the principle of a "Near Eastern market" expounded by Israeli president Shimon Peres after the Oslo Accords. An extremely wealthy businessman with interests in Saudi Arabia as well as the United States and France, Hariri was portrayed by his adversaries as the symbol of stateless liberalism. He privileged the reconstruction of the part of Beirut that had suffered the greatest damage during the war and, as a result, reinforced

the sense of inequity among those who did not live in the capital's historic neighborhoods. Waste was the focus of the accusations in *Dirty Hands,* a pamphlet by Najāh Wakīm written in
1998, which targeted the Horizon 2000 projects realized by the
Solidere Company. The company was controlled by Hariri and
was associated with a government agency, the Council for Development and Reconstruction. By the end of the decade, a quarter of the population was living under the poverty line, there were
long delays in the payment of government salaries and retire-
ment benefits, and the country was consuming beyond its means.
Georges Corm, both a judge and party to the affair (since he was
minister of the economy in Selim al-Hoss's government between
1998 and 2000), proved very critical on the matter.

Lebanon had lost the status it had enjoyed until the 1970s, that
of privileged financial intermediary between the liberal "Western
bloc" and the Arab world. Public debt rose from $2 billion in
1992 to $18 billion in 1999, then to $38 billion in 2004. The
debt was attributable, first, to the shifting of investments toward
the new El Dorados—the United Arab Emirates, Bahrein, Qatar,
Saudi Arabia, and even Egypt and Syria—and, second, to the lack
of will among political groups to strengthen the role of the state.
Nothing new came to light at the theoretical level to change that
reality nearly half a century after Mohammad Bāqir al-Sadr's
major work, whose intent was to find a specifically Muslim path
between liberalism and capitalism. The essays on poverty by
Majid Rahnema, who represented the old, disgraced order of the
shah's Iran, were ignored. And if the "Party of God" decried the
idea of making Lebanon an Arab Singapore or Hong Kong, it was
not only because of the malfeasance involved in its realization
but also because of the pacification it represented. Economic development was likely to undermine jihad, which was fostered by
conditions of scarcity. In practical terms, Shiites in both Iran and
Lebanon were as effective as anyone else at combining the market economy with a paternalism that guaranteed them the support of a clientele benefiting from their largesse. The "revolution

of the hungry" from the Baalbek-Hermel region, which remained one of the poorest in Lebanon, was an isolated case. Absence of development was not associated with a lack of means. Forms of luxury were sometimes justified on military grounds. That was the case, for example, for the 4x4s used to transport the mujahideen.

Social actors (the General Confederation of Lebanese Workers, the manufacturing unions, the unions of private school teachers, the League of Lebanese University Professors, the League of Secondary School Teachers, and the journalists' and magistrates' unions) were actively infiltrated. To obtain representative seats in the professional elections, the Hezbollah proved opportunistic, going so far as to ally itself with members of the Lebanese Forces, overlooking past relations established between that group and Israel, even though such relations were considered *the* uncrossable line. In 2000, during the legislative elections, the Amal-Hezbollah alliance won all twenty-three seats allotted to the South, without any easing of tensions. Amal's supporters accused the Hezbollah of ideological intransigence, while the Hezbollah's followers accused Amal of collusion with the Israelis, corruption at the highest echelons of the state and, via the Council of the South, politicking to achieve compromises. Basking in the role it had played in the liberation of a part of Lebanon, the Hezbollah took a clear lead over its objective ally.

VIETCONG ON THE LITANI

The Israeli policy of turning Lebanese public opinion and the Lebanese authorities against the Hezbollah by practicing violent punitive expeditions was a failure, as those responsible for it acknowledged. Nasrallah himself made reference to the Vietcong. In good times and bad, he repeated that every political action was subordinate to the struggle against the "Zionist entity." Such ought to be the state of mind of those who supported him: "The Hezbollah movement is a jihadist movement whose foremost objective is jihad against the Zionist enemy," and "every lucid

and sage political effort can and must decisively support that jihadist movement." In its speeches, official statements, and even
the cartoons it published on one of its websites,[2] the Hezbollah
sought to demonstrate that every concession the Arabs made
simply resulted in more humiliation and destruction. According
to Naʿīm Qāsim, "it is diplomacy that leads to lost causes and
continued occupation. It is diplomacy that has stolen our rights
in our region, has legalized Israel for sixty years, and has divided
Palestine. It is diplomacy that has made the Arab countries [slav-
ish followers] in their policy, not free and independent." Military
strategy targeted the Israeli forces established in Lebanon and
proved not only effective at the tactical level but politically beneficial: measured successes, capped by the Israeli withdrawal in
2000, pushed questions about the nature of the state to the background. At the same time, none of the Lebanese governments
managed to impel the international community to apply pressure
on Israel to apply UN resolutions, especially Resolution 425.
Lebanese leaders were thus restricted to the role of firefighters
and ambulance drivers for civilians fleeing the combat zones, and
the Lebanese army to the role of auxiliary to the Syrian army.

Intense diplomatic activity occurred after the Gulf War. Syria
and Lebanon agreed to participate in the negotiation process,
which was supposed to culminate in the resolution of conflicts in
the region. So too did Israel, under pressure from U.S. Secretary
of State James Baker. In accordance with the principle of "land
for peace," the United States sponsored a conference in Madrid
in October 1991. Although it was a failure, secret negotiations
between the Israelis and the Palestinians were conducted in Oslo
during the same period. They led to the accord signed by Arafat
and Yitzhak Rabin in Washington, D.C., in September 1993.
Jordan's recognition of Israel and the Wadi ʿAraba Treaty of
1994 marked a new phase. But two issues represented stumbling

2. www.hizbollah.tv (last consulted in May 2009. The site no longer
exists).

blocks: the creation of a viable Palestinian state with borders, since a capital (Jerusalem) would have to be shared and the "refugee" question resolved; and normalization between Israel and Syria. Members of the Hezbollah knew that the Syrians had undertaken several talks with the Israelis with the aim of reaching an accord based on the principle of "peace in exchange for the Golan Heights" (occupied since 1967). They were careful not to attack Damascus directly. Hence, when Naʿīm Qāsim mentioned the "September [1993] massacre," which left fourteen dead and some forty wounded following a demonstration in opposition to the Oslo Accords, only Lebanese leaders were targeted. The same was true for the incidents of March 1994 and July 1995. Part of the tension on the northern border of Israel can be attributed to the advances and retreats in the Syrian-Israeli negotiations. Syria knew that the Hezbollah supported Palestinian movements, which were slow to enter into Hafez al-Assad's good graces. Hamas opened an office in Damascus, but its leaders were sometimes tempted to transfer it to Tehran, where support seemed much more reliable.

By the end of the Lebanon War, the Hezbollah was engaging in clashes daily—sometimes several times a day—with Israeli troops and the SLA. Over the course of a decade, it had acquired the monopoly on fighting. A few rare negotiations took place through UNIFIL members or German mediators for the exchange of prisoners or of the mortal remains of soldiers. Such exchanges occurred in 1996 and 1998, and both times Israel agreed to pay the higher price. To limit the escalation of violence, which could always turn against them, the combatants in the "Party of God" generally avoided harming civilians, whether Lebanese or Israeli. But the Lebanese quietly demonstrated their opposition to Hezbollah initiatives, because they led to massive reprisals from Israel. For example, Hezbollah rescue workers were not always well received by the villagers after an Israeli bombing following a rocket launch. All the while, these same Lebanese were loudly voicing their support for "Resistance" against an "enemy" occupying part of their national territory, an enemy who did not hesitate to use munitions of depleted uranium and who disseminated antipersonnel mines. Public opinion was split, leaning now toward the media close to the government, now toward the Western (English- and French-language) media, and now toward the increasingly effective Hezbollah media. The Hezbollah's cameras filmed combat zones, noting any gain in terrain with a large number of flags, and observing any loss, material or human, on the enemy's part. The Lebanese ministers never took the initiative but managed crises as they could. They multiplied diplomatic efforts to obtain humanitarian support and provided aid to displaced persons, who on two occasions fled the southern part of the country by the tens of thousands.

Israel explicitly adopted the policy of the "iron fist." Any attack against its troops or territory was followed by a much more violent response, as a way of eliminating any inclination on the enemy's part to repeat it. That policy failed: not only did the attacks not end, they increased in intensity and effectiveness. Between 1982 and 2000, Israel lost nine hundred soldiers in Lebanon, with an average of twenty-five a year in the 1990s. In 1993, Operation Justice Rendered served as a response to a barrage of rockets launched over northern Israel, which was itself a reply to bombings. The Lebanese speak of the "Seven-Day War" (July 25–31) to characterize battles that took 132 lives, the most violent since 1990. Shimon Peres's warning was clear: "The Lebanese government must decide whether the Hezbollah represents it or not. If it represents it, Lebanon as a whole is in a state of war with Israel, and that means that the Hezbollah is seeking the destruction of the whole of Lebanon. The Lebanese government will have to cooperate with us to silence the Hezbollah and put an end to its activities." Despite the mass destruction of infrastructure, Israel failed to impel the Lebanese government to hobble the Hezbollah. An oral agreement prolonged the status quo ante, with a pledge not to bomb villages on either side of the border. Nasrallah rejected any coordination of his actions with the Lebanese government, seeing the proposal as a step toward "domestication," and he accused Israel of violating the oral agreement twenty times more often than did the Hezbollah.

The 1993 scenario played out again three years later. After an escalation in conflicts that extended beyond the "security zone," Katyusha rockets were sent over northern Israel, which replied by launching an operation baptized "Grapes of Wrath." Israel bombed highways, bridges, and power stations in addition to places where Hezbollah fighters were supposed to be hiding; they in turn continued to send rockets throughout the hostilities. State funerals commemorated about a hundred villagers, who died during the shelling of a UN base in Qana on April 18; Qana became a memorial that accused Israel of "genocide and terrorism." The UN General Assembly condemned Israel and demanded it immediately cease war operations. The next day, Shimon Peres and Warren Christopher in Jerusalem and Rafic Hariri and Hervé de Charrette in Beirut simultaneously announced a ceasefire. The April Accords of 1996 again sanctioned the defeat of Israel's military objectives and gave legitimacy to the Hezbollah's actions, even as they limited some of its modalities. The document, approved by the "Party of God," considerably increased the Hezbollah's diplomatic advantage, recognizing its right to continue "resistance" activities to liberate Lebanese territory. That right was recognized by France (which originated the idea of a supervisory mission) and by the United States, in addition to Lebanon, Syria, and Iran. The Lebanese government, for its part, won back part of the international credibility it had lost since 1975.

The conflict worsened as a series of events dashed the hopes that had surrounded the signing of the Oslo Accords and gave rise to increasingly divergent points of view between Israel and the United States on the one hand and the Arabs and the French on the other. In November 1995, a Jewish Israeli assassinated Prime Minister Yitzhak Rabin. In early 1996, at the end of an eight-month truce, Palestinian organizations rejected the peace process and committed two suicide attacks. Israel declared Syria politically and morally responsible for these actions and denounced the support Damascus was providing Hamas and the Islamic Jihad. A conference was held without Syria in Sharm el-Sheikh, Egypt, in February 1996. In opposition to the position of Egypt and Saudi Arabia, which France supported, the repressive option defended by Israel and the United States was adopted in the name of the exclusive fight against "terrorism," which was supposed to guarantee Israel's security and the defense of U.S. interests in their "zone of vital interest." The English-speaking nations' blockade on Iraq also increased, against the recommendation of the French, whose relations with Tel Aviv became more strained. Jacques Chirac, passing through Southern Lebanon on a tour of the Near East after he was elected president of France, called for the application of Resolution 425. The April Accords broadly adopted France's ideas, leading Nawaf Mūsawī, head of foreign relations for the "Party of God," to declare: "In 1996, a new era of French presence began in the region, thanks to the Hezbollah's resistance on the ground."

The Monitoring Committee (the United States, France, Syria, Lebanon, and Israel), responsible for examining actions and grievances, was required to operate with unanimous consent, which made its role difficult. It is crucial to note that, between 1996 and 2000, the cease-fire in no way prevented continued fighting. A polemic arose between Hariri and Nasrallah regarding the politicization of "resistance" and the de facto monopoly held by the Hezbollah in military matters. In addition, the party wanted to increase its control of aid to the refugees and put pressure on the government through street demonstrations. To quell these disagreements, the Hezbollah drew attention to periodic operations: for example, the ambush that thwarted an Israeli nocturnal operation around the village of Ansariye (1997), which proved that the mujahideen had informers in Israel; and the assassination of General Eretz Gerstein (February 2000). The conflict that led to the withdrawal of the Israelis and the SLA from

Jezzine and surrounding areas (May–June 1999) was an important episode in this regard. The subsequent interpretation proposed by the "Resistance" should not blind us to the fact that the residents at the time suffered from the fighting, and that Nadim Salem, the Greek Catholic MP of Jezzine, attempted to negotiate a solution during meetings held in Mar Roukoz. The government, which accepted the surrender of the SLA fighters, also had an implicit understanding with the Hezbollah, which continued its constant harassment in the occupied zone. There were likely some five hundred combatants, able to blend in with the population, who benefited from increasingly modern weapons provided by Iran via Syria, versus twenty-five hundred SLA members and fifteen hundred Israeli soldiers. Sheikh Nabil Kaouk, head of military operations, displayed military skills that were acknowledged by his enemies.

The South proved costly to Israel, which invested in the area's health sectors (the Marjayun Hospital) and in commerce. Lebanese workers crossed the border daily to earn their livelihood in Israel, and some even participated in its social security system. Part of the population was sympathetic to these programs, in both Christian and Shiite villages. Nevertheless, Ehud Barak, appointed Israel's prime minister after the 1999 legislative elections, was convinced that the situation could not continue. The SLA had lost half its members since 1990. Its aging commander, Antoine Lahad, was ill, and the assassination of Colonel Akl Hashim in January 2000 proved that its troops had been infiltrated by men devoted to the Hezbollah. When fears of repression arose, Nasrallah was reassuring: "Whether Muslims or Christians, most of the residents of the 'security zone' are an oppressed people . . . they are part of our family, and we are fighting for their freedom."[3] Barak then decided to resume negotiations in view of a rapprochement with the Syrians, who seemed to be the only ones capable of curbing the Hezbollah's autonomy. These

3. Remarks reported by Judith Harik.

failed after the Clinton-Assad meeting in Geneva in April 2000. In the weeks that followed, the prime minister of Israel decided to withdraw his country's troops from Southern Lebanon to honor his electoral promise. He attempted to negotiate a transitional period with the Lebanese government but was met with the argument that UN Security Council Resolutions 425 and 426 had to be strictly applied. He therefore made the decision unilaterally. The general staff of the SLA, with the exception of Lahad, was informed of Operation Twilight only after it was implemented, between May 22 and May 24. Six thousand Lebanese, most of them officers with their families, took refuge in Israel. Three years later, there were still two thousand of them, primarily in Haifa; the rest had returned to Lebanon or had emigrated to Europe or North America.[4]

The liberation of Southern Lebanon was accompanied by scenes of popular jubilation marked by the reuniting of families. Some episodes received wide attention, such as the unfurling of the Hezbollah's yellow flag over the ruins of Beaufort Castle. Khiam Prison, which had replaced al-Ansar camp in 1985, became a memorial bearing witness to the torture suffered by prisoners there (three thousand in fifteen years, including four hundred women) at the hands of the Israelis, and later, in 1995, of the SLA. The SLA leaders were convicted in absentia and sentenced to death or to life in prison. Despite Nasrallah's announcement, repeated many times, that he would "liquidate" the "collaborators," and despite a manifesto promising "the worst torments to the traitors," a different plan was adopted: no settling of accounts, no summary executions. The party, which alone controlled the territory, for the most part implemented the plan. Abuses were limited to burning down Lahad's house, destroying the statue of Haddad, dismantling the Voice of the South radio station, and profaning the graves of "collaborators" in Bint Jbeil.

4. A website justifies their action and commemorates their "martyrs": www.lebaneseinisrael.com/main.htm.

Credit for that restraint goes to Nasrallah. He took care not to alienate any part of the electorate on the eve of the legislative elections and to achieve a respectability that would mitigate the epithet "terrorist" attached to him. All the same, he criticized the clemency of the punishments meted out by the Lebanese justice system.

The Hezbollah portrayed that withdrawal as a military victory, even though there had been no final battle. That was primarily because the villagers spontaneously interceded en masse between the warring parties. The rare victims were attacked when they approached the Lebanese-Israeli border. But the myth of the Israeli army's invincibility was destroyed. Any withdrawal not associated with a negotiation could now be presented as a mark of weakness. The speeches of the Hezbollah's leaders—for example, Nasrallah's speech on May 26—provided ideological justification for military jihad and strategic justification for permanent guerrilla war conducted by trained men who blended in with the general population. Every new battle was presented as contributing to the "final" victory against Israel, whose demise appeared more imminent every day. Adopting an eschatological tone, these leaders declared that the existence of Israel was attributable only to its disproportionate power at a given moment and to betrayal, not to any intrinsic military weakness on Lebanon's part. The emphasis on the memory of the 1,276 "martyrs" who had contributed toward the advent of that day was intended to show that the language of force was the only appropriate one. 'Abd al-Ilāh Balqizīz immediately became the theorist of that strategy, a radical departure from that of Anwar al-Sadat in 1978: it was the first time the Tsahal had withdrawn from an occupied territory without receiving anything in exchange; force of conviction and of will had paid off. Three months later, after the failure of the Camp David Talks between Barak and Arafat, which Clinton had sponsored, the Second Intifada erupted from Jerusalem to Cisjordan and the Gaza as a whole.

The "Resistance" that the Hezbollah incarnated acquired a national dimension: the liberation of the South was the liberation of the fatherland. The condolences that Lebanese of all faiths expressed to Hassan Nasrallah on the occasion of his son Hādī's death in 1997 attested to the strong patriotic content of that message. According to Azani, on that day for the first time, Lebanese flags appeared at a ceremony alongside those of the Hezbollah. "Battalions of Lebanese resistance" also formed to unite Lebanese of all faiths. For a few months, these battalions participated in operations of moderate scope, so that, according to Naʿīm Qāsim, they would not be placed in danger unnecessarily. But by 2000, the Hezbollah was no longer taking the trouble to use the battalions as a symbol for the plural character of "national resistance," and the properly religious dimension continued to take precedence. Once the Blue Line was established on what would become the definitive border between Israel and Lebanon, areas of focus were identified to show that the Israeli "withdrawal" was not complete. According to Norton, that measure was taken after vigorous internal debates and consultation with Ali Khamenei, "who gave his blessing to continue the resistance, especially in the Israeli-Palestinian theater."[5] It was clear to the militants of the "Party of God" that the decision to end the fight against the "enemy" lay solely with the *walī al-faqīh*: "By virtue of his knowledge of religious science, the *faqīh* issues a fatwa on the necessity of jihad if certain conditions arise, and the authorization of reconciliation if other conditions arise . . . and if the *marjaʿ al-taqlīd* opposes the assessment on that subject, his opinion is not authoritative in the presence of the *walī al-faqīh*."[6]

President Emile Lahoud provided national support for the option of continuing the battle, pointing to the Shebaa farms. That

5. Augustus Richard Norton, *Hezbollah,* 5th ed. (Princeton, N.J.: Princeton University Press, 2009), p. 90.
6. *Wilāyat al-faqīh fī ʿassr,* pp. 41–42.

territory, rich in water and occupied by Israel since 1967, did not fall under Resolutions 425 and 426 but rather under Resolution 350. It was the object of a 1973 disengagement accord between Israel and Syria that was never implemented. After 2000, Syria declared it was Lebanese territory, while leaving the definitive borderline between the nations of Syria and Lebanon hazy. Other elements came to be added to that *casus belli,* including the essential question of water, focused on the source of the Wazzani River, and the villages of Ghajar and Nakheili. That led Hassan Nasrallah to say, during the visit by UN Secretary General Kofi Annan: "We are not going to wait indefinitely for international efforts to put an end to these violations. As we have done in the past, we will liberate even the smallest parcel of our territory." Among the arguments put forward were the violations of Lebanese airspace by Israeli aircraft and the prisoners being detained in the jails of the "Zionist entity." The new phase that had begun would show the altogether relative nature of each of those references.

THE COUNTERSOCIETY OF "RESISTANCE"

The concept of "countersociety," which Waddah Sharara borrowed from Annie Kriegel to characterize the Hezbollah's social project, is pertinent here. But the analogy is worth extending beyond the Communist model to that of French Catholicism at the turn of the twentieth century. It is apt at both the theoretical level—French Catholicism is an all-encompassing form by virtue of its refusal to compromise with what is not Catholic—and at the practical level: it is a set of effective institutions in the sectors of health, education and para-education, and the media. Religious orders, forced into exile between 1901 and 1914 by the anticlerical measures of republican governments, brought that concept with them to the Near and Middle East. The Hezbollah combined that framework with organizational models proper to the Iranian revolution, established in Lebanon with the aid of advisers. In the name of jihad, and in view of the advent of a Muslim society that alone would be capable of providing "justice" for all, the Hezbollah constituted a centralized social body within a state with a pronounced liberal bent that had imploded. But although that state was undermined by corruption and excessive debt, it was not totally absent, and cooperation existed between Hezbollah organizations and the Ministries of Health, Social Affairs, and Labor, as well as the Council of Development and the Council of the South. The Hezbollah thus specifically continued initiatives that had been taken within the Shiite community before the organization was founded. Mohammad Hussein Fadlallah, for example, built a network of social welfare, health, and education centers linked to one another through the Jam'iyyat al-mabarrāt al-khayriyya (Association of Benevolent Societies, 1978) and the Maktab al-khidmāt al-ijtimā'iyya (Bureau of Social Services, 1983). That network is the most important in the *dāhiya,* the southern suburbs of Beirut. Amal deployed its own network, and, according to Myriam Catusse and Joseph Alagha, these three groups, not counting the traditional notables or feudal chieftains, have networks that complement one another more than they compete.

The "Party of God" embraced an image of integrity and care for the most destitute, whereas their interlocutors—with the exception of Fadlallah—were presented as agents willing to compromise. The reality is more complex, but it is very difficult to grasp, since no researcher has access to the expenditures and receipts of the party, which may have as many as five thousand salaried workers in addition to its "combatants." The tuition at certain institutions of learning is comparable to that of their counterparts in other communities, which undercuts the principle that priority be given to the "disinherited." The movement's accounts are not made public. A veil of modesty is thrown over Iran's direct aid via the *bonyad* (clerical foundations), which Norton estimates at $100 million a year. The sums paid by sympathizers from the Lebanese diaspora are no better known than those collected through the payment of various religious taxes *(zakāt, sadaqāt, khums),* gifts collected during the Ashura celebrations, promotional receipts from different organizations affiliated with the Hezbollah, or the yield from investments abroad, including in the United States. The Hezbollah brushes aside these matters—worthy of observation and reflection—in favor of promoting the real effectiveness of its organizations, articulated around a network of committees and mosques, and the material progress allowed by their actions. It also regularly reminds people of the cause for which they were established.

The Hezbollah complex began in 1982 with al-Shahīd and al-Jarīh, which were intended to provide financial aid to hundreds of families of "martyrs" and the "wounded." The leaders of al-Shahīd quickly came to manage free clinics and two hospitals, as well as an institute for spreading the culture of martyrdom. They focus on health, politics, and education and participate in the social advance of the Shiite community within the context of war. Alongside them, Jihād al-Binā' is much more than a public works project devoted to the material well-being of a community long neglected by state services. That foundation has engaged in activities since 1985, and it took in hand the reconstruction of many buildings that had collapsed during the war, the repair of flood damage, the treatment of household waste, the transport of potable water, the installation of electricity (power stations and lines), and roadwork. It procures low-cost housing for people whose homes have been destroyed by bombs. In 2001 the Hezbollah still provided most of the potable water to the residents of the *dāhiya.* Outside the very urbanized coastal zones, it is also involved in agricultural development: loans, transfers, or gifts of tractors—all from Iran; the establishment of cooperatives; the development of a credit system; the provision of fertilizer; and the construction of training centers. But it also

applies pressure to occupy uncultivated lands left behind by displaced Lebanese and those of the diaspora. In the rural areas, it
has opened hospitals and medical centers, both permanent and
mobile, thus providing infrastructure in a territory where these
services were often nonexistent.

The religious communities grant their keenest attention to the
education sector and do not restrict their actions to gifts in kind
(books and supplies) and scholarships. The largest education
network remains that of the Catholic institutions, with 360
establishments. The Hezbollah's investment, the object of an excellent study by Catherine Le Thomas, is notable for its speed
and dynamism. Its central organization is the Ta'bi'a tarbawiyya
(Mobilization for Education), headed by Hajj Yūsuf Mer'ī, which
coordinates institutions that the Hezbollah founded or that it
runs, having co-opted existing units: *hawza 'ilmiyya* (religious
schools), *husayniyyāt* (places of worship), and the Association
for Learning and Education, headed by Mustafa Kassir, which
oversees fifteen al-Mahdī schools[7] (including the Imam Husayn
School, under the control of the Iranian Ismā'īl Khalīq until
1997). Linked to these is a second circle of institutions, that of
Imdād, which comprises private schools with a modern curriculum, some of them supervised or run directly by party cadres,
such as Hussein Hajj Hassan or Mohammad Yazbak. A third
circle is composed of elements that are autonomous but conso-
nant with the Hezbollah. The recruitment of teachers for the first
and second circles follows a dual set of criteria, which are not
always strictly applied: professional qualifications and a piety
consistent with the Hezbollah's reading of Shiism. Graduates of
these schools, it seems, usually go on to the Lebanese University,
Beirut Arab University, or the Islamic University of Lebanon.
Since 1994, the students have been supported by the Islamic

7. An educational complex was under al-Shahīd's jurisdiction before being taken over by Mobilization for Education in 2003.

Center for Orientation and Higher Education, which provides
them with grants and scholarships. In Lebanese higher education, which includes more than sixty institutions for barely 4.5
million residents, the Hezbollah therefore does not have a system
of its own. As Bruno Lefort has shown, it influences them from
further up the line, through the student branch of the Committee
of Higher Education, which is in charge of organizing forums
and supervising clubs or cultural events.

At the same time, the Center for Islamic Documentation and
Research has the mission of "Islamizing" curricula and of criti-
cizing "Western thought." The scope of the issues involved in
teaching a body of knowledge common to all Lebanese can be
understood, in particular, through the difficulties that historians
encountered in trying to produce a single textbook, as stipulated
by the Taif Agreement. While waiting for the supervising authorities to agree on that text,[8] the schools associated with the
Hezbollah use the *Nahnu wa-l-tārīkh* (History and Us) textbook
series provided by the Islamic Religious Education Association.
There is some ambiguity surrounding the term "history," since
one chapter is devoted to Adam and Eve. Antiquity holds a lesser
place in it than in other collections. Relations between Muslims
and the rest of the world, particularly with Jews and Christians,
are presented in terms of a conflict spanning many centuries, with
the "Crusades" serving as the frame of reference. Any conquest
in the name of Islam appears as a "liberation" or an "opening,"
whereas any "Muslim land" where an authority embracing Islam
no longer survives is an "occupied" country. The establishment
of Shiite Islam in Jabal 'Amil was a result of Husayn's death
and the demise of the Umayyad regime, which is called unrighteous. The fatwa attributed to Ibn Taymiyyah, which permitted

8. The textbook was published in the mid-2000s but was immediately
withdrawn from circulation. See Betty Sleiman, "Les processus de socialisation politique à travers l'enseignement de l'histoire au Liban," graduate
thesis for the Institut d'Études Politiques, Aix-en-Provence, under the directorship of Élisabeth Picard, thesis defense set for 2010.

"the spilling of blood of the Kesrewan Shiites," is an occasion
to point out the difficulties endured under the Mamluks. The
textbooks point an accusing finger at the Catholic religious communities of Europe. The rivalry between the Persian and Ottoman
empires serves as an opportunity to vaunt the superiority of the
Safavids. "Lebanon" is designated by name well before its founding as a nation, and, in various ways, the Shiite community turns
out to be the "root stock" there, having welcomed or endured
the successive arrivals of other faiths. The American, French,
and Russian revolutions take up considerable space and are used
to denounce the injustice of the old orders. Slavery is viewed
exclusively from the angle of the slave trade organized by Europe: nothing is said about slaveholding practices within the
Arab and Muslim world. And, finally, Israel becomes the ulti-
mate incarnation of a Western imperialism that must be ceaselessly combated.

The "'holistic' ambience" (Catherine Le Thomas) created by
Hezbollah institutions is favored by the control of space but also
of time. Words and gestures are charged with allusions specific
to the religious community and, increasingly, to the history of
the Hezbollah itself. No emphasis is placed on the structure
of the school day, where adjustments are sometimes made to the
time set aside for daily prayers; the debate, dating to the early
2000s, about replacing the Sunday day of rest with Friday has
been dropped. Priority is instead granted to the annual calendar,
with an emphasis on specifically Shiite rites surrounding the celebration of births (those of Muhammad, Imam al-Mahdī, and
Sayyida Zahrā), and above all, the ten days devoted to Ashura.
Sabrina Mervin recalls the prescription made by the "guide"
Khamenei, whose 1994 fatwa prohibited the *tatbīr* rite—which
resulted in bleeding caused by flagellation—and other mor-
tification practices. She adds that in 1999 the Hezbollah held a
congress to purify the "style" of *majlis* (assemblies) at the time of
Ashura and then established a permanent bureau "charged with
overseeing the content of the sessions, especially to expurgate

what are judged to be legendary [*ustūra*] accounts."[9] Specific liturgies mark the stages of life. The *taklīf*, for example, corresponds to the moment when nine-year-old girls take the veil. Commemorations of politico-religious events have grown exponentially: al-Quds (Jerusalem) Days, Disinherited of the Earth Days, Qana Massacre (1996) Days, Martyrdom of Hādī Nasrallah (1997) Days, Liberation (2000) Days, and Second Intifada (2000) Days. Remembrance is marked by a valorization of sites and the organization of "Resistance" tourism: the plan for a multimedia space in the *dāhiya*, a museum inside Khiam Prison (destroyed in 2006), a permanent exhibit near the ancient site of Baalbek, and panels on Beaufort Castle recalling the taking of that strategic stronghold.

It was during the 1990s that the Hezbollah became an impressive media force. Its leaders, such as 'Abbās Mūsawī, were aware early on of what was at stake, given the investment of the Lebanese Forces in that field of action. Hezbollah leaders enjoyed Iranian support from Kamal Kharazi. The Islamic political weekly *al-'Ahd (The Oath)* was founded in June 1984. Its circulation, five thousand according to internal sources, is said to have tripled during the 1990s. It altered its format in 2001 and changed its name to *al-Intiqād (The Critique)*. For party cadres, a theoretical review, *Baqiyyat Allāh (What Remains near God)* has existed since 1991. In 1988, alongside the Voice of the Disinherited and the Voice of Islam, Radio al-Nūr became the Hezbollah's foremost audio medium: in addition to news bulletins, it broadcasts analyses, sermons, and hymns, including those of al-Wilāya group, created in 1985.[10] In the midst of the conflict between Amal and the Hezbollah, the aim of that station was to "combat the preachers of discord and the enemies of humanity

9. Sabrina Mervin, "La religion du Hezbollah," in *Le Hezbollah: État des lieux*, ed. Sabrina Mervin (Arles: Sindbad/Actes Sud, 2008), p. 197.

10. That group, linked to the Hezbollah, has a website: http://welaya-hlb.com.

and Islam." Eleven years later, those in charge of al-Nūr obtained a license from the Lebanese state, created a website, and soon joined the Arab States Broadcasting Union, at whose festivals and competitions they garnered several awards.[11] Al-Manār TV station was launched in June 1991, during the Madrid Conference. In 1994, the Public Information Center (Wahdat al-iʿlām al-markazī) coordinated all communication activities, and three years later the Hezbollah became the majority shareholder (55 percent) of Lebanese Communication Group, which merged al-Manār and al-Nūr. Al-Manār Satellite TV, launched in 2000, benefited from its coverage of extraordinary events for Arabic-speaking viewers: the battles preceding the Israeli withdrawal from Southern Lebanon and those of the Second Intifada. Nevertheless, according to a U.S. investigation reported by Norton, in the mid-2000s al-Manār was only the sixth most-watched Arabic station, far behind al-Jazīra and al-ʿArabiyya.

The Hezbollah's effort to provide an all-encompassing system, though very effective, has its limits. The two hours weekly devoted to religious education in the schools is equivalent to that of other institutions; the textbook *Al-islām risālatunā (Islam Is Our Message)* does not reflect the interpretation of Shiism specific to the Hezbollah; and Koran clubs as well as recitation contests are common in the Sunni world as well. The exaltation of "martyrdom," based on the link between the death of Husayn at the hands of Yazīd and the death of the mujahideen at the hands of the Israelis—in forms as diverse as plays, video clips, testaments, and eulogies—though of great internal effectiveness, has been met with uneasiness in Sunni circles. The "Party of God" leaders are aware of the problem, and the religious programs on Satellite al-Manār (on average, three hours of daily broadcasts) have been modified so that a general Muslim audience will not be

11. In 2005, al-Nūr employed more than a hundred people, and its network covered Lebanon, the Occupied Palestinian Territories, Israel, and a part of Jordan and Cyprus.

disturbed by overly pronounced Shiite references. In the fields of education and culture, offerings based exclusively on revolutionary Shiism and on a nationalism of resistance to a single enemy have a mobilizing effect but have proved inadequate. It has therefore been necessary to compromise with exogenous cultural elements. Since 1994, the programmers of al-Manār and al-Nūr have opened their doors to sports, entertainment, fictional programs, and domestic how-to shows. Singing is taught in small kindergarten groups, and profane spectacles (puppet shows, for example) are also held. The practice of sports, including swimming, and mastery of cutting-edge technologies are encouraged at the primary and secondary levels. The line between interest in a subject for its own sake and training for war is undoubtedly difficult for consumers to grasp. The case of al-Mahdī scouts, created in 1985 and counting more than forty thousand members, is telling. The scouting movement, engaged in questions of health, the sciences, and the environment, is also a means to identify those most likely to assume military-related duties, as the leftist Egyptian daily *Rose al-Youssef* demonstrated in an article published in August 2006. March-pasts with a display of arms have certainly disappeared, and signs of allegiance to Khomeini are more discreet, as are the summer camp "drill instructors"; but the pledge to "liberate al-Quds" and obedience to God in line with the *wilāyat al-faqīh* remain.

Within a decade, the Hezbollah acquired in Lebanese society something more than respectability: a reputation synonymous with pride. That pride served as a model for the Palestinians who rejected the path Yasser Arafat had taken. The stones thrown at Prime Minister Lionel Jospin of France by students of Birzeit University, who criticized him for having dared to link the Hezbollah's activity to "terrorism," are evidence of that. Yet the legacy of the 1980s is not the only one at issue. The Hezbollah is accused of being involved in actions extending beyond the borders of Lebanon. Some are acknowledged, such as active support

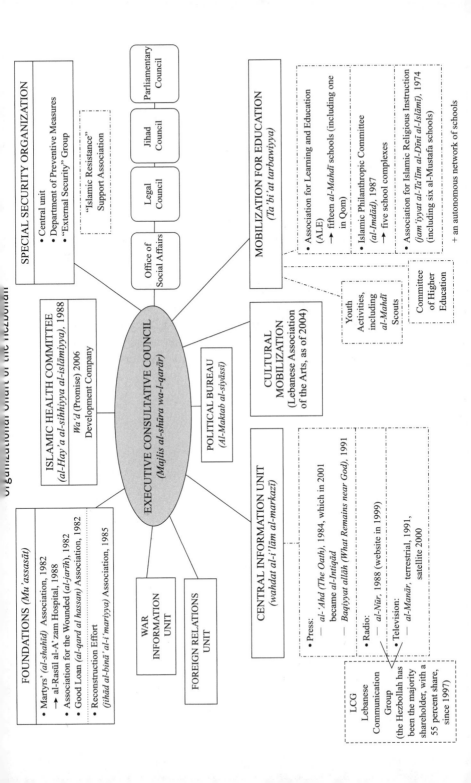

Organizational Chart of the Hezbollah

SPECIAL SECURITY ORGANIZATION
- Central unit
- Department of Preventive Measures
- "External Security" Group

"Islamic Resistance" Support Association

Parliamentary Council | Jihad Council | Legal Council | Office of Social Affairs

ISLAMIC HEALTH COMMITTEE
(al-Hay'a al-sihhiyya al-islāmiyya), 1988

Wa'd (Promise) 2006 Development Company

FOUNDATIONS (Mu'assasāt)
- Martyrs' (al-shahīd) Association, 1982
  → al-Rasūl al-A'zam Hospital, 1988
- Association for the Wounded (al-jarīh), 1982
- Good Loan (al-qard al hassan) Association, 1982
- Reconstruction Effort
  (jihād al-binā' al-i'martiyya) Association, 1985

EXECUTIVE CONSULTATIVE COUNCIL
(Majlis al-shūra wa-l-qarār)

WAR INFORMATION UNIT

FOREIGN RELATIONS UNIT

CENTRAL INFORMATION UNIT
(wahdat al-i'lām al-markazī)
- Press:
  — al-'Ahd (The Oath), 1984, which in 2001 became al-Intiqād
  — Baqiyyat allāh (What Remains near God), 1991
- Radio:
  — al-Nūr, 1988 (website in 1999)
- Television:
  — al-Manār, terrestrial, 1991, satellite 2000

LCG Lebanese Communication Group (the Hezbollah has been the majority shareholder, with a 55 percent share, since 1997)

POLITICAL BUREAU
(Al-Maktab al-siyāssī)

CULTURAL MOBILIZATION
(Lebanese Association of the Arts, as of 2004)

Youth Activities, including al-Mahdī Scouts

Committee of Higher Education

MOBILIZATION FOR EDUCATION
(Ta'bi'at tarbawiyya)
- Association for Learning and Education (ALE)
  → fifteen al-Mahdī schools (including one in Qom)
- Islamic Philanthropic Committee (al-Imdād), 1987
  → five school complexes
- Association for Islamic Religious Instruction (jam'iyyat al-Ta'līm al-Dīnī al-Islāmī), 1974 (including six al-Mustafa schools)
  + an autonomous network of schools

for Hamas and the Islamic Jihad. Others are concealed. Even though Mughniyah's name has been mentioned, the Hezbollah denies being behind the attack on the Israeli embassy in Buenos Aires (1992) and on a Jewish community center in the Argentine capital in 1994. It also denies any involvement in an anti-American attack in Saudi Arabia (1998). In any event, these accusations carried little weight in Arab public opinion at the turn of the 2000s. The Hezbollah, strengthened in Lebanon by the Israeli withdrawal, enjoyed a wider margin for maneuvering vis-à-vis Damascus. Bashar al-Assad had just succeeded his father, Hafez; and, to impose his authority in that high-responsibility position—to which he was not destined until his elder brother's fatal automobile accident—he had to face down his uncle as well as the Sunni opposition. That act of subjugation has not failed to have repercussions in Lebanon, where part of the Sunni community finds the Syrian crackdown increasingly difficult to bear.

A Model of Recovered Pride,
a Contested National Party

When the fervor associated with the liberation of the South subsided, the situation became more strained. In September 2000, in an action that elicited hopes in some quarters and indignation in others, the Assembly of Maronite Bishops publicly raised the question of the Syrian presence in Lebanon. For the Hezbollah, that was intolerable. On one hand, Israel continued to occupy the Shebaa farms as well as the Kfarshouba Hills; on the other, Syria did not maintain an occupation force in Lebanon but was a friendly power that had placed thirty thousand soldiers at the country's disposal to avert any risk of a new civil conflict. The Hezbollah embraced the same asymmetrical position regarding Lebanese prisoners and the missing: there were six hundred cases in Syria, half that number in Israel, yet the party's military-diplomatic discourse and actions took only those in Israel into account. The persistence of a national agreement vis-à-vis the sole "enemy" remained de rigueur. Emile Lahoud, head of state beginning in 1998, was an officer close to the Syrians who participated in the ouster of General Aoun in 1990. From his place of exile in France, Aoun promoted the rise of the future Free Patriotic Movement (FPM) and took satisfaction in the adoption of the Syrian Act, which attested to a shift—without immediate effect—of U.S. policy in the Middle East. The risk of a schism within Lebanon over the "Resistance" was limited only so long as the opposition was not joined by major actors from Sunni and Druze circles. The first signs of such a development were perceptible in 2000, and the fracture came about soon after February 14, 2005, the date of Rafic Hariri's assassination. From then on, two poles openly faced off: one centered on the Hezbollah, the other on the Future Movement backed by the Druze leader Jumblatt, with the Christians dispersed between the two. The fact that no official festivities were held in May 2006 to commemorate the liberation of the southern part of the country was one sign of that rift within the nation.

The United States' almost unconditional support of Israel, whose leaders never adopted the means to promote the creation of a viable Palestinian state, served the Hezbollah's cause. The failure of the Camp David negotiations between Arafat and Barak, overseen by President Bill Clinton in summer 2000, reinforced that orientation. At that time, the Israeli prime minister broke the taboo on negotiating the status of the old city of Jerusalem. For the head of the Palestinian Authority, however, the accord had to entail at minimum the complete and total recognition of sovereignty over the Esplanade of the Mosques. Al-Aqsa Intifada erupted two months later, and the negotiations, which resumed in Taba in January 2001, were without effect. That allowed Hamas's rise to power and Ariel Sharon's victory in the Israeli legislative elections in February. In the meantime, George W. Bush was elected president of the United States, and he did not intend to grant priority to the Middle Eastern scene. The attacks of September 11, 2001, led not to a diplomatic about-face but to a further step toward a polarized representation of geopolitics: friends versus enemies. Within the context of war, "terrorism" became Washington's principal interpretive grid. The United States targeted the nations comprising the "Axis of Evil," which included Iraq and Iran. On September 16, 2001, Secretary of State Colin Powell declared: "The Hezbollah is a threat to the region, just as al-Qaida is a threat to the world."[1] The American Israel Public Affairs Committee applied pressure to have the Hezbollah placed on the Department of State's list of foreign terrorist organizations. At the time of the intervention in Afghanistan in October 2001, however, Iran kept a low profile, since its government was not displeased to be rid of the neighboring Taliban regime. At the same time, contacts between the United States and the Hezbollah—though denied by the Bush administration—may have been established through Kofi Annan and European Union envoys to urge the "Party of God" to renounce its military branch. Its refusal, linked to the Israeli leaders' positions, left the participants within the register of violence, which reached its peak in 2006.

THE LOSS OF A MONOPOLY ON STREET DEMONSTRATIONS, THE GAIN OF A POLITICAL ALLY

Within a decade, the Hezbollah had managed to put its stamp on street demonstrations. The only exception to its near monopoly on mass mobilizations was the crowd that gathered during Pope John Paul II's visit in 1997. In political matters, by contrast, the few opposition demonstrations held by Aounists were quashed, and some of their followers imprisoned. The "Party of God" owed its success to three factors: its organizational skills, the obligingness of the Syrian army, and the Hezbollah's rallying cries before 2000. That popularity did not translate into a corresponding number of seats in parliament because of the electoral system, anxieties relating to the representation of a state vulnerable to manipulation by Iran, and the political power of Rafic Hariri, head of the Future Movement. After his electoral victory in 2000, that businessman was once again named prime minister.

1. Colin Powell, "CNN Interview on Anti-Terrorism Campaign," American Rhetoric Online Speech Bank, n.p., http://www.americanrhetoric.com /speeches/colinpowellcnn91601.htm.

Twenty-two MPs opposed his appointment, including nine in the Hezbollah. The dissension was obvious. In February 2001, Hariri conducted a government delegation to Paris to reassure partners and potential supporters about Lebanon's restored stability. But the assurance that Lebanon would give Israel no pretext for disrupting that stability was undercut by the Hezbollah: it launched an operation, which led to Israeli reprisals. Hariri, whose relationship with Lahoud was in a sorry state, planned to resign, but he reversed that decision after going to Damascus and Anjar. Bashar al-Assad and Ghazi Kanaan still held all the cards, as Ariel Sharon, who had just prevailed in the Israeli legislative elections, was aware. Sharon therefore decided to attack the Syrian military bases in Lebanon but did not manage to undermine his enemies' determination.

The Hezbollah continued to conduct periodic operations in the disputed zones of Shebaa and Ghajar and to launch rockets when the Israeli response was considered disproportionate. In January 2004, the "Resistance" obtained a further symbolic victory during an exchange of prisoners and mortal remains: Israel released twenty-three Lebanese and four hundred Palestinians in exchange for the bodies of three soldiers and a lieutenant colonel captured in Beirut. The event was well timed within a context that had become less favorable for the "Party of God." The reasons that Mohammad Raad* and Mohammad Fneish were obliged to resign from the Consultative Council in 2001 have not been clarified (there is now only one noncleric on the council: Khalil Hajj Hassan). The polemic with Nayif Krayem, who was forced to resign his post as director of al-Manār because of a suspected allegiance to Fadlallah, left its mark. At the same moment, Gibran Tueni, editor of the major daily *al-Nahār*, was formulating increasingly vigorous criticisms against the discourse of the "Resistance." Finally, skirmishes between the Hezbollah and partisans of Amal occurred during the Ashura celebrations in 2002 and 2003, and al-Tufaylī reappeared on the scene.

These factors need to be put in perspective. The Hezbollah's predominance over Amal was still apparent during the municipal elections of 2004: in the territory as a whole, the proportion of seats obtained in local governments was 2 to 1 in favor of the Hezbollah. Although increasingly restrained, the majority of the population's support for the "Resistance" against Westerners was real. Rafic Hariri himself defended the Hezbollah when Washington asked him to freeze its accounts, and Monsignor Nasrallah Boutros Sfeir* hailed it as a movement working for the country's liberation. Nevertheless, the Maronite patriarch also encouraged a "national" line that regularly assembled MPs in Qornet Chehwān, between Beirut and Jounieh. The Hezbollah tried to circumscribe the risk. At a meeting held at a ski resort in the Lebanese Mountains in late August 2001, Nawaf Mūsawī and Mohammad Kamati met with members of the Islamic-Christian National Dialogue Committee and representatives of the Qornet Chehwān Union.

Signs of a shift were visible in a gesture of reconciliation between the Druze and the Maronites: during the summer of 2001, Walid Jumblatt received Patriarch Sfeir in Chouf. The past was not forgotten, and the material questions were far from settled—the amounts the inhabitants of Chouf received from Jumblatt to rebuild their homes seemed laughable—but a step had been taken. At the political level, foundations were laid for a possible joint opposition to the control exercised by Damascus. Distrust, increasingly apparent, marked relations between the Syrians on one side and Harari's Future Movement and its allies, particularly Jumblatt's PSP, on the other. The increase in tensions was perceptible in August 2004, when Bashar al-Assad let Hariri know that any interference with the three-year extension of Lahoud's presidential term would be viewed as opposition to Syria. The response came from France and the United States, which pushed through UN Security Council Resolution 1559. That text defended Lebanon's independence and called for disarming the militias and withdrawing "all the remaining foreign forces." The genesis of the resolution is unknown, but speculations about the friendship between Hariri and Chirac have circulated. In any event, the Hezbollah leaders declared that the resolution did not apply to them, since they represented a "force of resistance" and not a "militia"; as for the Syrians, they did not consider themselves "remaining foreign forces." The day after the UN resolution was adopted, the Lebanese parliament voted to extend Emile Lahoud's presidential term, and he named Omar Karami to form a new government.

Among the twenty-nine MPs voting against the extension was the Druze Marwan Hamadeh, the victim of a failed assassination attempt in October. Walid Jumblatt then decided to defy the Syrians, once again raising the issue of the assassination of his father, Kamal Jumblatt. He also strengthened his contacts with France. The Hezbollah took offense at these publicly declared positions, and the electoral campaign promised to be spirited, with no way to envision the outcome. But on February 14, 2005, Rafic Hariri and MP Bassel Fleihane were assassinated. A suspect was arrested the same day, but the machinations behind the attack were all too obvious. The Karami government's investigation bogged down, and the funeral was the occasion for a large gathering on Martyrs' Square. Day after day, Lebanese people, at first only a scattering, then in increasingly large numbers, shouted "Liberty, Sovereignty, Independence," demanding the truth about the attack and about the departure of members of the government. The demonstrators did not spare the Syrian regime, using a slogan that played on the president's name—"Assad fi Lubnan, Arnab fi-l Jūlān" (lion in Lebanon, rabbit in Golan)—to condemn the instrumentalization of Lebanon in the Syria-Israel showdown. On March 8, to shouts of "Labbayka ya Nasrallah" (at your service, Nasrallah), the Hezbollah and its allies Amal and the Syrian Social Nationalist Party (SSNP) responded with a huge counterdemonstration aimed at reminding people who was in control of the streets. Hassan Nasrallah invited Bush and Chirac to observe that, in addition to those on Martyrs' Square protesting the Syrian forces in Lebanon, there were Lebanese protesters on Riyadh al-Solh Square, who defended that presence. But on March 14, Martyrs' Square, where students had chosen to set up camp, was invaded by a flood of people and rebaptized "Freedom Square" for the occasion. Among the participants, Bahia Hariri, sister of the assassinated prime minister, met with unreserved approval from the crowd. The rallying cry of the Christian Right, defended by Pierre Gemayel thirty years earlier, was appropriated by the majority: "Lubnān awwālan" (Lebanon first).

It was an astonishing event: the "Cedar Revolution" was no longer just a half-hearted slogan for its promoters, Samir Frangieh* among them. Syria banned Lebanese newspapers from appearing in that country the next day. Omar Karami resigned, throwing in the towel even before he had formed a second government. The movement was democratic and peaceful, calling for change without resorting to force. It belonged to the same context as Egypt's Kefaya (Enough) Movement. The disillusionment was on a par with the hopes. Bombs exploded in majority-Christian neighborhoods, more to incite disorder and anxiety than to kill. A month later, under Franco-American pressure, an international inquiry into the assassination of the prime minister opened, and Syrian troops left most of Lebanese territory. Modest demonstrations of approval accompanied the dismantling of Syrian bases near Batroun and the removal of a poster of Bashar al-Assad on Corniche Beirut. Only the Hezbollah hailed the "accomplishment" of the Syrians, who were said to have become the "center of national life" in Lebanon. On April 19, during his going-away ceremony, Nasrallah offered a Kalashnikov to Rustom Ghazali, Ghazi Kanaan's successor as Syrian head of intelligence in Anjar as of 2003. In the months following the forced withdrawal of its soldiers, Syria retaliated with economic sanctions, without meeting with disapproval from the Hezbollah. Damascus sought to cut off Lebanon by blocking its trucks on the borders, knowing there was no outlet on the Israel side. The *mukhābarāts* (information services) remained active among Syria's allies, as did the members of the major powers' secret services. Farouk al-Sharaa would later declare: "The conflict will continue in Lebanon so long as some [Lebanese] continue to pursue international oversight."

General Aoun returned to Lebanon on May 7 and was greeted by a crowd that included members of all the religious communities. Through the voice of Jumblatt, a powerful adversary of Aoun's in 1988, the pro-sovereignty March 14 camp invited the former head of state not to disregard what his compatriots had endured during his exile and not to attempt to co-opt a popular movement. The pro-Syrian March 8 camp kept a low profile. Aoun's return could not have been negotiated without the Lebanese and Syrian authorities. His first gestures were intended as signs of reconciliation. The visit he made to Samir Geagea in prison did not have the same political weight as his meeting with President Lahoud, which preceded his contacts with Omar Karami and Suleiman Frangieh Jr.* The gesture of the "unifier" was not to the taste of the March 14 leaders, and that new factor changed the entire game plan during the May–June legislative elections. The short electoral campaign began an interlude during which confessionalist reflexes once more came into play. A temporary consensus took shape between the Future Movement, the PSP, and the Amal-Hezbollah coalition. These parties and their allies extricated themselves from a difficult situation in the face of Michel Aoun's Free Patriotic Movement, which, while attracting 70 percent of Christian votes, obtained only 21 of the 128 seats in parliament, though it had hoped for at least two-thirds of the 64 seats reserved for Christians. During the discussions preliminary to organizing a national unity government, Aoun demanded in vain a correction to his parliamentary representation through a sufficient number of high-ranking ministerial posts. He placed himself in opposition to the political class as a whole, the Hezbollah included. The "Party of God" agreed to send two of its members to Fouad Siniora's government, without making the rejection of any negotiation with the "enemy" a preliminary condition.

For six months, a wave of assassinations struck the leaders of the March 14 alliance (Samir Kassir, Gibran Tueni) and members of the political Left (Georges Hāwī), producing a climate of fear. What these men had in common was that they had all criticized the Syrian occupier and its Lebanese allies, including the Hezbollah. Just before the beginning of summer, Samir Geagea was released, having been granted amnesty along with members of a radical Sunni group that had been behind the 1999 barracks massacre of Lebanese soldiers. The head of the Lebanese Forces joined the March 14 camp, which was coping with the country's economic and political troubles. That led to a first resurgence of the popular wave that had brought that camp to power. The international investigation continued: four Lebanese security high officials, including the powerful general Jamil al-Sayyid, were arrested.[2] The Hezbollah declared Israel responsible for the attack on Hariri, but its leaders believed that Lebanon had to maintain full control over the proceedings, given the danger of a foreign takeover. Their position led to an acute institutional crisis. Siniora attempted to circumscribe it by promising never to call the military branch of the Hezbollah a "militia."

A national dialogue committee was established on the principle of unanimous resolutions. The discussions were long and arduous. They focused on regulating relations with Syria by exchanging ambassadors and drawing borders, and on disarming the Palestinian militias. Many implicit or unspoken views undermined these official exchanges, and no concrete accord was reached. Among the issues left hanging were, first, the establishment of a special international tribunal and, second, a national defense strategy, which entailed arming the Hezbollah. Signs of a

---

2. At the request of the special tribunal, they were released on April 30, 2009.

rapprochement between Aoun and Nasrallah appeared. During the demonstrations held by the "Party of God," photographers never failed to hang up portraits of the "Raīs" (Aoun), who was likely to be the most qualified candidate in the coming presidential election.

On February 6, 2006, after violent demonstrations linked to the publication of caricatures of Muhammad in a Danish newspaper, an FPM-Hezbollah *wathīqat al-tafāhum* (memorandum of understanding) was signed in Haret Hreik, the Hezbollah-controlled neighborhood where General Aoun had been born. The event, celebrated in the reception area of Saint Michael Church, came as a surprise. It was a result of six months of secret negotiations between Gibran Bāsīl and Ziyād ʿAbs for the FPM and of Ghālib Abū Zaynab and Abū Qūmātī for the Hezbollah, and it allowed the "Party of God" to emerge from a kind of political isolation, even while enjoying the broadest community support. There is no mention of jihad in the text of the "strategic allies," to borrow Naʿīm Qāsim's expression, but the agreement does make reference to a resolution of the "Palestinian question." That would entail continuing the fight against Israel, to which the issue of disarming the "Resistance" was subordinated. Included as well was the resolution of all matters relating to Lebanese prisoners and the construction of a more equitable state by means of a consensual democracy based on a new electoral law. One of the major points of convergence between the two movements concerned the refusal to settle Palestinian refugees in Lebanon. This was a delicate matter because it was recruited for so many different causes. The United Nations claimed there were 400,000 Palestinians in Lebanon, but, according to the most serious estimates, there were only 250,000, despite a high fertility rate and the arrival of new refugees in 1967 and 1970. A small minority had enjoyed Lebanese citizenship since 1948; another small group had been massacred during the wars; and the vast majority had emigrated to other destinations.

The memorandum of understanding was presented as a working document for all the Lebanese parties, which until that time had acknowledged the failure of national dialogue, and as a basis for a national unity government. It united the "two cleanest leaders [zaīms] of the Arab world" (Aoun and Nasrallah), both from the working class, against corruption and familial clientelism. Its aim was to reconcile the Lebanese with one another and Lebanon with "its Arab surroundings," that is, with Syria. General Aoun proposed to bury past grievances with that country on condition that the prisoner issue be settled. The text sealed an objective alliance between the two fiercest opponents of the 1989 Taif Agreement, but they continued to have different motivations, which showed that they were counting on a convergence of minorities throughout the Arab world, where the majority Sunnis were pervaded by a Wahhabism linked to the discourses of two major doctrinaire figures of the twentieth century: *Sayyid* Qutb and Abū-l 'Ala' Mawdudi. The memorandum of understanding ignored the Hezbollah's ideological and organizational dependence on Iran, which had been strengthened by the victory of Mahmoud Ahmadinejad in the Iranian presidential election (Ahmadinejad would call for the destruction of the state of Israel, portrayed as a "black and dirty microbe" and a "savage animal") and the Israeli withdrawal from Gaza, unilaterally decided on by Israel.

A FORCE UNVANQUISHED BUT ON THE DEFENSIVE

During the Beirut summit in spring 2002, the divisions within the Arab world burst forth once again. At that time, King Abdallah of Saudi Arabia relaunched the "proposal" that his brother had pushed through twenty years earlier during the Fez summit: peace between Israel and the Arab League states, in exchange for Israel's withdrawal from all the occupied territories. Ariel Sharon's government, involved in a test of strength with Yasser Arafat(who was under siege in the Palestinian Authority Mukataa in Ramallah), ignored the proposal. Arafat's fate elicited no unified response from the Arabs. On the contrary, the Syrians decided to prohibit his speeches from being retransmitted to Beirut via satellite. That cacophony served the political line defended by the Hezbollah, whose leaders again declared that no negotiated solution with the "Zionist entity" could be considered. They also acknowledged that the Hezbollah was providing light arms to Hamas, the chief Palestinian movement opposing the Oslo Accords. In the months that followed, however, that position was undermined by the Iraqis. Because they were Shiites, the Hezbollah leaders offered no support to Saddam Hussein, who had persecuted their coreligionists and expelled some of them. But in Nasrallah's view, the Iraqi regime's disappearance would occur only at the cost of a U.S. presence. On the eve of hostilities, he proposed a reconciliation between the existing power and the opposition forces, which garnered, at best, polite disapproval from the Iraqi Shiites. After the fall of Saddam Hussein, the Hezbollah's secretary general—to shouts of "Death to America"—declared his support for all forms of "resistance" against the "occupation," but without choosing sides between the two antagonistic Shiite organizations on the Interim Governing Council: the Supreme Council for the Islamic Revolution and al-Da'wa Party.

The front was no more united among the Western powers. The "antiterrorist" campaign launched by the Bush administration after the attacks of September 11, 2001, targeted a vast constellation of movements that embraced Islam. Alongside al-Qaeda and other Sunni radical elements, Washington strategists had their eye on the Hezbollah, with the active support of the pro-Israel lobby. Without consulting its partners, the United States outlined a proposal for reconfiguring the Near and Middle East, whose map had been drawn by the British and French colonial powers after World War I. In October 2002, the United States urged the European Union to put the Hezbollah on a financial blacklist, but France blocked the move. The United States did not participate in the Paris II meeting, which was intended to raise massive financial aid for the Lebanese, whose debts had reached a new high. In the forefront of the dispute between the United States and France was a disagreement about how to resolve the crisis with Iraq. After Bush imposed his views, Chirac ventured an attempt at rapprochement at the Évian Summit. The area of agreement between the two men was Lebanon. France felt that the Land of Cedars ought to recover the place it had held before the war. For the United States, Syria no longer constituted a bulwark against Iraq, which was now under U.S. control, and so became once more a convenient pariah, since it harbored no fewer than ten Palestinian organizations engaged in intifada, including Hamas. Khaled Meshaal, the leader of Hamas, met with Nasrallah from time to time in the Syrian capital.

Anxieties were keen among the authoritarian Arab regimes, caught between accusations from abroad ("You are not democratic") and those from within ("You are no longer fighting Israel"). The weight of that dual criticism was increased by Arab fears of an axis connecting Tehran and the southern suburbs of Beirut via Baghdad and Damascus. In the name of Arab identity and Sunnism, Egyptian president Hosni Mubarak and Abdallah, king of Jordan, agreed to oppose what they called a "Shiite crescent" run by Iran. The reality was more complex. Iran was no more opposed to the fight against partisans of al-Qaeda than was Syria. Iran did play a role in Iraq, but the clerics of Qom, though they had close ties to their counterparts in Najaf, were also in a rivalry with them. The leader of the Najaf clerics was Ayatollah Sistānī, who had never issued a call to arms against the coalition led by the United States. For its part, Syria did not omit to recall that it stood ready to open new peace negotiations with Israel, provided that the Golan as a whole was on the table. The most solid alliance was the one between Tehran and the *dāhiya;* it was further strengthened when Mahmoud Ahmadinejad came to power. Vito Romani has seen clearly that the election of the new president of Iran reestablished an ideological missing link between the *walī al-faqīh* and the Hezbollah.[3] As a result, Iran increased its presence in Lebanon, with the creation of twin cities, billboards vaunting Persian investments, and the return of the Iranian flag as a joint symbol in Hezbollah demonstrations. The hostility of the Hezbollah's discourse against the United States reached a higher pitch in late spring 2006, when the issue of uranium enrichment reached the United Nations. Hamas's victory in the Palestinian legislative elections further exacerbated tensions.

The war of summer 2006 was directly linked to the Israeli-Palestinian conflict. Since the withdrawal from Southern Lebanon, the average number of Israeli soldiers killed every year had fallen from twenty-five to three. But the Hezbollah intervened along the northern border of Israel every time the situation became particularly tense in the Occupied Territories. On July 12, Hamas faced an offensive of Israeli troops after taking a noncommissioned officer hostage. In support of its ally, the Hezbollah attacked an Israeli patrol, killing eight and taking two hostages, which it intended to exchange for prisoners. The recovery operation failed. The Israeli response, supported by the United States after the House of Representatives passed a resolution, was the application of a plan to stamp out the Hezbollah's military potential via air raids and a ground offensive in Southern Lebanon, which was portrayed as a "death trap." The Lebanese were unanimous in condemning the mass bombings. Hundreds of thousands of residents from the South, primarily Shiites, fled to Beirut and points farther north or to Syria. Often lodged in schools, they were sometimes warmly received, but at other times tensions arose. Such was the case in the majority Sunni neighborhood of the ʿAbd al-Qāder secondary school, run by the Hariri

3. Mahmoud Ahmadinejad was the candidate supported by Khamenei, who issued a religious opinion asking those he serves as *marjaʿ* to vote for him.

Foundation, and in some majority-Christian regions, where, at the request of their hosts, Hezbollah militants were obliged to put away their flags. The United States used diplomatic efforts to delay a cease-fire agreement and provided munitions to the Israeli air force, thus demonstrating Washington's desire to cooperate with a significant weakening, if not the complete destruction, of the Hezbollah's military apparatus. Nothing of the kind occurred. The Israeli ground forces, though again occupying part of Southern Lebanon, made no headway, and the number of rockets falling on Israel, including for the first time Haifa, did not diminish. Israel acknowledged failure after a bombing in Cana (July 30), which had also been attacked in 1996. Washington then joined with Paris to pass UN Resolutions 1701 and 1702, which authorized the massive reinforcement of UNIFIL (from two thousand to fifteen thousand men) and the deployment of the Lebanese army on the Lebanese-Israeli border.

According to Norton, neither of the two enemies seems to have taken into account the determination on the other side. The thirty-three-day war (July 12–August 14) culminated in more than eleven hundred dead on one side (and, according to various estimates, two hundred Hezbollah fighters), more than a hundred and sixty on the other (including forty-three civilians), as well as considerable material damage in the target zones, including the neighborhood of Haret Hreik, site of Hezbollah headquarters, where more than 250 residential buildings were destroyed. In the Winograd Commission Report, Israel acknowledged strategic errors, which gave rise to resignations within the army and the government. Within that tragic context, a joke circulated in Egypt: "If the Jews start fighting like Arabs, they are doomed." The Hezbollah wavered only briefly after it orally accepted Resolution 1701, including the agreement that any person caught with weapons in the designated area would be subject to arrest. On September 24, Nasrallah, before an extraordinarily large crowd, celebrated "divine victory" *(nasr ilāhī)*. All the allies of the "Party of God" were invited, as were political and religious dignitaries and Arab trade union leaders. In a rousing speech, the party's secretary general called for the construction of a new state. Fouad Siniora's efforts to find a resolution to the war via a seven-point plan were swept aside. Minister of Defense Elias al-Murr, victim of a failed assassination attempt, was determined to prevent any new provocation directed at Israel, but his warnings went unheeded. When the public learned of a truck crammed full of weapons that the Lebanese authorities had seized, it was outraged; the very existence of the truck demonstrated how limited were the means of the UNIFIL and the Lebanese army for applying the UN resolutions.

In the media, the Hezbollah won the "sixth Arab-Israeli war," to borrow al-Jazīra's expression. Al-Manār, whose offices were completely destroyed, interrupted its programming for only two minutes, having found a relay station somewhere unknown to the Israelis. Standing before the cameras, Israeli prime minister Ehud Olmert appeared by turns sure of himself and hesitant, declaring without proof that "Nasrallah is already in flight." By contrast, every one of Nasrallah's statements was carefully calibrated to produce an effect. In his speech of July 15, 2006, for example, he asked his listeners to "watch the Israeli warship sink before your eyes"; shortly thereafter, a military vessel located a few kilometers from the Lebanese shore was the target of a ground-to-ground missile. Again a week later, knowing he had broad support among Arabic speakers, he communicated his "surprise" at the reproaches formulated by the governments of Saudi Arabia, Egypt, and Jordan. These states, along with Kuwait, Bahrein, Morocco, and even Iraq, had criticized the capture of the two Israeli soldiers; they were disavowed by Syria, Sudan, Algeria, Yemen, and the Palestinians. The secretary general of the Hezbollah appeared stronger and more alluring than ever. The novelist Percy Kemp, once Elie Hobeika's éminence grise, attested to this in an article in *Libération;* and, even before the end of the war, the journalist Joseph Samāha, disappointed with the coverage of the Lebanese press, put together his own editorial staff, drawing especially from leftist circles, and founded a new daily, *al-Akhbār*.

The Hezbollah proclaimed the "end of the age of defeat" in late summer. ʿAbd al-Ilāh Balqizīz published an augmented edition of his book, which had originally appeared in 2000, giving it a new title. *The Resistance and Liberation of Southern Lebanon* became *Hezbollah: From Liberation to Dissuasion (1982–2006)*. Once again, in reference to the Hezbollah's "victory," he reprimanded the Arab regimes that had agreed on principle to bargain with Israel. A hundred thousand dollars may have been dedicated to a full-scale advertising campaign to promote an interpretation of events consistent with that representation. Distinguished artists from the Arab world and extras (children and adults) in traditional Gulf Arab dress appeared in a video, *Nasr al-ʿArab (The Arabs' Victory)*. That shows how much the Hezbollah wanted to create an Arab consensus around it. Dissenting voices were rare, but they did exist. For example, there was the mufti of Tyre, Ali al-Amine,* who was distressed to see a "victory" celebrated after so much death and destruction.

THE ISLAMIC STATE AS INACCESSIBLE HISTORICAL IDEAL

The three years following the 2006 war crystallized the antagonism between politico-religious forces in Lebanon. The Hezbollah leaders, true to the rhetoric adopted in the early 1990s, denounced all opposition to their foreign political activities by equating it to "treason," since, in one way or another, its aim was to valorize a possible acknowledgment of the "Zionist enemy" supported by U.S. "imperialism." Officially, they called for abandoning confessionalism, but unofficially they sought to replace the dual power-sharing arrangement (between Muslims and Christians) with a tripartite arrangement (among Shiites, Sunnis, and Christians) in all leadership posts. General Aoun, ignoring that demand, supported the Hezbollah in the name of an alliance "baptized in blood." He did not omit to attack the Taif

Agreement—even while hoping to reestablish the preeminent place of the Christians—and promoted a rapprochement with Damascus and Tehran. In response, the parliamentary majority adopted a contrapuntal rhetoric, denouncing submission to the *wilāyat al-faqīh* on the one hand and the Damascus agenda on the other. That fed recurrent accusations that parliament was "on the payroll of the United States and working for the Zionist project." Support and pressure from Washington, and from Riyadh and Paris, were no illusion, but the aims of these various governments were not interchangeable. The Hezbollah cadres knew that. They did not intend to seize power under the present circumstances but rather to shut down debate on a number of subjects. The large-scale demonstrations, the long months of negotiations around a system of governance that included a blocking minority, and the vacant presidency beginning in November 2007 illustrate that choice of strategy, which would culminate in armed conflict in May 2008.

The confrontation between the two camps erupted openly in autumn 2006. The "Party of God," which portrayed itself as the instrument of a restored Arab and Muslim pride, accused the Siniora government of having played into the hands of the Israelis and even of having provided them with crucial military information. By way of response, Jumblatt asserted that, since 2005, the Hezbollah had been "involved in one way or another in some, if not all, of the assassinations" of politicians or literary figures. No evidence emerged to support the assertions on either side, but the impending adoption of the proposed by-laws for an international tribunal exacerbated tensions already aggravated by reconstruction, the ethnic-religious civil war in Iraq, and the issue of uranium enrichment in Iran. On October 31, Nasrallah launched an appeal for a national unity government; it looked like an ultimatum. A week later, Nabih Berri began "consultations," which faltered over the question of a blocking minority demanded by the Hezbollah—and by Bashar al-Assad. On November 11, on the eve of the vote to accept a special tribunal, the

Amal and Hezbollah ministers, along with a Greek Orthodox ally, declined to participate further in the Siniora cabinet. They were attempting to take away its legitimacy, since, according to the Taif Agreement, all the major communities had to be represented in the government. Three grounds were invoked: incompetence, corruption verging on injustice, and the fact that the government was "on the payroll of the United States and Israel." Those who resigned pledged to return only on the condition that they obtain a blocking minority. Supported by the president of the country, they hoped to paralyze Lebanese institutions. The parliamentary majority denounced a path that could lead to anarchy, demagogy, intimidation, and "obscurantism." On November 21, MP Pierre Gemayel, son of Amine and a member of the March 14 alliance, was assassinated. UN Security Council Resolution 1757 ratified the creation of the international special tribunal, despite the nonratification of the decision by the Lebanese president. The rift was complete.

The FPM and the Hezbollah conducted a joint "civil disobedience" campaign. It took the form of roadblocks with burning tires, demonstrations—which occasionally took a violent turn—and, especially, the installation of an enormous encampment in the central city, resulting in the shutdown of two hundred businesses and fifteen months of unemployment for hundreds of people. During that time, the Hezbollah interfered with foot traffic on the Grand Serail, behind Nejmeh Square: the prime minister and part of his cabinet were obstructed but not knocked down. During a meeting on December 10, Na'īm Qāsim's speech on the struggle of good against evil roused more enthusiasm than General Aoun's, which focused on necessary state reforms. The parliamentary majority lamented the unnatural alliance, and a Sunni-Druze summit was held at the Druze community house in Beirut to issue a warning against taking to the streets. Ali al-Amine, Shiite mufti of Tyre, supported the statement. The Public Liberties and Democracy Defense Commission, chaired by Sinane Barrage, denounced the occupation of the central city, where,

according to statements from Aounist ranks as well, the "camp-
ers" were soon receiving daily remuneration. Sharp tensions
gripped the Maronites, whom the patriarchate had trouble ap-
peasing. Clashes erupted between Sunnis and Shiites at Lebanese University, leading Nasrallah to go on television and issue
a fatwa calling for calm. Even more serious skirmishes took
place in Tripoli between Sunnis—themselves divided because of
the Hezbollah's support for the Sunni sheikh Yakan's Islamic
Action Front—and Alawites. Attacks targeted officers, and
threats loomed over Arab and Western embassies. That poison-
ous climate, against the backdrop of social protests, was punctuated by references to the bloodshed that one group had caused
the other during the war.

The camps also faced off behind the scenes. The parliamentary majority denounced the organization of "security zones"
or "enclaves of extraterritoriality," which cobbled together a territory in which the state could no longer intervene, especially
around the airport, zones considered the "strategic depth" of the
southern suburbs. A policy of purchasing plots of land under
false names was implemented in Majority-Christian and -Druze
zones. Iranian funds, under the indirect control of Iranian ambassador Muhammad Reda Shibani, may have been used to establish continuous property zones controlled solely by the Shiite
community, between Chouf and the southern suburbs of Beirut
on the one hand, and between Southern Lebanon and the Bekaa
Valley on the other. During the same period, the journalist Emile
Khoury revealed to the Lebanese public the content of a declaration by Iran's supreme leader that had been published in the Iranian newspaper *Keyhan*. In it Khameini had claimed that, since
the Shiites of Lebanon represented 40 percent of the population
and owned 40 percent of the property, their actual power ought to
correspond to that share. Furthermore, young Christians in the
FPM, followers of Suleiman Frangieh Jr., and Sunnis sympathetic
to the discourse of the "Resistance," were accused of training in
camps in the Bekaa under the Hezbollah's leadership. Aoun's

reply was to invoke the right of self-defense, and he denounced the "illegitimacy and unconstitutionality" of the government, which he held responsible for the country's economic deterioration. The Hezbollah targeted the UN, accusing Terjé Roed-Larsen of showing bias regarding Resolution 1559 in his annual reports, which noted an increase in the deliveries of weapons from Syria. The Hezbollah denounced information "coming from the enemy camp" but refused to provide its own. In addition, in January 2007, when Paris Conference III convened donors and lenders—this time with the United States in attendance—to save the country from bankruptcy in exchange for normalization, Nasrallah cranked up the pressure by accusing Siniora of selling off Lebanese independence. The Hezbollah used the same refrain to denounce the imprisonment of the four officers suspected of involvement in the assassination attempt on Rafic Hariri, and the attitude of Saudi Arabia, accused of creating an obstruction by pushing Saad Hariri to adopt an intransigent position on the system of governance and on the electoral law.

The fight against the Sunni group Fatah al-Islam, retrenched in the Palestinian camp of Nahr al-Bared at the edge of Tripoli, led to an interruption in the action on the political front. That clash was a result of an attack on a Lebanese army barracks that caused the deaths of several soldiers. It took no fewer than three months for troops poorly equipped in weapons and munitions to stamp out the insurgents. The operation commander, General François al-Hajj, was assassinated a few months later. Accusations flew on both sides: according to one camp, the group was supported by Syria; according to the other, by the Future Movement. When a bomb killed six members of UNIFIL in June, an accusing finger was also pointed at Sunni radicalism. But during the summer, both Walid Eido (a Sunni) and Antoine Ghanem (a Maronite) were assassinated. The March 14 alliance, which had a narrow parliamentary majority, thereby lost two new members. The speaker of parliament, Nabih Berri, refused to convene the MPs to resolve the crisis, on grounds that he was not certain he could achieve a two-thirds majority. The League of Arab States attempted in vain to play the role of mediator. In autumn 2007, on al-Quds Day, Hassan Nasrallah delivered a speech that scandalized the parliamentary majority: he attributed to Israel responsibility for the assassination of Hariri and other majority figures. In accordance with a Machiavellian plan, Israel had supposedly eliminated its own henchmen to shift the accusation onto Syria. The crisis reached an even higher pitch in November, when Emile Lahoud stepped down, without any agreement having been reached on a candidate likely to succeed him.

The conflict of spring 2008, which marked the final stage of deterioration and anticipated the fighting in the streets, was predicted by the *Observer* in late April. In January, new clashes had pitted Sunnis against Shiites or Christians—in Zahlé, for example. On February 14, two demonstrations shook Beirut: that of the March 14 alliance, which commemorated Rafic Hariri's assassination, and that of the March 8 alliance at the funeral of Imad Mughniyah—the main link between the Hezbollah and the Pasdaran—who had been assassinated two days earlier in Damascus. On one side, Nasrallah exalted the heroism of the "martyr," in order to appear a greater threat than ever to Israel: "Imad Mughniyah left behind thousands of Imad Mughniyahs. . . . If you want that kind of open warfare, so be it, you shall have it." The March 14 alliance denounced the risk of establishing a "totalitarian system," along with "the threat of chaos, misfortune, and ruin." The Grand Mufti of Lebanon, Mohammed Rashid Kabbani, convened a summit of Muslim authorities to ease tensions between communities by appealing to Muslim brotherhood and the separation between "religion, a factor of unity," and "politics." In April, the Hezbollah abducted the Frenchman Karim Pakzad and questioned him for several hours. But what provided the spark was the government's decision to suspend a security officer at the Beirut airport and to cut off the Hezbollah's illegal telephone communication network, which extended from the southern outskirts of Beirut and to Jbeil and

Hermel. The Hezbollah denied the scope of the network and saw the move as a direct attack on its military capacities. With its allies, the Shiites in Amal and Emir Arslan's Druze, it seized West Beirut neighborhoods by force, sweeping aside Hariri's militia security force and destroying the building that housed the Future TV station. Other clashes occurred in Chouf, where Jumblatt's supporters disarmed Hezbollah fighters. Jumblatt, convinced he would not have the upper hand for long, ordered his followers to release their prisoners. The army stepped in only after the fact. It seemed passive both in Beirut and in Tripoli, Lebanon's second largest city, where, according to statements reported in the press, Sunni-Alawite clashes were accompanied by acts of torture. The death toll was high: eighty in only a few days. Aoun, who had called for people to take to the streets and overthrow the government, explained that the "agreement" with the Hezbollah had made it possible to spare the Christians. His opponents retorted that he was agreeing temporarily to the status of *dhimmis* (protected persons) at the expense of legal status, that of equal citizens protected by the state.

For months, the Arab League had proved powerless to bring the positions of the two camps closer together. This time, the reaction of the influential nations was effective, since the latent state of war in Iraq since the U.S. occupation of 2003 roused fears of a conflagration, to such an extent that some considered sending Arab troops into Lebanon. In an unprecedented declaration following the first battles, Grand Mufti Kabbani openly attacked the "Hezbollah leaders," urging them to "fear God, since the Sunni Muslims of Lebanon can no longer tolerate their maneuvers, and the Lebanese in general are no longer prepared to tolerate new political and military forays." He said he regretted "that an Islamic country would finance these aggressive acts . . .; what was taken to be a resistance has turned into disobedience and invasions of the streets of Beirut by an outlaw group." Then he launched an appeal to the Arab and Muslim world. Fadlallah, unlike Qabalān, who railed against the "submission of the authorities to the American Zionist plans," spoke out on May 16 to mark his distance from those who had prevailed on the ground and to recall that "Lebanon is a country of consensual compromises and not of political victories." Neither of the government's two decisions was implemented. Sheikh Hamad ben Jāssem al-Thānī, emir of Qatar, though suspected by the parliamentary government of serving Syrian-Iranian interests more than Lebanese ones, stepped in to allow the leaders to find a peaceful resolution. The almost deserted encampment in the center of Beirut was removed. The Doha Agreement of May 21 proposed a consensus candidate, made adjustments to the electoral map, and included a joint pledge not to resort to arms for political ends. General Michel Suleiman, chief of staff, was elected president of Lebanon on May 25, and he named Fouad Siniora prime minister. Siniora, vilified by the FPM, Amal, and the Hezbollah, managed with some difficulty to constitute a national unity cabinet on July 12. The principle of the one-third blocking minority was applied to the composition of the cabinet, accompanied by a promise not to use it.

The divorce between the two camps was less notable in their acts than in their discourse. In the months following the 2006 war, the parliamentary majority launched two media campaigns, one to promote individual choice versus group decisions, the other to oppose "the culture of death at the expense of our right to life." With a debt estimated at $40 billion (the largest debt per capita in the world), Lebanon could not afford the luxury of a new war, which, in any event, a majority of Lebanese opposed. Nasrallah responded in substance that the military jihad had to continue to fulfill all its sacred duties, and he denounced those whose "only concern is to speechify, write, dance, or make poetry," since a "culture of life [that] consists of turning an enemy into a regional neighbor" was untenable. A year after the war, he explained to his listeners that "the region of Baalbek-Hermel in particular and of the Bekaa in general is not a rear base. It is a front line, like all the regions north and south of the Litani."

Even within the Shiite community, however, the Hezbollah per-
ceived signs of demobilization: in 1998, al-Inmā' Group opened
a first amusement park, Fantasy World, in the *dāhiya,* and new
sites were planned for Sidon, Tyre, Bint Jbeil, and Nabatieh. The
party gave its backing after the fact and, like the clerics in Iran, it
displayed a trend toward openness that manifested itself, for
example, in the adoption of colored clothing for women. By contrast, it retained the initiative in elaborating a culture of "resistance," with an annual calendar of events enhanced by contri-
butions from artists in the fields of music and theater and by
iconographic representations (posters) and media outlets (websites, videos). Its promoters knew how to orchestrate special
events, such as ceremonies for the return of the last Lebanese
prisoners detained in Israel and the exchange of mortal remains.
One such ceremony, on July 12, 2008, held with the backing and
collaboration of all the Lebanese authorities, sanctified the Druze
Samir Kantar, perpetrator of a triple murder, including that of a
little girl. Kantar was prepared to resume jihad after thirty years
in prison. On that occasion, President Suleiman congratulated the
"resistance heroes returning from the occupied lands." He viewed
the welcome they received as "proof of this nation's attachment to
the dignity of its sons, living or dead." But most significant was the
outpouring of gratitude from popular gatherings in the South and
in Beirut: "We know that when the *Sayyid* [Nasrallah] promises,
he keeps his promises."

That culture of "Resistance" fed on the war that Israel was
waging against Hamas in Gaza in late 2008 and early 2009. It
found no outlet for action, however, except demonstrations
that called on the Arab world—and the world outside—to react
against the use of violence, which had caused more than four
hundred deaths in three weeks. Within that context, the Hezbollah showed it had lost its margin for maneuvering, and the active
presence in Beirut of the deputy speaker of the Iranian parliament, then of the president of the Supreme National Security
Council of Iran and the Iranian deputy minister of foreign affairs,

changed nothing in the matter. With the exception of a few rockets launched by small Palestinian groups, it seems that no attack
was conducted from the southern border of Lebanon to "re-
lieve" Hamas fighters in Gaza. The scenario of summer 2006 was
not repeated. Several factors explain that change: the Hezbollah's
need to fend off accusations that it was only an armed group in
the service of Iran (and to a lesser degree, of Syria); the presence
in Southern Lebanon of a stronger UNIFIL and of the Lebanese
army; Tehran's caution, given the prospect of normalization raised
by the advent of a new U.S. administration; and the desire to
show that Israel, once again the loser in the media war, was capable only of resorting to violence, primarily against children,
women, and the elderly. Tehran even took the initiative, forming
a criminal court representing some fifteen nations to try "twenty-
nine Zionist figures" on charges of war crimes.

Hamas and the Islamic Jihad did not benefit from effective
armed support during the weeks of war but they could boast of
having resisted Israel by force of arms. They received the con-
gratulations of the Hezbollah's secretary general and of the
authorities in Iran, where Meshaal and his companions were
greeted with wreaths of flowers to celebrate a "divine miracle"
and the "beginning of the end of Israel." In the Arab world, however, Nasrallah lost some of his aura because of his accusations
against Egyptian president Mubarak, whom he portrayed as a
henchman of Zionism:

> Some Arab regimes, in this case those that signed the so-called peace
> accord with Israel, are the active accomplices of the Israeli aggres-
> sion against Gaza. In July 2006, they implored Israel to root out the
> Hezbollah. Today they continually ask Israel to annihilate Hamas,
> the Islamic Jihad, and the other resistance organizations. This is
> shameful! These regimes orchestrated Palestinian dissension in order
> to destroy the Resistance, just as they pressed the previous Lebanese
> government to make the two accursed decisions last May 5. . . .
> Some television stations ought to baptized 'al-'Ibriyya' [the Hebrew]
> and not 'al-'Arabiyya' [the main Saudi satellite station].

Nasrallah appealed to the Egyptians to "take to the streets by the millions" to get the Rafah Border Terminal opened, which the Cairo government interpreted as an invitation to overthrow the regime and as the use of "Palestinians' blood" to achieve "political gains." An official Egyptian communiqué of January 30 called Nasrallah an "agent" obedient "to Tehran's orders," and the polemic extended to the financial issues associated with rebuilding the destroyed neighborhoods of Gaza.

It was within that context that Lebanon relaunched the "national dialogue" on its defense strategy. One camp believed it was necessary to restore the state monopoly on the legitimate use of force; the other, that it was imperative to endorse the armed role of the "Resistance," so long as the Israeli-Arab conflict had not ended and no central strong state had been built. The latter position weakened after the battles of May–June 2008, which prompted three hundred personalities from civil society (journalists, academics, businessmen, human rights militants) to sign a petition that clearly placed them in the first camp:

> The Lebanese people initiated its Intifada on February 14, 2005, without anyone's help. They succeeded in putting an end to the Syrian occupation of Lebanon, which the entire world, including Israel, had endorsed and sponsored. That people is today capable of protecting their right to a free and dignified life, of building a state worthy of them, and of once again providing proof that right does not submit to might. The pro-sovereignty forces, which have agreed to participate in dialogue in a last attempt to preserve civil peace, are called upon to give absolute priority to the question of disarming the Hezbollah. The equation is simple: to maintain these arms means the end of Lebanon.

In Doha, the participants believed they could resolve the issue by distinguishing between a "security issue" and a "strategy issue," but Mohammad Raad remained inflexible: "The Resistance is not the object of any discussion or of any formula." In his May 25 speech, Nasrallah echoed that view. He ratified the Doha Agreement, "which stipulates that one must not resort to the weapons of Resistance to realize political gains," but, adopting an accommodating reading, he defended the return to an agreement in force when Hariri was prime minister: a "Resistance" without hindrance, a "state" centered on economic and institutional questions.

Under pressure from the Hezbollah, the ministerial declaration was adopted. A formula that linked the "people," the "army," and the "Resistance" was retained, but with the omission of the original reference specifying "within the framework of the state." That weakened the line the Aounists had adopted. Since that time, the Hezbollah members of parliament have supported an internal regulation that stipulates that attacks on MPs or political parties are forbidden, a measure that Nabih Berri has zealously applied to eliminate any shred of debate on the subject of disarmament or of the "Resistance" in the minutes of parliamentary sessions. The Hezbollah means to continue to mobilize the masses around the theme of "Resistance" as a "national constant," and, from time to time, of "open war" against Israel, in anticipation of its final defeat. To prevent losing control of the military jihad by delegating its weapons to the state, it incurs the risk that Sunni groups will strengthen their own armaments. That state possesses an army of only about forty thousand underequipped men; but, since 2006, it has availed itself of the UNIFIL to secure its southern border. The occupation of the Shebaa farms has ceased to be a decisive argument; when the United States outlined the plan to settle the problem diplomatically in June 2008, Mūsawī, Qāsim, Fneish, and Trad Hamadeh hastened to declare that there was no linkage between it and the question of disarmament. Boutros Harb, in a plan he submitted for negotiation in February 2009, defended the idea of a "civil resistance" integrated into a broad defensive deployment that would include the Hezbollah. Despite Qāsim's initial pledges, and in Nasrallah's absence, the Hezbollah has refused to put any proposals in writing. It asserts, through the voice of Raad, that there is "no way to debate the question of disarming the Resistance before the liberation of the last occupied plot of earth in Lebanon." The reason is clear: the horizon of its action is a jihad to liberate Jerusalem. All negotiation is rejected because it can lead only to concessions to Israel. Under these circumstances, Nasrallah has made Mughniyah the "commander of the two victories," that of 2000 and that of 2006, and a "martyr." Mughniyah's feats of arms in the 1980s and 1990s and his responsibilities within Iranian institutions are hushed up, and the denials that Mughniyah belonged to the Hezbollah are forgotten.

The Sunni-Shiite conflict continues to widen, despite proclamations of unity in the name of Lebanon or of Islam against Israel, the meeting between Raad and Hariri, and the inauguration of al-Amine Mosque in October 2008. Contrary to all promises made since the war, the arsenal of the "Resistance" has been directed against other Lebanese. The Sunnis of Beirut feel betrayed and humiliated—in denouncing the attacks on places of worship, sheikhs speak of *naaqs* (inferiority)—and trust will be reestablished only slowly. The Hezbollah, which initially wanted to shift responsibility onto government militias to justify its "limited operation," is now trying to make people forget about it. Yet evocations of the original *fitna,* common during the Iran-Iraq War (1980–1988) but subsequently repressed, are resurfacing, and not only within the ranks of radical groups visible in Northern Lebanon. Anathemas and appeals from the Sunnis not to pray for the Shiite "heretics" are no longer unusual. Rumors of Shiite proselytism are circulating from the Persian Gulf to Syria and Morocco. This is not only a clash between regional powers, Saudi Arabia and Egypt against Iran and Syria. The Egyptian Muslim Brotherhood demonstrated its undying support for Nasrallah during the 2006 war but in the end sent no volunteers to Lebanon; the Lebanese branch of the brotherhood is divided, and its relations with the Hezbollah have deteriorated, despite an attempt at rapprochement. Furthermore, the "Islamic resistance" may serve as a model for Hamas, but in the Occupied Territories it serves as a foil for the PLO, whose members took

to the streets en masse in Gaza, shouting a contemptuous "Shiites, Shiites" during one of the rare opposition demonstrations
following the dismissal of the representatives of the Palestinian
Authority in June 2007. For the Sunnis, the decision of the "Resistance" to take up arms against Lebanese citizens in May 2008
proves that it is impossible to trust the Shiites in general and the
Hezbollah in particular. The preacher Hassan Saïd al-Shahal, for
example, appealed internationally for "moral and material" aid
"because the Sunni community needs to make up for its short-
falls in every area." The Sunnis' distrust is explicitly linked to
the practice of *taqiyya* (dissimulation). In response to the end-
less claims that the Sunnis were responsible for Husayn's death,
some Sunnis accuse the Shiites of having played a role in elaborating the *isrāʾīliyyāt,* tales that combine narratives borrowed
from Judaism and from the canonical Muslim tradition, portrayed
in this polemical context as a forgery by Jews, supposed converts
to Islam. This provides a way for the Sunnis to view their adversary as a *kāfir* (heretic).

The rapprochement between Amal and the Hezbollah, and
Fadlallah's qualified support, represent the reflex of a religious
community that feels threatened. In addition, the Hezbollah can
avail itself of the support of the Committee of Bekaa Ulema and
of Sheikh ʿAfīf al-Nābulsī, head of the Jabal ʿAmil Ulema Association. A minority of Shiites, however, has rejected Iranian influence, has tenaciously defended the National Pact and the Taif
Agreement as a "permanent and stable point of reference," and
has called for a political power not dependent on clerical oversight. Three men embody that minority: Ibrahim Shams al-Dīn,
Ahmad al-Assaad, and Sheikh Mohammad Haj Hassan. Shams
al-Dīn is a state minister, son of the late vice chair of the SISC.
He runs the foundation bearing his father's name and published
his father's "political testament," in which Mohammad Mahdī
Shams al-Dīn denounces the process of Iranization. The Lebanese
Shiites, he writes, must not "conceive in their nation a political
or economic project of their own that would distinguish them

from others." Ahmad al-Assaad is from a family of notables from the South, president of the Lebanese Option Gathering and the son of Kamal al-Assaad, who was speaker of the Lebanese parliament. He garnered more than thirty thousand supporters at the start of the legislative election campaign, but his coreligionists seem unlikely to identify in great number with views that invite the "West" to apply Resolution 1701 more rigorously and to "create democracies in the Middle East" to fight "Islamist movements [that] have nothing to do with Islam." Mohammad Haj Hassan, who possesses more modest financial means, is head of the Free Shiite Movement and has adopted a rhetoric of Arab identity against the "Persian monster," embracing the authority of Najaf against that of Qom. For example, he believed himself justified in announcing in Cairo, in April 2008, that "the Hezbollah has arrived at one of the last episodes in its long run. It aspires to found its religious republic, whose allegiance would be to Iran." The Sunnis know that this is an opportunity to be seized, as attested by the meeting between Ahmad al-Assaad and Misbāh al-Ahdab, Sunni MP of Tripoli, and Saad Hariri's visit to Ayatollah Sistānī.

The Hezbollah remains a very popular movement within the Shiite community. That attachment is attributable to an ideological commitment, the effectiveness of the Hezbollah's training of the younger generations, and its support of families. After the 2006 war, every family with a casualty in the conflict received $10,000 to $12,000 in cash, an initiative that reproduced at a large scale the one that followed the 1996 bombings. Architects, engineers, and doctors have spared no efforts to meet the needs of the population, and tens of thousands of free meals have been served. The increasing efficiency seems to have been made possible only by professionalization and the outsourcing of services such as electric power. This does not mean, however, that the "Party of God" has embraced a liberal approach. It never calls for bids, and in autumn 2006, when European cities offered their skills and financial support to rebuild the Haret Hreik neighborhood, the offer was declined. The party exerts its control over geographical space and over the media, where any form of critique elicits a reply. The author of *The Bee Road,* Rami Alleik, a former Hezbollah militant who may have converted to Christianity, has been able to constitute a network of working groups (in Beirut, Chhim, Nabatieh, and 'Amchit) baptized "Lebanon Ahead" in the aim of "building a new Lebanon," but he has trouble gaining access to the airwaves. The Hezbollah also clearly exerted its pressure in June 2006 after a televised broadcast in which a comedian made jokes at the expense of the Hezbollah's secretary general. Within a few hours, tens of thousands of party sympathizers took to the streets to protest, sometimes violently, that attack on "honor." Editorial cartoonists refrain from poking fun at Nasrallah. (By contrast, the party's adversaries use Hezbollah symbols, such as the Kalashnikov, to condemn weapons used "to defend weapons," according to the slogan in use in May 2008.) Nasrallah is the only political personality not portrayed by a puppet on the Lebanese television program corresponding to the French "Guignols de l'Info" (News Puppets). The practice of self-censorship is strong, and al-Manār TV has been no more successful than others in treating the news as something other than propaganda. For the thirtieth anniversary of the Islamic revolution, the station had a series of special programs. One of them, broadcast on February 9, 2009, welcomed the representatives of the Iranian religious communities, including the apostolic Armenians, who, along with their Shiite fellow citizens, celebrated the anniversary of the revolution and its economic, social, and political advances. The Sunni currents considered radical were not welcome, and the future form of the Lebanese state was left in suspense.

DOCUMENTS OF THE HEZBOLLAH

II

OPEN LETTER

February 16, 1985

*This document was presented at a press conference on Febru-
ary 16, 1985, in the* husaniyya *of the Shiyāh neighborhood. It
was published in the weekly newspaper* al-ʿAhd, *founded eight
months earlier. We present an original and, for the first time,
complete [French] translation. According to Régis Blachère—
whose translation of the Koranic passages is used here[1]—the
term "Hezbollah" ought to be rendered literally as "Faction of
God." In the rest of the work, we have preferred to leave it as
is or to render it as "Party of God," now in common use. The
same is true for terms used increasingly in European languages
(*ummah, jihad . . .) *and for certain proper names that will be
easily identifiable.[2]*

This is an original and complete translation. [My translation from the
French.—trans.]

1. [I cite from the N. J. Dawood translation of the *Koran* (New York:
Penguin, 1956), modifying it when necessary to conform to the French
version—trans.]

2. Our thanks to Jean-François Petillot, experienced Arabist and brilliant
pedagogue, for his proofreading and for the long discussions of summer
2007. The authors assume responsibility for the errors and infelicities that
remain.

IN THE NAME OF GOD, THE COMPASSIONATE, THE MERCIFUL

Those who take Allah, his Prophet, and the believers as their protector [and allies] . . . for the Faction of Allah produces Victors (5:56).[3]

This open letter, which the Hezbollah addresses to the disinherited[4] of Lebanon and of humankind, sets forth its conception and its program on the occasion of commemorating the martyred sheikh Rāgbib Harb*—may God be pleased with him— symbol of the Muslim resistance, on the 26th day of Jumāda I in the year 1405 of the Hegira, which is to say, February 16, 1985.

In tribute to the torch whose flame flared bright—illuminating the path of the disinherited in Lebanon toward a free and dignified life—and who annihilated, at the cost of his pure blood, the omnipotence of the Zionist entity as well as its myth. In tribute to the guide who lit the way, who dedicated himself to his people, for whom he was a model in jihad, and who never refused them his inspiration, until his death as a martyr in view of victory; he was the witness to the tyranny and arrogance of the imperialists. In tribute to the symbol of the triumphant Muslim resistance and of the magnificent uprising—worthy of the great battles in the Husayn saga—that our people are pursuing in Southern Lebanon and in Western Biqā [Bekaa]; in tribute to the one who dashed the dreams of America in Lebanon and who stood up to the Israeli occupation, raising the banner of action under the authority of the jurist-theologian commander *(wilāyat*

---

3. [Translation modified to conform to the French.—trans.].

4. The Arabic uses a different term for "disinherited," borrowing a word used during the Iranian revolution of 1978–1979, which combines the notions of humiliation and purity, and that therefore conveys the exclusive right to wage the battle to overthrow the order, unjust or unrighteous because it does not abide by the "law of God." That usage illustrates a vein running through the entire document. In a given society, these "disinherited" stand opposed to the "oppressors" or the "arrogant" and, by extension, to the "imperialists" at the international level.

al-faqī al-qāʾid),[5] whom Rāghib was always fond of describing as the guide of the Muslims, namely, Rūh Allāh Al-Khumayny [Rūhollāh Khomeini]; in tribute to the martyred sheikh Rāghib Harb—may God be pleased with him—we offer, to commemorate his memory, this open letter to the disinherited of humankind, spelling out the revolutionary Muslim political line that the glorious martyr incarnated, along with his brother martyrs. This line, therefore, will become a clear program and a precise guide for all the mujahideen in Lebanon. We implore the Lord— glory and exaltation be His—to bestow steadfastness upon us, to make our steps sure, and to grant us victory over the unrighteous peoples.

Peace, mercy, and God's blessing be upon on you.

Say: "This is the truth from your Lord. Let him who will, believe in it, and him who will, deny it." For the unrighteous We have prepared a fire which will encompass them like the walls of a pavilion. When they cry out for help they shall be showered with water as hot as molten brass, which will scald their faces. Evil shall be their drink. (18: 29)[6]

WHO ARE WE, AND WHAT IS OUR IDENTITY?

O free disinherited . . . We are the sons of the faction of God in Lebanon. We greet you, and, through you, we address humankind in all its components: individuals and institutions, parties and associations, political bodies, humanitarian groups and media . . . omitting no one. We are careful to make our voices heard by everyone, so that they may understand our views, adopt our perspective, and inform one another of our plans. We are the sons of the faction of God, and we consider ourselves an integral part of the Muslim nation in the world, facing the most arrogant assault of imperialism, from the West and from the East, whose aim is to

5. This term is so central that it is the object of a series of articles in *al-ʿAhd* beginning in 1984.

6. [Translation modified.—trans.]

drain it of the prophetic charge with which God has graced it. God graced it therewith so that it might become the best community that has appeared to humankind: it enjoins the good, forbids evil, and believes in God, and [arrogant imperialism has the aim] of alienating its property, its wealth, of exploiting the energies and skills of its children to take power in all its affairs.

We are the sons of the faction of God. He granted victory to our vanguard in Iran. That vanguard has once again founded the nucleus of the central state of Islam in the world. We are enlisted under the orders of a single leadership, wise and just, represented by the power *(walī)* of the jurist-theologian uniting all conditions. That leadership is at present incarnated by the imam, the supreme ayatollah Rūhollāh Musavi Khomeini—may his shadow remain—who launched the revolution of the Muslims and who instigated their glorious rebirth. On these foundations, we in Lebanon are not an organized party closed upon itself, nor do we confine ourselves within a narrow political framework. . . . On the contrary, we are a community connected to Muslims from every corner of the world, solidly bound to Islam, the principle of faith and well-established policy, whose message God has perfected through the hand of the seal of His prophets, Muhammad—peace and blessings upon him—He who bestowed on the universe a religion through which they can worship Him: *This day I have perfected your religion for you and completed my favour to you. I have chosen Islām to be your faith* (5:3).

On the basis of that state of affairs, whatever assails the Muslims in Afghanistan, in Iraq,[7] in the Philippines, or anywhere else assaults the body of the Muslim nation, of which we are an indivisible part. We take great pains to confront that fact, based on a legal obligation and in light of an overall political conception, determined by the authority [*wilāyat*] of the jurist-theologian commander. As for our culture, its fundamental sources are the

---

7. The weekly *al-ʿAhd* several times demonstrated its support for Iran in the war against Iraq and the "global powers."

noble Koran, the infallible Sunna, as well as the laws and fatwas promulgated by the jurist-theologian, our source of imitation. This is absolutely clear and available to all without exception. There is no need for theorizing or philosophizing: what is necessary is commitment and application.

As for our military capacities, no one can imagine their scope, in that no military group can be distinguished from our faction as a whole: each of us is a warrior when called to jihad, and each of us receives his combat mission in accordance with his legal assignment, within the space of action conforming to the authority [*wilāyat*] of the jurist-theologian commander. God is with us, He supports us as His subjects, and He strikes terror in the hearts of our enemies and makes us victorious over them, thus sanctifying His supreme victory.

THE IMPERIALIST WORLD HAS COME TOGETHER TO MAKE WAR ON US

O free disinherited: the nations of the iniquitous imperial world, in the West and in the East, have come together to combat us; they have begun to set their agents against us, and they are attempting to discredit us and slander us with lies. They treacherously attempt to introduce a fracture between us and the honorable disinherited. They keenly endeavor to minimize and dilute the chief acts in our confrontation with America and its allies. Through its local agents, America has sought to instill the belief that those who put an end to its arrogance in Lebanon, who forced it to leave completely disabused, and who foiled its plot against the humble in that country, were only a handful of fanatics, terrorists having no other business than to blow up establishments selling alcoholic beverages, gambling dens, pleasure houses, and so on. But we were certain that such propaganda could not fool our Muslim nation. The world and all its components know that anyone who dreams of confronting America and the imperialists throughout the world does not seek refuge in such marginal activities, which divert him from the essential.

AMERICA IS THE SOURCE OF ALL OUR ILLS

We wish to eradicate what God condemns . . . and the first root of that evil is America. All endeavors that impel us to commit marginal actions are without usefulness, unless their aim is to confront America. The imam guide Khomeini has certified it on several occasions: America is truly the source of all our ills, it is perfidy incarnate. When we combat it, we are only exercising our legitimate right to restore the dignity of our nation and to defend Islam. We proclaim with the greatest clarity that our community fears only God, that it accepts neither defeat nor aggression nor injustice. America and its allies in the Atlantic Alliance, as well as the Zionist usurpers established on the sacred Muslim land of Palestine, all offend us. They debase us. As a result, we are permanently set to fight, ready to repel aggression, to defend our honor, our existence, and our religion.

Truly they have destroyed our country, devastated our villages, slaughtered our children, and humiliated us.[8] They made us slaves under the authority of criminal executioners, who perpetrated terrorist acts against our community. They continue to support these butchers, the allies of Israel; they deny us the right of self-determination in accordance with our will. Their bombs fell like rain on our families during the Zionist invasion of our country and the siege of Beirut. Their planes have continually attacked civilians, night and day, striking our families, our children, our wives, and our wounded. . . . The districts run by the servile Phalangists were spared by the enemy and were used to orient their forces.

We have shouted to alert the world's conscience, but we have received no compassion and have found no support. That international conscience, which failed us during the days of the

---

8. It is possible to translate the Arabic expression as "they raped our women." But it is not clear that the author or authors of the text wanted to convey this explicitly, for reasons of honor.

ordeal, was activated when the criminal Phalangists, allies of Israel, were besieged in Zahlé, in the Bekaa, and on the day of the siege of Dayr Al-Qamar in Chouf.

That dumbfounded us. The universal conscience was stirred only at the request of the most mighty and to respond positively to the interests of the imperialists. In a single night, therefore, the Israelis and the Phalangists massacred thousands of our fathers, children, wives, and brothers at Sabra and Shatila, and no organization, no state authority pronounced the slightest condemnation for that atrocity, committed in coordination with the NATO forces, which had withdrawn from the camps a few days before—a few hours even. These forces, put to flight, had agreed to place these camps under the protection of the wolf [Israel], responding favorably to the maneuver of the American fox Philip Habib. These awful crimes led us to the following absolute certainty: *You will find that the most implacable of men in their enmity to the faithful are the Jews and the pagans* (5:82).[9]

CONFRONTATION IS OUR ONLY ALTERNATIVE

Following from these premises, it is our opinion that we will repel aggression only by means of sacrifice. . . . We will recover our honor only through the sacrifice of our blood. Freedom is not granted, it can only be recovered through the efforts of our souls and spirits. As a result, we place honor, freedom, and religion above a wayward life and a continual subjection to America and its allies, as well as to the Zionists and their allies the Phalangists. . . . We have risen up to liberate our country, to drive out the colonizers and invaders, and to be able to dispose of ourselves. Our patience has been pushed to the limit, our ordeal has lasted for decades, since before that we saw only predators, toadies, and the impotent.

9. The verse continues: *"and that the nearest in affection to them are those who say: 'We are Christians.' That is because there are priests and monks among them; and because they are free from pride."*

THE ARRANGEMENT BETWEEN ZIONISTS
AND PHALANGISTS

Hundreds of thousands of victims fled, including half a million Muslims forced into exile. Such is the approximate result of the crimes committed by America, Israel, and the Phalangists. Nearly all their neighborhoods were destroyed in Al-Nab'a [Nabaa], in Bourj Hammoud, in Dekwaneh, in Tel al-Zaatar, in Sibniyé, in the neighborhood of Ghourané and the region of Jbeil, where our surviving loved ones continue to suffer ordeals, without any international agency coming forward to protect them. The Zionist occupation has continued, it has brought Muslim lands—as much as a third of Lebanese territory—under its fist, with the prior cooperation and full agreement of the Phalangists, who rejected any attempt to block entry by the incursion forces.

They have joined in the realization of a series of Israeli plans allowing the Zionist project to succeed. They paid the asking price in order to reach the heights of power. That is how the butcher Bachir Gemayel obtained the presidency, by appealing to Israel and the oil-producing monarchies, and by counting on the submission—to the Phalangists—of the leading Muslim MPs. He succeeded in burnishing his ignoble image in an operating room called the "Public Salvation Committee." Yet this was nothing but an American-Israeli bridge, crossed by the Phalangists to impose an authority on the gathering of the disinherited. But our people have ceased to tolerate that defeat, and the dreams of the Zionists and their allies have been annihilated.

In spite of everything, America sank deeper into its folly, and Amine Gemayel succeeded his buried brother. His first measures were to destroy the houses of exiles and to commit exactions against the Muslim mosques. He gave the army the order to bomb the suburban neighborhoods of the disinherited. The NATO forces were invited to stand beside him and against us. The shameful May 17 agreement was signed, the accord that led to Lebanon's subjection to Israeli control and American colonization.

OUR CHIEF ENEMIES

Our people could no longer bear all that perfidy and therefore decided to confront the infidels as a whole: America, France, and Israel. Our people inflicted a first punishment on them on April 18, then again on October 29, 1983. And so a war against the Israeli occupation forces truly began. Two of its important military command headquarters were destroyed with the aid of the popular armed Muslim resistance, inflicting a defeat on the enemy and leading to its decision to flee. For Israel, that outcome constituted a first in the history of the war between the Arabs and the Israelis. We proclaim that the sons of the faction of God now know perfectly well who their chief enemies are in the region: Israel, America, France, and the Phalangists.

OUR OBJECTIVES IN LEBANON

The following objectives are part of an escalating confrontation with our enemies:

- to definitively drive Israel out of Lebanon, a first step toward the definitive disappearance of Israel and the liberation of al-Quds [Jerusalem] from occupation;
- to definitively drive America, France, and their allies out of Lebanon; to put an end to the influence of any colonial state whatsoever in the country;
- to hand over the Phalangists to a legal authority and to have them all tried for the crimes they committed against Muslims and Christians with the encouragement of America and Israel;
- to act in such a way that the sons of our people as a whole may decide their own fate and choose in complete freedom the system they want, knowing that we do not conceal our commitment to a Muslim power and that we invite everyone to choose an Islamic system, which alone guarantees justice and dignity for all and

which alone bars any possibility of a new colonization
of our country.

O FRIENDS

Our objectives in Lebanon, like our enemies, are therefore clearly
determined. As for our friends, they include all the destitute
peoples of the world; they represent all those who make war on
our enemies and those who take care not to harm us. Individuals,
parties, associations . . . we address ourselves to them especially,
saying: You, warriors and members of organizations, whoever
you may be in Lebanon, and whatever your ideas may have
been, we agree on major objectives: to rid ourselves of American
omnipotence over the country and of the Zionist occupation
pressing on the necks of human beings, and to combat all takeover attempts by the Phalangists with respect to the government
and the administration, even if our styles and the levels of our
confrontations differ.

Come then. We stand above the polemics existing between us
in insignificant matters, and we throw open the doors of emula-
tion in order to realize great plans. It is not important that one
party predominate; the essential thing is that the masses be an
integral part of it. It is not important to increase the number of
military parades before citizens but rather to increase the number of actions against Israel. And it is not important to fashion
fine ideas and hold conferences; the essential thing is to emancipate Lebanon from American schemes.

Your dreams do not originate in Islam. . . . That in no way
prevents us from aiding one another to realize these objectives. In
fact, we sense that the reasons that motivate you from the standpoint of combat are fundamentally Muslim grounds; they have
their source in the injustice and humiliation to which the despots
subject you. . . . These reasons, even if they were forged from
ideas that are not Muslim, will recover their essence when you
see that it is revolutionary Islam that is engaged in the forefront of the battle and that resists crime and injustice. We can-

not accept harassment, provocation, or insults to our dignity or our *ummah* from you. There is no ambiguity [that is a pledge on our part], that is best. We will also be vigilant in seeing that you do not prevent us from reaching our objectives. Then you will find us open toward you. We will draw nearer to you every time your thinking draws closer to our own, every time we see you are free to decide, every time the interest of Islam and of the Muslims justifies an evolving relation with you, to strengthen them.

O disinherited followers, you aspire for what is right, but you miss. The one who aspires toward what is right and misses is not the same as the one who aspires for what is illegitimate and achieves his goal. That is why we extend our hand to you and tell you sincerely: our nation accepts the invitation of God, and it pleases God and his Prophet to invite you to live with them.

WE ABIDE BY ISLAM, BUT WE DO NOT IMPOSE IT BY FORCE

O free disinherited! We are the *ummah* that obeys the message of Islam and that wants the humble and the folk to learn that heavenly message, since it lends itself to the realization of justice, peace, and security in the world. And God—exalted be He—says: *There shall be no compulsion in religion. True uprightness is now distinct from aberration. He that renounces the Tāghout[10] and puts his faith in God shall grasp a firm handle that will never break. God hears all and knows all. God is the Patron of the faithful. He leads them from darkness to the light. As for the unbelievers, their patrons are the Tāghout, who lead them from light to darkness. They are the heirs of the Fire and shall abide in it forever* (2:256–257).[11]

10. The "Tāghout" are supposedly the idols of pre-Islamic Arabia (Mohammad Ali Amir-Moezzi, ed., *Dictionnaire du Coran* [Paris: Robert Laffont, 2007], p. 56).

11. [Translation modified.—trans.]

As a result, we do not want to impose Islam on anyone, just as we refuse to have others impose their convictions and their systems on us. We do not want Islam to govern by force in Lebanon, as political Maronitism currently does in Lebanon. Nevertheless, we are convinced by Islam as doctrine and as regime, spirit and authority. We invite everyone to learn what it is and to respect its law, just as we invite everyone to adopt it and abide by its precepts at the social, political, and individual level.

If our people are allowed to choose freely the form of their political system in Lebanon, they cannot fail to wager on Islam. That being the case, we call for the founding of an Islamic regime based on the free and direct choice of the people, not on the imposition of force as some imagine. We declare that we set our hearts on having Lebanon be an indivisible part of the political map opposing America, international imperialism, and global Zionism, and on seeing that map governed equitably by Islam. Said aspiration is that of the nation, not the ambition of one party; it is a popular choice, not that of a coterie.

THE MINIMUM REQUIREMENT CONCERNING OUR ASPIRATION IN LEBANON

By virtue of that, to achieve the objective, the minimum we can accept on the part of those who might want to take in hand the lawful realization of that ambition is that they emancipate Lebanon from its compliant attitude toward the West and the East, that they definitively drive out the Zionist occupier from its lands, and that they found the order freely decided upon by the people. Why do we oppose the present system? Here are our visions, our plans for Lebanon. In the light of these, we oppose the established order for two principal reasons:

- it participates in building the global power and constitutes an element on the political map hostile to Islam;
- it is fundamentally unjust, neither reformable nor modifiable, and it must be extracted by the roots.

The unrighteous are those who do not judge according to God's revelations (5:45).[12]

OUR POSITION TOWARD THE OPPOSITION

It is in light of the two preceding considerations that we position ourselves in relation to the opposition in general within the Lebanese regime. We maintain that any opposition that operates within the lines imposed by the imperialist powers is only a formal opposition and is definitively linked to the regime in place. Any opposition that situates itself within the framework of conserving and preserving the established constitution and forming an obstruction to any effort toward changing the system at its root is also a formal opposition. It does not work for the interests of the toiling masses. Similarly, any opposition that operates from within positions from which the regime wants it to operate is a short-lived opposition, which is nothing but a handmaiden of the established order. Moreover, it is mad from our point of view to aspire toward political reform in light of the corrupt confessional system. It is just as mad to form any government, or for any person to participate in any ministry whatsoever, that represents an element of the unjust order.

WORDS FOR THE CHRISTIANS OF LEBANON

O noble disinherited, it is to you we turn in addressing these words to the Christians of Lebanon, the Maronites in particular. The policy conducted by the Maronite political leaders through the "Lebanese Front" and the "Lebanese Forces" does not allow the achievement of peace and stability for the Christians of Lebanon. In fact, it is a policy based on clannishness, religious discrimination, and an alliance with the colonizer and Israel.

12. [Translation modified—trans.] The verse cited begins as follows: *We decreed* [*in the Torah*] *for them* [*those who practice Judaism*] *a life for a life, an eye for an eye, a nose for a nose, an ear for an ear, a tooth for a tooth, and a wound for a wound. But if a man charitably forbears from retaliation, his remission shall atone for him.*

The Lebanese ordeal has proved that religious discrimination has been the principal cause of the great explosion that has dismantled the country. The alliance with America, France, and Israel was of no use to the Christians on the day they needed their support. Consequently, it is time for the fanatical Christians to put an end to that allegiance, to the chimera of a monopoly of privileges at the expense of others. They must abide by the heavenly invitation, using reason rather than weapons and the virtue of consensus rather than confessionalism.

We are aware that the Messenger of God, the Messiah—prayer and peace be upon Him—is innocent of the atrocities committed by the Phalangists in His name and in your name, and innocent of the mad policy on which your leaders rely to govern us and you. Similarly, the Prophet Muhammad—may God bless him and grant him peace—is also innocent of what is attributed to the Muslims who do not abide by God's law and who do not implement his prescriptions on you and on us. You have therefore been able to assess matters and have learned that your interests lie in what you decide of your own free will and not in what is imposed by fire and the sword. In view of that, we reiterate our invitation to reply to God's word:

> Say: "People of the Book, let us come to an agreement: that we will worship none but God, that we will associate none with Him, and that none of us shall set up mortals as deities besides God." If they refuse, say "Bear witness that we have surrendered [muslim] to God." (3:64)[13]

O Christians of Lebanon, if you find it intolerable that some Muslims participate in government affairs. . . . By God, so is it also for us, because they participate in a power unjust to us and against you, a power not founded on the principles of religion

13. Note that Régis Blachère links this verse to an invitation to the "Jews of Medina"—not to the Christians—to guide them toward Islam.

and on the law, which was made perfect by the seal of the two prophets. You wanted justice; is it not established by God in the first place? It is He who, from Heaven, sends the message of Islam, spread by the prophets to guide men in accordance with what is fair and to offer them all what is their right.

If some people deceive you, making you fear our reaction to the crimes committed by the Phalangists against us, be assured that it will never happen. The men of peace among you have never ceased to live with us, without any molestation of their purity. And if we fought the Phalangists, it was because they prevented you from seeing the truth, they were for you an obstruction on the path toward God. They wanted to corrupt that straight way on earth, they were swollen with pride.

We wish you well and invite you to convert to Islam in order to find fulfillment in religion and for eternity. If you refuse, we will have no choice but to incite you to keep the promises you made to the Muslims, so that you will not participate in any aggression against them. O Christians, free your thoughts from the remnants of confessionalism and emancipate yourselves from your bond of obedience to your tribal group, closed upon itself. Be clear-sighted about what we are inviting you to have in Islam; for in Islam lies your salvation, your happiness, the good of religion, and eternity. Our invitation is addressed to all the destitute who are not Muslims. As for those who are of the Muslim faith, we enlist them to apply Islam fully and to place themselves above fanaticism, which religion abhors.

We certify to all that ours is the era of the advent of Islam and of what is right, the advent of the overthrow of apostasy and illegitimacy. Therefore, join the side that is right before what shall come to pass:

> On that day the unrighteous man will bite his hands and say: "Would that I had walked in the Apostle's path! Oh, would that I had never chosen so-and-so for my companion! It was he that made

me disbelieve in God's warning after it had reached me. Satan is ever treacherous to man." (25:27–29)[14]

OUR HISTORY WITH THE IMPERIALISTS

O humble and honorable oppressed . . . As for our history with the imperialists, we can sum it up in these terms: we are convinced that the confrontation on principle between America and the Soviet Union goes far back in time and is irreversible. . . . The two poles have failed to bring about happiness among men; in fact, the ideology presented to men, though it varies—depending on whether it is capitalist or collectivist—shares a materialist content and has not succeeded in curing the ills of humankind.

Neither Western capitalism nor Eastern socialism has managed to establish the rules of a just and stable society. They have not been able to strike the balance between the individual and society, or between human instinct and the general interest. Both sides have come to admit this and have mutually recognized that reality. They have realized that there was no longer any reason for a clash of ideas between the two camps. Beyond differences of principle, therefore, the two vie for world opinion in terms of influence and interests.

In light of that observation, we note that the ideological battle between combatants is over. It has been replaced by conflicts of interest and influence between world powers, now dominated by America and the Soviet Union. As a result, the oppressed countries have become the site of the confrontation, and their peoples serve as fuel to that end. We consider that battle between the two giants a natural consequence of the material motivations that impel them to act. We cannot accept that confrontation to the detriment of the interests of the disinherited and their countries. We are confronted with every sort of voracity and with other kinds of meddling in our affairs.

14. [Translation modified.—trans.]

And, while we condemn America's crimes in Vietnam, Iran, Nicaragua, Grenada, Palestine, Lebanon ... we also condemn the Soviet invasion of Afghanistan, its interference with Iran's affairs, its support of the conflict with Iraq, and so on. In Lebanon and in the land of Palestine, we are concerned in the first place with the confrontation with America, given that, among the world powers, it exerts the chief influence; and second, [with that] with Israel, master of international Zionism. Therefore, the confrontation with America's allies, the member states of the Atlantic Alliance entangled with them, whose support of America is injurious to the populations of the region, is our affair. And we warn the nations that have not yet served American interests not to become involved in that venture at the expense of our community's freedom and interests.

PUTTING AN END TO ISRAEL'S EXISTENCE

As for Israel, we consider it the American beachhead in our Muslim world. It is the enemy usurper that must be combated until right is restored, against the despoiling of our people. That enemy represents a great danger for future generations and for the destiny of our nation, especially since it is quite specifically considering the possibility of expansionism, moving from the first stage, its occupation of Palestine, to attempt to build a Greater State of Israel from the Euphrates to the Nile.

Our battle against the usurper Israel is grounded in an ideological and historical analysis, according to which that Zionist entity is our enemy from its birth and constitution, and that it is established on a land stolen at the expense of the rights of a Muslim people. Our confrontation with that entity must therefore not cease until its disappearance. That being the case, we recognize no cease-fire agreement with it, no truce, no peace treaty, whether isolated or not. We firmly reject every plan for mediation with Israel. We consider the intermediaries an enemy organ, since their mediation will serve only to recognize the legality of the Zionist occupation of Palestine. On the basis of that position on principle, we reject the Camp David Accord, we reject the Fahd plan, the Fez plan, the Reagan plan, the Brezhnev plan, the Franco-Egyptian plan, and any plan that recognizes even partially the Zionist entity.

In that context, we condemn all deviant states and institutions that pursue solutions involving renunciation in the face of the enemy and that accept the "land for peace swap." We consider that a betrayal of the blood of the Palestinian Muslim people and of the sacred cause of Palestine. Furthermore, the Jews have in recent times encouraged the colonization of Southern Lebanon and the emigration of the Jews from Ethiopia—among other societies—to the interior of occupied Palestine: we consider all that a part of Israel's plan for expansion within the Muslim world and a tangible indicator of the danger resulting from any recognition of that entity or coexistence with it.

THE MUSLIM RESISTANCE, A RISING FORCE

Even as we mention the case of the usurper Israel, we must also mention the phenomenon of Muslim resistance, which has been set in motion from the occupied Lebanese zones, to effect a historical and cultural reversal of the course of the battle against the Zionist enemy. The noble Muslim resistance has achieved victories, and by its military heroism has continually given rise to skirmishes and to heroic acts against the attacking Zionist forces. By the faith of its combatants, it has shattered the myth of Israel's supposed invincibility; it has been able to push the usurping entity to a true impasse, because of the current depletion of its military, human, and economic forces, which compelled its leaders to recognize the difficulty of the confrontation with the Muslims.

With the aid of God—His kingdom come—that Muslim resistance must continue, develop, grow, and unite all Muslims in every region of the world to permit their backing, their aid, their support, and their participation, until we can extirpate the cancer cell. We insist on [the] Islamic character [of that resistance] only because that is in keeping with the clearly Muslim reality perceptible in the defensive battle, in the objective, continuity, and breadth of the confrontation . . . and in no case does that belie patriotism: on the contrary, it reinforces it. . . . Conversely, if one dilutes the Islamic character, then patriotism becomes much more fragile.

APPEAL FOR BROAD MUSLIM PARTICIPATION

We seize this opportunity to launch an open call to all the sons of Muslims in the world. We invite them today to join their brothers in Lebanon, on the basis of that appeal, for the honor of battle against the occupying Zionists, whether directly or through their active support of the mujahideen. Fighting Israel is among the responsibilities of all Muslims everywhere in the world; it is not only the responsibility of the sons of Jabal ʿāmil [Jabal ʿAmil] or the eastern Bekaa.

For the first time in the history of the battle against the enemy, by the blood of its martyrs and the jihad of its heroes, the Muslim resistance was able to drive the enemy to the decision to reverse direction and withdraw from Lebanon—and without any American pressure. On the contrary. Without a doubt, the Israeli decision to withdraw brought to light a real uneasiness on the part of America and marked a historic turning point in the course of the battle against the usurper Zionists.

The mujahideen, taken as a whole, have confirmed that if the nation is allowed to freely guide itself, miracles can happen, and the predicted outcomes can be reversed. Women, whose weapons are stones and boiling water; children, whose weapons are shouts and bare fists; old men, whose weapons are fragile bodies and heavy sticks . . . the young, whose weapons are rifles and the personal desire associated with their faith—all have participated in the resistance.

THE GOVERNMENT POLICY OF SUBSIDIES
AND TALKS LEADING TO BETRAYAL

Let us pause for a moment on the gesticulations that can be seen on official occasions, gesticulations whose aim is to make people believe that the authorities support the resistance to the occupation, and let us clearly state that the people reject them and have contempt for their authors. . . . Although a few declarations from a handful of government leaders have been published, no one is fooled. The masses have realized that these declarations do not represent the position of the authorities as a whole, especially since no one can say that the authorities have ever used their army to earn the honor of participating in liberation.

As for financial support for the resistance, it is absolutely nil. The mujahideen have not received arms or munitions or supplies of weapons or anything resembling them. Our people reject a policy of subsidies billed to the resistance. The day will come when all who have trafficked in the blood of the heroic martyrs, all who have sought glory at the expense of the mujahideen's wounds, will be judged.

We attest that the policy of bargaining with the enemy is a major betrayal of the resistance, which the established order claims to sustain and support. The insistence of the authorities on undertaking talks with the enemy could only have been a result of the conspiracy aimed at recognizing the Zionist occupation plan and at granting immunity for the crimes against the rights of the disinherited in Lebanon. Parenthetically, let us recall that the Muslim resistance has announced its refusal to feel bound by any result emerging from the talks. On the contrary, it is convinced of the need to pursue jihad until the Zionists evacuate the occupied zones, the first step toward their disappearance.

THE INTERNATIONAL FORCES AND
THEIR EQUIVOCAL ROLE

The international forces that global imperialism seeks to place in Muslim territories, in the zones that will be evacuated by the enemy, will consequently represent a security barrier. They will constitute an obstruction to the resistance's movement and will guarantee the security of Israel and its invasion troops: these are complicit forces, which we reject. As a result, we could be obliged to treat them in the same way as the Zionist invasion forces. May everyone know that the restraints of the order imposed by the Phalangists are not binding for the mujahideen of the Muslim resistance in any way whatsoever. States must therefore reflect carefully before venturing into the mire where Israel drowned.

THE REGIMES RESPONSIBLE FOR THE ARAB DEFEAT

As for the Arab regimes that rush to reconcile with the Zionist enemy, they are impotent regimes incapable of standing firm with the *ummah's* ambitions and aspirations. Bloodless, they cannot conceive of confrontation with the Zionist usurper of Palestine, inasmuch as they grew up in the shadow of colonial control, which played the preeminent role in the advent of these corrupt regimes. Some of these backward powers, especially the oil-producing monarchies, have no scruples about welcoming American and British military bases in their countries. They are not ashamed to appeal to foreign experts to help them with official duties. They carry out the policies that "White House" circles decide, squandering and redistributing wealth to the colonial powers by every means.

Some of them claim to be defending Islamic legitimacy so as to veil their betrayal and justify their submission to America's will. At the same time, they absolutely forbid the dissemination of even a single revolutionary Muslim book in their countries. And because of the defeatist policy conducted toward Israel by these backward regimes, Israel managed to convince many of them that it had become a reality and that it was impossible not to recognize it and not to admit the necessity of guaranteeing its security. That defeatist policy encouraged the late Sadat to commit an enormous act of betrayal: to reconcile with Israel and to conclude a shameful agreement with it. That policy of defeat was also conducted by the Gulf Solidarity Committee, the Jordanian-Egyptian axis, Iraq, and Arafat's organization.

The defeatist policy vis-à-vis America is what governs the position of the backward leaders regarding the hateful war imposed on the Islamic Republic of Iran. They shamelessly support the collaborationist Saddam, financially, economically, and militarily, thinking that the "Zionized" order of Tikrīt[15] is capable of putting an end to the Islamic revolution and of preventing the spread of its revolutionary character and concepts. That defeatist policy is what impels the backward regimes to return people to ignorance, to weaken them, to dissolve their Muslim solidarity, to quash all the Muslim movements that have stood up to America and its allies in their countries. That same policy serves as defense against the fear of the disinherited's awakening. It forbids them access to political affairs, an eventuality that would represent a great danger for the perpetuation of their de facto regimes, first, by raising the consciousness of these peoples with respect to the widespread corruption of their governments and their equivocal relationships, and second, by arousing these people's sympathies for liberation movements in every corner of the Muslim world and beyond.

From our point of view, the backward Arab regimes represent an obstacle to the growth of the consciousness of the Muslim peoples and to their unity. We consider them responsible for the obstruction of attempts to pursue the fight and to keep open the wound in the Zionist enemy's side. We place great hope in the Muslim peoples, who have begun to protest unequivocally

15. Saddam Hussein's native city.

in most of the Muslim countries. They have been able to infiltrate the revolutionary world to acquire experience, especially the world of the victorious Islamic revolution. The day will come when the crumbling regimes will collapse under the blows of the disinherited, just as the throne of the tyrants in Iran collapsed. At this hour, when we are waging a ferocious battle against America and Israel and against their schemes in the region, it is our duty to advise these backward regimes not to conduct an action against the movement of the resurgent *ummah* resisting colonization and Zionism. These regimes must therefore learn the lesson of Islamic resistance in Lebanon, namely: persevere in the armed struggle against the enemy until its complete defeat. Similarly, we advise these regimes not to associate themselves with new proposals for submission or with hostile plans that target the Islamic revolution under way. Their potentates will meet the same fate as Anwar Sadat, Nurī al-Saʾīd [Nuri Saïd],[16] and others.

THE INTERNATIONAL FRONT FOR THE DISINHERITED

We turn to all the Arab and Muslim peoples to tell them clearly that the experience of the Muslims in Iran—henceforth governed in accordance with Islam—can no longer be ignored by anyone. It has been confirmed without the shadow of a doubt that the heart, stripped bare and propelled by the will of faith, is a power, thanks to God the Immense, that breaks through all the barriers of the tyrannical and oppressive regimes. Furthermore, we invite these peoples to become closely united, to outline their objectives, to rise up and shatter the chain constricting their will, and to overthrow the collaborationist governments that rule them. We implore the disinherited throughout the world to constitute an international front that unites all their liberation movements. They would thereby be able to coordinate their efforts globally, to make their movements effective and to concentrate

16. Nuri Saïd, head of the Iraqi government, was executed in July 1952 during the revolution led by Aref.

on their enemies' weaknesses. If all the nations and regimes of the colonial world are today at war with the disinherited, it is up to the disinherited to come together and confront the machinations of the forces of imperialism in the world.

All the oppressed peoples, especially the Arab and Muslim peoples, must understand that only Islam is fit to embody the idea of resistance against tyranny. The proof has been given: modern ideologies, without exception and for all time, have been subordinated to the interest of the agreement between America, the Soviet Union, and others. It is therefore time to understand that all the Western philosophies regarding the originality of man and his instincts cannot respond to his aspirations or to the elimination of injustice, aberration, and ignorance. Only Islam brings about man's awakening, his progress; only it offers him something new, since

> [the lamp] is lit from a blessed olive tree neither eastern nor western. Its very oil would almost shine forth, though no fire touched it. Light upon light; God guides to His light whom He will. (24:35)

GOD WITHIN MUSLIM UNITY

O Muslim peoples, beware of the perverse colonial division that seeks to break up your unity so as to sow schisms among you and to exacerbate the sectarianism between Sunnis and Shiites. Know that colonization was not able to control the wealth of the Muslims until it had endeavored to rend apart and partition their ranks. . . . It provoked the Sunnis against the Shiites and incited the Shiites against the Sunnis. Subsequently, colonization entrusted that mission to its minions, the unworthy leaders and ulema, whose authority it imposed on believers. Yet God is God for the unity of the Muslims. That is truly the rock on which the schemes of the imperialists founder, the hammer that destroys their unrighteous machines. You must therefore not settle for the "divide and conquer" policy being conducted in your countries and your tribes. You must resist it by clinging to the noble Koran:

Cling one and all to the faith of God and let nothing divide you (3:103). Have nothing to do with those who have split up their religion into sects. God will call them to account and declare to them what they have done (6:159).

O LEARNED MEN OF ISLAM

Your special responsibilities, learned men of Islam, are very great; they are equal to the catastrophes that preoccupy the Muslims. You are the best positioned to perform the duty of guiding the *ummah* to Islam . . . to make it aware of what the enemies are planning to do, so as to conquer it, rob it of its wealth, and enslave it. You are certainly aware that the Muslims regard you as the guardians of fidelity to the Messenger of God—peace and blessings be upon Him—and the heirs of the prophets and messengers of God. . . . Be therefore the model that allows them, first, to rise above the glitter and glamour of life here below, and second, to aspire to paradise and martyrdom for God. The Messenger of God is an excellent model for you: he was hungry among men, he sated himself among them, he was at home with those who prayed in the mosque, and he guided their ranks on the paths of jihad. He was their refuge during missions. They were reassured by his directives and his presence, unshakable in their trust. O learned men of Islam . . .

The guide Imam Khomeini has insisted on several occasions on the need for the skills of the learned Muslim and has directed his attention toward purifying himself before asking the same of others. He has said this in several of his statements: if the people knew that the owner of a shop was not honorable, they would say that such-and-such is not honorable; if they knew that a merchant was swindling people, they would say that such-and-such is an imposter; if they knew—God forbid—that a man of religion was not honorable, then they would say that the religion would not be good. Therefore, learned men of Islam . . . regarding these things, and many others as well, your responsibilities are vast. Call upon God in the fulfillment of them. Proclaim God All-Powerful,

following the invitation of Imam Alī—prayer and peace be upon him: "We do not ask You for a light load, rather we ask You for a strong back." And you will see that the *ummah* will respond favorably to your appeals, to your orientations and conduct. Know that the colonizer was well acquainted with your position within the *ummah*. That is why he vigorously addressed his attacks against the breasts of the learned mujahideen. He organized a Satanic plot to conceal the noble imam Mūsa al-Sadr, after discerning that he was an obstacle to hateful projects . . . and he killed the Muslim philosopher Sheikh Mortada Motahhari.*
The great Muslim *marjaʿ*, the noble ayatollah Mohammad Bāqir al-Sadr, was executed because some sensed the peril he incarnated with these words: "Unite in Imam Khomeini as he united with Islam." The colonizer is waiting for the opportunity to do harm to any learned man of Islam who performs his Muslim duty the best way possible.

Furthermore, colonization assails the Muslims through the preachers of leaders who do not fear God, who issue fatwas in areas where they are unwarranted, who deem conciliation with Israel lawful, who forbid destroying it and justify the treachery of the unrighteous leaders. The colonizer would not have acted thus had he not known the importance and influence that the man of religion exerts over the people. Your special responsibilities, learned men of Islam, are therefore to educate the Muslims to abide by the laws of religion, to clarify the political line that will guide them on the right path and lead them toward consolation and exaltation. Concern yourselves with the religious institutes *(hawzas)* in such a way that they may produce leaders faithful to God and attentive to the victory of religion and the nation.

A LAST WORD ON THE SUBJECT OF INTERNATIONAL INSTITUTIONS

Finally, we must speak of the international institutions and agencies, such as the UN and the Security Council, among others. Let us observe that these institutions are not in general the forum for the oppressed nations. They are ineffective because of the global imperialist states' control over decisions, whether in applying them or in paralyzing them. The right to veto that a few nations possess is proof of our argument.

As a result, we do not expect these institutions to produce anything that serves the cause of the humble oppressed. We invite all nations preoccupied with the subject to develop a proposal to abrogate the veto of the imperialist powers. So too, we invite them to construct a proposal to ban Israel from the United Nations, with the recognition that it is an illegal usurper hostile to human aspirations.

O noble disinherited . . . here are our proposals and objectives, there the rules likely to guide us. Whoever accepts us accepts the law, and God is the law. As for those who reject us, we shall wait until God decides between us and the unrighteous community.

Peace, mercy, and God's blessings upon you.

Hezbollah/Faction of God

POLITICAL CHARTER

November 30, 2009

In the name of God the Beneficent, the Merciful. Praise be to God, Lord of Worlds, prayer and peace on the seal of the prophets, our lord Muhammad, and on his holy family and his noble companions, and on all the prophets and messengers.

God All-Powerful says in his glorious Book: "Those that fight for Our cause We will surely guide to Our own paths. Surely God is with the righteous" (26:69).

And the All-Powerful says: "Believers, be devout toward God and seek the right path to Him. Fight valiantly for His cause, so that you may triumph." (5:35)[1]

The purpose of this document is to put forward the political vision of the Hezbollah. It includes our views and our positions, hopes, ambitions, and fears. It emerges in the first place from the good we have experienced, from our top-priority actions, and from our sacrifice to the vanguard. In an extraordinary political age rife with change, it is no longer possible to apprehend these changes without noticing the specific position occupied by our

This is an original and complete translation. The authors thank Amin E. and Abdellatif I. for their valuable assistance. [English translation based on the French version—trans.]

1. [Translation modified—trans.]

Resistance, or the number of actions carried out in the course of our itinerary. These changes will need to be placed within the context of a comparison between two antagonistic paths and the growing discordance that characterizes them:

1. The ever-widening path of Resistance and refusal,[2] based on military victories and political successes; the popular and political implantation of the model of Resistance, the constancy of political options, despite the magnitude of the threat and the size of the challenges . . . in the aim of shifting the power relations of the regional equation in favor of the Resistance and those who support it.

2. The path of the American-Israeli domination and imperialism in its various dimensions, alliances, and direct or indirect extensions. This path has witnessed military retreats and defeats, political failures that, one after another, have uncovered a failure resulting from American strategies and schemes. All of which culminated in a situation of stagnation and regression, and in a powerlessness within our Arab and Islamic world to control events and the path of development.

These facts must be understood within a broader international landscape, which in turn reveals the American impasse and the decline of the hegemony of a single pole in favor of a plurality, whose shape is not yet altogether stable. The collapse of the American and global financial markets and the stagnation and incapacity that the American economy now faces make the crisis of the global imperialist regime even more far reaching. It is the reflection of a renewed structural crisis in the arrogant capitalist model, a crisis that has reached its peak.

For that reason, it is possible to say that we are positioning ourselves within a context of historical changes that prefigure

2. "Refusal" must be understood as the rejection of any agreement with Israel (see below).

the decline of the United States of America as a hegemonic force, the decomposition of the single-pole hegemonic regime, and the beginning of an accelerated and historic deterioration of the Zionist entity.

Resistance movements lie at the heart of these changes. They appear as an essential strategic fact in this global landscape, having played a central role in the developments or in the impetus for changes that have occurred in our region.

For more than two and a half decades in Lebanon, the Resistance—and within it, the Islamic resistance—was a pioneer in the confrontation against hegemony and occupation. It held firm to that choice during a time that seemed to be both the beginning of the American era, marked by efforts to incarnate it, and the end of History. In light of the circumstances and the power relations in force at that time, some considered the choice of Resistance a delusion, a lack of political awareness, or a tendency counter to rational and real necessities.

In spite of that, the Resistance persisted in its jihadist path, conscious of the righteousness of its cause and of its capacity to build victory, thanks to faith and confident surrender to God the All-Powerful, thanks to membership in the *ummah* as a whole, the commitment to Lebanese national interests, trust in its people, and the erection of humane values in [the realms of] law, justice, and freedom.

During the course of its long jihad, through its aforementioned victories, from the defeat of Israel's occupation of Beirut and of the mountain, then its flight from Saydā, Tyre, and Nabatieh, then the acts of aggression of July 1993 and April 1996, to liberation in May 2000 and then the July 2006 war, that resistance planted the roots of its loyalty and of its model even before achieving victories. The stages in the development of its plans have accumulated, one on top of another: the force of liberation, then the force of equilibrium and confrontation, then the force of dissuasion and defense. To that let us add its role in domestic politics, as a pillar contributing to the construction of a powerful and just state.

Parallel to that, the Resistance was able to develop its political and humanist position. A Lebanese national value, it was also considered a shining Arab and Islamic value; it has now become a global and human value. The inspiration of its model and the reproduction of its achievements, on the basis of two factors—experience and deontology—are leading to freedom and independence in every corner of the Earth.

Although recognizing these promising changes and witnessing the stagnation of the enemy, which has resulted from the powerlessness of his war strategy and his incapacity to set his own conditions in imposing compromises, the Hezbollah does not underestimate the magnitude of the challenges and dangers that remain. It does not minimize the difficulties of the path of confrontation, the sacrifices required by the path of Resistance and [by efforts] to restore rights and contribute to the awakening of the *ummah*. Nevertheless, before [doing] all that, it can avail itself of greater clarity in its choices, more determination in its will, more trust in God, in itself, and in its people.

Within that context, the Hezbollah will define the essential lines that constitute the intellectual and political framework for its vision and its positions in face of the challenges raised.

CHAPTER 1
Hegemony and the Awakening
First: Western and American Hegemony and the World
After World War II, the United States became the party responsible for the central and privileged plan of hegemony. Under its leadership, that plan underwent a vast development—unprecedented in history—of the means of domination and submission. To accomplish this, it put to use the complex yield from ventures in various realms and at different levels: scientific, cultural, epistemological, technological, economic, and military. These ventures are sustained by a politico-economic scheme that sees the world solely as a collection of open markets governed by their own laws.

What is most dangerous about the concept of Western hegemony in general, and American hegemony in particular, is the founding belief that the world belongs to them and that they have the right to rule because of their superiority in several domains. For that reason, the Western—and especially, American—expansionist strategy, coupled with a capitalist economic plan, is global in nature, a strategy of boundless appetite and greed.

The domination of wanton capitalist forces, represented primarily by international networks of monopolies, composed of transnational and even transcontinental companies and of various international institutions, financial in particular—all of which receive military support—led to an increase in fundamental antagonisms and conflicts that are no less significant: conflicts of different identities, cultures, and civilizations, in addition to the conflicts between poverty and wealth.

Wanton capitalism has transformed globalization into an instrument for differentiating and destroying identities and has imposed the most dangerous alienation: cultural, civilizational, economic, and social. That globalization reached its most dangerous pitch in becoming a military globalization via the bearers of the Western plan for hegemony. We have witnessed its manifestations in the Middle Eastern region, beginning with Afghanistan, Iraq, Palestine, and Lebanon. It was Lebanon's fate to be the victim of Israeli aggression in July 2006.

Especially between the last decade of the twentieth century and the present, the American plan for hegemony and domination reached dangerous levels never before known. It has continued to grow since the breakup of the Soviet Union, which represented a turning point. By American calculations, this was a historic opportunity to become the only power to conduct globally the plan for hegemony, in the name of historical responsibility and of the idea that there is no difference between the world's interests and American interests. That involves promoting hegemony as being in the interest of other nations and peoples, not portraying it as an exclusively American interest.

That process reached its apogee when the New Conservative movement seized the reins of George W. Bush's administration. That movement expressed its vision in the document "The Project for the New American Century," composed on the eve of the American elections in 2000 and implemented after George W. Bush's administration took power in the United States of America.

What that document—which quickly became the Bush administration's working plan—insisted upon most was neither strange nor surprising, namely, the problematic of rebuilding American capacities, which reflected a new strategic vision for American national security. It became quite apparent that said national security was based on the constitution of military capacities, considered not only as a method of dissuasion but also as a powerful means of action and intervention, whether in preventive operations that launch anticipated attacks, or therapeutically, to deal with crises once the operations are completed. After the events of September 11, the Bush administration once again found the conditions favorable for exerting the greatest ascendancy and the greatest influence, by putting into practice its strategic vision of sole hegemony over the world, under the slogan "the global war on terror." In that way, the administration undertook initiatives, considered successful at first, in accordance with the following scheme:

1. Militarize its relations and policies to the maximum degree.
2. Avoid depending on multipolar frameworks and make strategic decisions on its own. Coordinate when necessary with allies it can count on.
3. Quickly put an end to the war in Afghanistan, then move to the next stage, the most important in the plan for hegemony, namely, the takeover of Iraq, considered the principal center of gravity for establishing a new Middle East that would be equal to the demands of the

post–September 11 world. That administration had no
scruples about using every means: falsification, imposture,
and obvious lies to justify its wars, particularly against
Iraq and all those—states, movements, forces, and
personalities—that resist its neocolonialist project.

Within that framework, the Bush administration decided to
conflate "the concept of terrorism" and "the concept of resistance" to remove the human and legal legitimacy of the Resistance. It thereby legitimated the multiple wars it was waging
against the Resistance, in the aim of obliterating the last rampart
of peoples and states that defend their right to live in freedom,
dignity, and honor, their right to unrestricted sovereignty, to construct their own experiment, and to maintain their role and place
in the movement of human History from the civilizational and
cultural point of view.

The label "terrorism" has become a pretext for American hegemony by means of certain instruments: pursuit, arbitrary
arrest, and the abandonment of the most elementary principles of
fair trials, as is the case in the Guantanamo prison; direct interference in the sovereignty of states, which has transformed them
into a registered trademark for arbitrary charges and punitive
measures against entire peoples; [and] the accordance to itself of
an absolute right to wage destructive and devastating wars, which
do not distinguish the innocent from the guilty and also make no
distinction between children, the elderly, women, and the young.

Thus far, the American terrorist wars have cost several million
human lives, not counting the overall destruction, which affects
not only stones and infrastructure but the very structure and
foundations of societies. These societies have therefore been bro-
ken apart, and the result has been interference in the process of
development through a retrogressive operation that has reproduced unending civil conflicts based on religion, community, and
race—not to mention the target represented by the storehouse of
these peoples' cultures and civilizations.

There is no doubt that American terrorism is the foundation of all terrorism in the world. The Bush administration transformed the United States into a danger that threatens the world as a whole at every level. If a worldwide poll were to be taken today, the United States would appear as the most despised state in the world.

The fiasco of the war against Iraq, the evolution of the Resistance in that country, the regional and international discontent at the effects of that war, the failure of the so-called war on terror, particularly in Afghanistan—which has seen the return in force of the Taliban, the acknowledgment of their role, and efforts to come to an agreement with them—and, likewise, the total failure of the American war, via Israeli instruments, against the Resistance in Lebanon and Palestine, have all culminated in the erosion of American prestige at the international level and in a strategic retreat in the United States' ability to take action and to become entangled in new ventures.

Despite what has been presented, that does not mean that the United States will easily leave the scene. On the contrary, it will do everything necessary to protect what it calls "its strategic interests," because the policy of American hegemony is motivated by ideological considerations and intellectual projects fed by extremist orientations, in alliance with a military-industrial complex whose greed and lust have no limits.

Second: Our Region and the American Scheme

Although the disinherited world as a whole bows under the yoke of that imperialist hegemony, our Arab and Islamic world bears the heaviest burden, for reasons relating to its History, its civilization, its resources, and its geographical location.

For centuries, our Arab and Islamic world has been exposed to interminable and savage colonialist wars. But the most recent phase began with the settlement of the Zionist entity in the region, within the context of a scheme whose aim was to break the region up into entities fighting among themselves and rejecting one another on various pretexts. That colonialist phase reached its apogee when the United States succeeded the former colonizers in the region.

The central and chief aim of American imperialism is represented by domination in all its forms—political, economic, cultural—of the populations and the theft of their wealth. Foremost among these is the theft of oil resources, the chief instrument for controlling the direction of the world economy, by every means not subject to rules or moral and human norms, including the use of excessive military force, direct or indirect.[3]

To realize its aims, America has adopted general policies and working strategies. The most important of these are:

1. To provide all means for guaranteeing stability to the Zionist entity, as an advanced base and center of gravity for the American colonialist project and [with the aim of] breaking up the region; to support that entity by every means and for all time, and to provide it with a security network for its existence, allowing it to play the role of a cancerous cell that cuts off the *ummah's* capacities and potentialities and destroys its possibilities, hopes, and aspirations.

2. To destroy the spiritual, civilizational, and cultural possibilities of our peoples and to work to weaken their morale by promoting media wars and psychological warfare that take as their targets our peoples' values, as well as the symbols of their jihad and resistance.

3. To support the vassal regimes and despots in the region.

4. To hold, by sea, land, and air, the geostrategic positions in the region that constitute nodal points, whether autonomous or interdependent; to deploy military bases at vital points of articulation in the service of its wars and in support of its agents.

---

3. "Indirect" must be understood as through the intermediary of Israel.

5. To prevent any renaissance [*nahda*] in the region that would allow it to possess the means of power and progress and would permit it to play a historic role at the global level.

6. To sow discord [*fitna*] and divisions in all their forms, particularly doctrinal discords between Muslims, in order to produce internal, interminable civil conflicts.

It is clear that every conflict today, whatever it might be, wherever it might be in the world, can be apprehended only within a strategic global perspective. The American danger is not a local danger or one specific to one region rather than another. As a result, the front of engagement against that American danger must also be global.

It is beyond doubt that that confrontation is difficult and delicate; it is a fight of historic scope, and, as a result, it is a generations-long fight that requires the favorable use of every virtuality. Our experience in Lebanon has taught us that difficult does not mean impossible. On the contrary, dynamic and reactive peoples by themselves, and a wise leadership aware of and ready for every possibility, can count on achieving multiple feats, can build victory after victory. As such, that question is valid vertically, across History, and is so horizontally as well, across geographical and geopolitical space.

American imperialism has left our *ummah* and our peoples no other choice but that of Resistance, in the aim of a better life, a better human and humane future governed by fraternal relations, both diverse and unified, where peace and harmony reign. Such were the strokes drawn by the movement of the prophets and the great reformers across History, and such is the future, in accordance with the prospects and desires of the righteous and transcendent human spirit.

CHAPTER 2
Lebanon

First: The Nation

Lebanon is our homeland, the land of our fathers and forefathers. It is the homeland of our children, grandchildren, and of all the generations to come. For its sovereignty, its dignity, and its honor, for the liberation of its soil, we have offered the dearest sacrifices and the worthiest martyrs. We want that homeland to belong to all Lebanese equally, we want it to embrace them, encompass them, rise up through them and through what they bring to it.

We want it to be unified and united as a land, a people, a state, and as institutions. We reject every sort of division or "federalism," overt or covert. We want it to be sovereign, free, and independent, worthy, honorable, invincible, strong, and powerful, a factor in the regional equations, contributing in an essential way to the construction of the present and the future. So has it always been present in the production of History.

One of the most essential conditions for the establishment and perpetuation of a nation of this kind is that it have a just, powerful, and strong state, a political system that truly represents the will of the people and their aspirations for justice, freedom, security, stability, prosperity, and dignity. That is what all Lebanese desire, what they work for, and we are among those Lebanese.

Second: The Resistance

"Israel" represents a constant threat to Lebanon, as state and as entity, and an imminent danger because of its historical claims on the land and water of Lebanon—the only model of a coexistence between followers of heavenly messages, in accordance with a specific formula, and a nation that opposes the idea of a racist state, represented by the Zionist entity. Furthermore, the existence of Lebanon on the border of occupied Palestine, in a region troubled by conflict with the Israeli enemy, has forced this country to assume Lebanese-national and Arab-national responsibilities.

The Israeli threat to that nation began with the implantation of the Zionist entity in the land of Palestine. This is an entity that has ceaselessly voiced its claims on Lebanese land. It wants to annex parts of it and lay its hands on its resources, on its water in the first place. It has progressively attempted to act on these claims.

That entity began its aggression in 1948, beginning on the borders and moving to the interior of the nation, from the massacre of Hawla in 1949 to the attack on the Beirut International Airport in 1968. Between these occurrences were long years of aggression against the border regions, their lands, inhabitants, and wealth. This was a first step toward direct occupation, by means of repeated invasions—up to that of March 1978—of the border region and toward subjection to Israeli security and its political and economic power within the framework of a global scheme, in anticipation of the subjugation of the nation as a whole during the 1982 invasion.

All that unfolded with the complete support of the United States of America, as the so-called international community and its institutions turned a blind eye, under a suspicious cloak of official Arab silence and in the absence of the Lebanese authority, which had abandoned its land and its people in the grip of massacres and the Israeli invasion, having failed to assume its responsibilities and state duties. Within the context of that great national disaster—the people's suffering, the absence of a state, and the world's abandonment—those Lebanese who are true to their homeland have found no recourse other than their law and the vindication of their national, moral, and religious duty to defend their land. Their choice was to launch a popular armed resistance to confront the Zionist danger and the constant assault on their lives, their property, and their future.

In these difficult circumstances, during which time the Lebanese were without a state, the measures to recover the homeland by means of armed resistance began by liberating the land and emancipating political decision making from the hands of the Israeli occupation. That was the first step toward restoring the state and building its constitutional institutions. Most important was the reestablishment of the national values on which the state was founded. Foremost among these: national sovereignty and dignity, which gave the value of freedom its true dimension. These were no longer mere slogans: the Resistance sanctified them thanks to the liberation of the land and of man. These national values have become the cornerstone for the construction of modern Lebanon. They have reserved a place for that country on the world map and have restored to it the consideration it ought to have as a country to be respected. Its sons are proud to belong to it, because it is the land of freedom, culture, science, and diversity,[4] just as it is the land of vitality, dignity, sacrifice, and heroism. All these dimensions combined were crowned by the Resistance by means of what it accomplished: the 2000 liberation and the historic victory in the July 2006 war. The Resistance provided a living experiment in defending the homeland, an experiment that has become a lesson inspiring peoples and nations to defend their lands, to protect their independence, and to preserve their sovereignty.

That national feat by the Resistance was achieved with the assistance of a faithful people and a national army. It obstructed the enemy's objectives and handed that enemy a historic defeat. The Resistance—its fighters, its martyrs—and alongside it Lebanon, its people and its army, emerged the victors. That is the beginning of a new phase for the region. The Resistance, by its role and function, is the central axis for dissuading the enemy, for ensuring the protection of independence and of the nation's sovereignty, for defending its people, and for pursuing the liberation of the rest of the occupied lands.

4. These terms are found in the thinking of the founders of Lebanon in 1943. The Hezbollah writers have added a second series of qualifiers.

That role and that function are a permanent national necessity so long as the Israeli threat and the enemy's claims on our lands and water persist, given the absence of a strong and powerful state and the imbalance in power relations between the state and the enemy—an imbalance that generally impels weak states and peoples, faced with the claims and threats of tyrannical and strong states, to seek out methods to make the best of the potentialities and capacities available. The constant Israeli threat imposes a defensive method on Lebanon, based on the pairing of a popular resistance that defends the homeland against any Israeli conquest, and, as its complement, a national army that protects the homeland and consolidates its security and stability. The success of that procedure was recently demonstrated: it lay behind Lebanon's victories and supplied the means to protect the country.

That method, established within the framework of a defensive strategy, constitutes a protective shelter for Lebanon, after the failure of the wagers made on other protections, whether international, Arab, or those negotiated with the enemy. The option of Resistance allowed Lebanon to liberate its land, restore its state institutions, protect its sovereignty, and achieve true independence. Within that framework, the Lebanese—their political forces, social strata, intellectual elites, and economic organizations—are engaged in preserving that method and adhering to it, because the Israeli danger places Lebanon in all its components in peril. That requires the broadest participation possible among the Lebanese, who must assume the responsibility for defending the homeland and for supplying it with the means of protection.

Both the success of the Resistance's experience in its confrontation with the enemy—the failure of all schemes and of all wars to put an end to that Resistance, to restrict its choices and take away its weapons—and the persistence of the Israeli threat and its danger to Lebanon make it incumbent on the Resistance to persevere in its efforts to possess the instruments of power and to strengthen its potential and capacities. It will thereby be able to perform its duty and fulfill its national responsibilities: contribute toward pursuing the mission of liberating those of our territories that are still under occupation—the Shebaa farms, the Kfarshouba plain, and the Lebanese village of Ghajar; secure the return of the remaining prisoners, of the missing, and of the martyrs' bodies; and participate in the defense and protection of the land and the people.

Third: The State and the Political Regime

Political confessionalism is the chief problem of the Lebanese political regime, preventing its reform, evolution, and continuing modernization. The establishment of the regime on confessional foundations represents a serious hindrance in the realization of a true democracy, in light of which an elected majority can govern and an elected minority [can constitute] the opposition, one that offers the possibility of a healthy sharing of power between the majority and the opposition, or between the different political coalitions. As a result, the essential condition for setting in place a true democracy of that kind is the suppression of the regime's political confessionalism, and that is what the Taif Agreement stipulated, requiring, to achieve that end,[5] the formation of a national supreme council.

While waiting for the Lebanese to accomplish that historic and delicate feat—namely, the suppression of political confessionalism—through national dialogue, and so long as the political regime rests on confessional foundations, consensual democracy remains the principal rule for exercising power in Lebanon, because it is the actual embodiment of the spirit of the Constitution and the essence of the coexistence pact. *Consequently, any approach to national issues based on a majority-*

5. It is specified in the Taif Agreement that this "national committee" must "study" and "make proposals" in that direction and not itself "achieve" that end (see also clause 95 of the Lebanese Constitution).

minority equation is dependent on the satisfaction of the historical and social conditions necessary for the application of true democracy, in which the citizen will become a value in himself.[6]

The will of the Lebanese to live together, with their dignity respected and with equal rights and duties, makes constructive cooperation an imperative, in view of laying the foundations for real cooperation, which would constitute the most suitable method for protecting their diversity and complete stability, after a period of instability caused by various policies rooted in a propensity for monopoly, elimination, and exclusion.

Consensual democracy represents a political method propitious for real participation by all, and a factor of trust that reassures the nation's constituent parts. It contributes significantly toward the implementation of the construction phase of a peaceful state that all citizens [will] feel was built for them.

The state we aspire to build with other Lebanese is the following:

A state that preserves public liberties and provides all the conditions proper for their exercise.

A state that is vigilant about national unity and cohesion.

A powerful state that protects the land, the people, sovereignty, and independence, [one] that has a strong, powerful, and well-equipped national army, effective security institutions looking after the people's safety and interests.

A state whose structure is built on modern, effective, and mutualist institutions, based on qualifications, jobs, and clear and well-defined concerns.

6. That expression—which we italicize—appears word for word in the memorandum of understanding of February 6, 2006, between the Free Patriotic Movement and the Hezbollah (point 2: "Consensual Democracy"). It was adopted in the Manifesto of the Free Patriotic Movement of May 2005: "[the belief of the Free Patriotic Movement is] that man as an individual is a value in himself."

A state that commits itself to applying the laws to all, within the context of respect for public liberties, for the equity of rights, and for the duties of citizens, whatever their faith, region, and orientation.

A state that satisfies the conditions for sound and just parliamentary representation, which can be realized only through a modern electoral law that allows the Lebanese voter to choose his representatives in the absence of all financial influence, all sectarianism, and all pressure, and that realizes the broadest representation possible of every category of Lebanese people.

A state that relies on persons with scientific qualifications and technical skills, and on persons of integrity, whatever their religious allegiance, and that sets in place, without deal-making, strong and effective tools for purging the administration of corruption and of the corrupt.

A state that satisfies the conditions of an independent supreme judicial power, removed from the control of politicians, in which capable, upright, and free judges exercise their delicate responsibilities to establish justice among the people.

A state in which the economy is based primarily on the productive sectors, one that works to stimulate and strengthen them, particularly the agricultural and industrial sectors, by giving them the share falling to them, through proposals, programs, and aid that allow them to improve production and sales. These make it possible to provide adequate and sufficient employment opportunities, especially in the rural areas.

A state that adopts and applies the principle of balanced development among the different regions and that works to repair the economic and social fractures among them.

A state that is concerned about its citizens and that works to offer them adequate services such as education, health care, and the environment needed to assure a dignified life, one

that alleviates the problem of poverty, provides employment opportunities, and so on.

A state that cares for the rising younger generations, that aids
in directing their energies and developing their talents by
guiding them toward humanist and national goals, and
that protects them from decadence and depravity.

A state that works toward strengthening the role of women
and fostering their participation in all realms, to take
advantage of their specificities and influence and to respect
their station.

A state that grants suitable attention to the place of education, especially with respect to the public schools, that
strengthens the Lebanese University in all its aspects
and applies [the principle of] compulsory and free
education.

A state that adopts a decentralized administrative system that
grants major administrative powers to the various administrative units (prefecture, district, municipality),[7] in order to
increase the opportunities for development and facilitate
business and citizen action, yet without allowing that
administrative decentralization to turn subsequently into
a sort of "federalism."

A state that fights to end emigration, that of the young and of
families and that of brains and skills, within the context of
an overall and practical plan.

A state that is concerned about its emigrant citizens everywhere in the world, that defends and protects them, that
uses to its advantage their dissemination, their status, and
their positions to serve national causes.

The establishment of a state with these characteristics and
conditions is a goal for us and for every faithful and loyal Lebanese. We in the Hezbollah are going to deploy all our efforts, in

7. In the original text: *Mohāfaza, Qada', Baladiyya.*

cooperation with the various political and popular forces that share that vision with us, to realize that eminent national goal.

Fourth: Lebanon and Lebanese-Palestinian Relations

One of the catastrophic consequences of the appearance of the Zionist entity on the territory of Palestine and of the expulsion of its populations has been the question of Palestinian refugees. They were displaced to Lebanon to live temporarily as guests among their Lebanese brothers while awaiting their return to their own homeland and region, from which they were excluded.

Because of that refuge, what the Palestinians and the Lebanese have equally suffered has its true and direct cause in the Israeli occupation of Palestine and the catastrophes and disasters that resulted from it and that affected all the peoples of the region. Its misdeeds were not committed solely against the Palestinians. And likewise, the suffering of the Palestinian refugees in Lebanon has not been limited to the pain of forced exile and refuge. To it have been added: the savage Israeli assaults and massacres, which have destroyed stones and men, as was the case of the camp in Nabatieh, which was entirely destroyed; the cruel living conditions in the camps, where the circumstances led to the absence of even the minimum requirements for living in dignity; the loss of civil and social rights; and the inability of the successive Lebanese governments to fulfill their duties in that regard.

That abnormal situation now constrains the responsible Lebanese authorities to assume their responsibilities and to build Lebanese-Palestinian relations on sound, solid, and legal bases that take into account just law, the scales of justice, and the common interests of the two peoples. The [Palestinian] presence and [Lebanese-Palestinian] relations must no longer be governed by whims, passions, political calculations, internal disputes, and international interference.

We maintain that the success of this mission depends on the following:

- direct Lebanese-Palestinian dialogue;
- the capacity of the Palestinians in Lebanon to agree on the choice of a single authority of reference to represent them in that dialogue, moving beyond the disagreements current in the general Palestinian context.
- the granting of civil and social rights to the Palestinians of Lebanon, as befits their human situation and in view of preserving their personality, their identity, and their cause.
- adherence to the right of return and rejection of naturalization.

Fifth: Lebanon and Arab Relations

Lebanon, Arab in its identity and allegiance, professes its identity and its allegiance as a natural and original condition of the structure of Lebanese society. Living space, geopolitics, strategic depth, policies of regional complementarity and national interests[8]—as strategic determinants of the political position of Lebanon and its major interests—require that it commit itself to the righteous Arab causes, to the vanguard of the Palestinian cause, and to the struggle against the Israeli enemy.

Similarly, there is a clear need to combine efforts to overcome the conflicts that are tearing Arab ranks apart. The incompatibility among strategies and the disparity of alliances, despite their seriousness and intensity, do not justify the swerve toward policies targeting one or another, or the adherence to external proposals founded on exacerbating the division, on provoking religious fanaticism, and on stirring up factors that parcel up or chip away at the *ummah*, leading to its depletion, which benefits the Zionist enemy and the execution of American schemes.

The evolution of political organization, founded on reducing or regulating the conflicts and on keeping them from erupting

---

8. "National interests" must be understood as the interests of the "Arab nation."

into open battles, is an option that deserves to be adopted. Its intent is to bring to fruition a qualitative and responsible convergence of approaches to national questions;[9] to seek common denominators, in order to strengthen them and provide opportunities for constructive exchange at the governmental and popular levels; and to bring into being the largest possible joint framework that can serve our causes.

It is there that the choice of Resistance constitutes a key necessity and an objective factor for hardening the Arab position and weakening the enemy, regardless of the nature of the strategies or political wagers adopted.

As a result of everything that has been presented, the Resistance does not consider it a handicap to generalize the benefits of the Resistance option, in order to reach the various corners of the Arab world, so long as the results are placed within the context of an equation that will weaken the enemy and strengthen and harden the Arab position.

Within that framework, Syria has adopted a distinct and unyielding position in the battle with the Israeli enemy. It has supported the resistance movements in the region, has stood beside them under the most difficult circumstances, and has worked for the unification of Arab efforts to ensure the interests of the region and to face the challenges.

We affirm the necessity of adhering to the special relationship between Lebanon and Syria; it is a shared political, security, and economic need. It is prescribed by the interests of the two countries and the two peoples, by geopolitical obligations, by the imperatives of Lebanese stability, and by the shared challenges to be faced. We therefore extend an invitation to put an end to the negative atmosphere that has warped relations between the two countries in recent years and to reestablish as soon as possible these relations within a normal situation.

---

9. "National questions" must be understood as questions relating to the "Arab nation."

Sixth: Lebanon and Relations with Islam

Our Arab and Muslim world faces challenges that affect the various components of our societies. As a result, it is incumbent on us not to underestimate their danger. Thus, the sectarian dissensions and community tensions fabricated from whole cloth, particularly between Sunnis and Shiites; the invention of ethnic disagreements between Kurds, Turkomans and Arabs, Iranians and Arabs; . . . the intimidation and terrorizing of minorities; the constant hemorrhaging of Christians from the Arab East, especially from Palestine and Iraq even more than from Lebanon—all these threaten the cohesion of our society, reduce its immunity, and increase the impediments to its awakening and evolution.

Religious and ethnic diversity represents a source of wealth and social vitality; instead, it has been misused, employed as a factor for fragmentation, dissension, and societal collapse.

The situation resulting from that misuse was caused by a convergence between premeditated Western policies (American in particular), and fanatical and irresponsible practices and conceptions internal [to the Arab and Muslim world], combined with an unstable political environment.

It is urgent to take these truths into account, and it is necessary to insert them—as a key concern—into the programs of [political] forces and into the principal orientations, including those of the Islamic movements charged with containing these challenges and with remedying these problems.

The Hezbollah insists on the importance of cooperation between Muslim states in every realm. That is what procures them their strength in the form of solidarity against imperialist schemes and societal protection against cultural and media conquest. That is what incites them to make the most of their resources through the exchange among these states of different benefits.

Within that framework, the Hezbollah maintains that Iran, [inasmuch as it is] Islamic, is an important central state in the

Islamic world. It is Iran that, through its revolution, brought down the shah's regime and its American-Zionist schemes. It is Iran that sustained the Resistance movements in our region and courageously and determinedly took the side of Arab and Islamic causes, foremost among them the Palestinian cause.

The policy of the Islamic Republic in Iran has been clear and constant in support of the primary cause, the central and most important one for Arabs and Muslims, namely, the Palestinian cause, ever since the announcement of the victory of the blessed Islamic revolution under the leadership of the *walī al-faqīh* Imam Khomeini (may God sanctify him) and the opening of the first Palestinian embassy on the site of the former Israeli embassy. That support has persisted in all its forms to this day, under the leadership of the *walī al-faqīh* Imam Khamenei (God grant him long life). It has led to remarkable victories, for the first time in the history of the struggle against the Zionist conquerors.

The invention of discord on the part of certain Arab parties with the Islamic Republic of Iran represents an attack on us and on the Palestinian cause, which serves only "Israel" and the United States of America.

Iran, which formulated its political doctrine and constructed its living space on the basis of the "centrality of the Palestinian cause," the antagonism with "Israel," the confrontation of American policies, and the complementarity of the Arab and Islamic environment, is justified in demanding the will for cooperation and brotherhood. One must deal with Iran as if it were a jumping-off point, a strategic and important center, a sovereign, independent, and liberating model supporting the current Arab-Muslim pro-independence project, and a power that immunizes the states and the peoples of our region.

The Muslim world is strengthened by its alliances and the cooperation of the states. We affirm the importance of the advantage to be drawn from the elements of political, economic, and human forces present in every state among the states of the

Islamic world, based on reciprocity, assistance, and noncompliance to the imperialists.

We recall the importance of unity among Muslims—as the All-Powerful said, "Cling one and all to the faith of God and let nothing divide you"[10]—and of suspicion toward what divides them, namely, sectarian provocation, especially between Sunnis and Shiites. We are counting on the lucidity of the Muslim peoples to block the machinations of conspiracies and sedition at that level.

Seventh: Lebanon and International Relations

In accordance with the Hezbollah's vision and methodology, the criteria for discord, conflict, and combat rest for the most part on the loftiest politico-moral principle, [pitting] the arrogant against the disinherited, the oppressor against the oppressed, the haughty occupier against those who aspire to freedom and independence.

In the same way, the Hezbollah believes that mono-hegemony destroys the global balance and global stability, international peace and security.

The American administration's unlimited support for "Israel," the fact that it has incited attacks and provided cover for the Israeli occupation of Arab territories, combined with the hegemony of the American administration over international institutions, the polarized character of the criteria for promulgating and executing international decisions, the policy of interfering in the affairs of other societies, the militarization of the world, the adoption of the logic of itinerant wars in international conflicts, and the provocation of disturbances everywhere in the world place the American administration in the position of an enemy to our *ummah* and our peoples. All of which makes it principally and primordially responsible for the disorder and disruption produced in the international system.

As for European policies, they fluctuate between powerlessness and ineffectiveness on the one hand and, on the other, the

10. Koran 3:103.

unjustified embrace of American policies. That leads to an intensification of the Mediterranean tendency in Europe, to the benefit of the hegemony of the pro-NATO tendency, with its colonialist backdrop.

The embrace of American policies—particularly during the era of [America's] historic defeat—constitutes a strategic error that will only lead to more problems, difficulties, and complications in Euro-Arab relations.

Europe bears a particular responsibility because of the legacy of colonialism, which caused colossal damage to our region. Our people are still suffering from its impact and consequences.

Because some European peoples have a history of resistance to the occupier, the duty of Europe, moral and human before being political, requires that it recognize the right of peoples to resist the occupier, based on the distinction between resistance and terrorism.

In our opinion, the need for stability and cooperation in Euro-Arab relations requires the implementation of a more independent, more just, and more objective European rapprochement. It will be difficult to construct a common living space—from the standpoint of both politics and security—without that transformation, which guarantees treatment for the sources of dissension that create crises and instability.

Conversely, we observe with a great deal of attention and consideration the efforts toward independence and liberation, and the rejection of hegemony, in the countries of Latin America. We perceive vast areas of agreement between their proposals and those of the Resistance movements in our regions, leading to the construction of a more just and better balanced international order.

The conjunction of that experience with our own constitutes a promising reason for hope at the global level, based on a universal human identity and a shared political and moral backdrop. In that context, the slogan "unity of the disinherited" will remain one of the foundations of our political thought, constructing our conception, our relationship, and our positions with respect to international affairs.

CHAPTER 3
Palestine and Negotiations for Compromise
First: The Palestinian Cause and the Zionist Entity

Ever since it desecrated Palestine and banished the country's residents in 1948, the Zionist entity, with the approval and support of the forces of international hegemony at the time, has represented a direct assault and a grave danger affecting the Arab region as a whole, as well as a true threat to its security, stability, and interests. The harmful effects have not been confined to the Palestinian people or to the states and peoples neighboring Palestine. The attacks, tensions, and wars endured by the region, as a result of aggressive Israeli proclivities and practices, are only proof of and witness to the scope of the injustice affecting the Palestinian people, the Arabs, and the Muslims, following from the crime against humanity committed by the West when it implanted that foreign entity in the heart of the Arab and Islamic world, so that it would be a hostile [means of] penetration and the vanguard of the Western imperialist scheme in general, and a base for domination and hegemony over the region in particular.

Zionism is a racist movement, in theory and in practice. It results from an authoritarian and tyrannical imperialist mentality. In its essence, it is a project of expansionist implantation and Judaization. The entity produced by it has risen up, has strengthened and maintained itself, through occupation, assault, massacres, and terrorism, with the support, approval, and sponsorship of the colonialist states, particularly the United States of America. That nation is linked [to the Zionist entity] by a strategic alliance that has made it a true partner in all the wars and massacres, and in all its terrorist practices.

The battle that our *ummah* is waging against the colonialist Zionist scheme in Palestine stems for the most part from our duty to defend ourselves against the imperialist Israeli occupation, the assault and injustice that threaten our existence and take aim at our rights and our future. It does not stem on our part from religious, racist, or ethnic clashes, even though those who carry out that imperialist Zionist scheme have never had any scruples about using religion and religious feeling as a means to realize their aims and objectives.

The recognition of the Jewish identity of the "State of Israel" demanded from the Palestinians, the Arabs, and the Muslims by the American president Bush, his successor, Obama, and with them the leaders of the Zionist entity, is the most obvious proof of that.

The natural and inevitable consequence is that that artificial usurper is experiencing an existential dilemma that poisons its leaders and henchmen, given that it had an unnatural birth, that it is an entity incapable of living and perpetuating itself, and that it faces disappearance. The historical responsibility not to recognize that entity is incumbent upon the *ummah* and its peoples, whatever the pressures and challenges may be, as it is incumbent on them to persist in the work of liberating the entire usurped land, of restoring the rights that were stolen, however much time and however many sacrifices are required.

Second: Al-Quds and al-Aqsa Mosque

The entire world grasps the importance and sanctity of al-Quds[11] and al-Aqsa Mosque. Al-Aqsa Mosque is the first of the two *qibla,* the third holy site, the site of the nocturnal journey of the messenger of God (prayers and the blessings of God be upon him), and the crossroads for the prophets and messengers (the prayers of God be upon them). No one denies the majesty of that site, among the most sacred points of reference for the Muslims, nor its profound connection to Islam, as one of the most important Muslim symbols on earth.

11. The term "Jerusalem" does not adequately render what a speaker of Arabic understands upon hearing the term "al-Quds."

The city of al-Quds, which holds Muslim and Christian holy sites, enjoys an exalted place among Muslims and Christians equally.

The continued Israeli occupation of that holy city, accompanied by plans and proposals for Judaization; the expulsion of its sons; the confiscation of their houses and properties; the encirclement of them by Jewish neighborhoods, by strips and blocs of colonies; their suffocation by the racist wall of separation, combined with the continued American-Israeli efforts aimed at establishing [Jerusalem] as an eternal capital of the Zionist entity with international recognition: all these constitute aggressive measures, which are rejected and condemned.

Furthermore, the dangerous, repeated, and persistent attacks against blessed al-Aqsa Mosque, the excavation work undertaken around it with the aim of destroying it, represent a real and grave danger threatening its existence and continued survival and augur harmful consequences dangerous to the region as a whole.

The obligation to save, liberate, defend, and protect al-Aqsa Mosque is a religious duty and a human and moral responsibility incumbent on every free and honorable son of our Arab and Islamic *ummah* and on all free men of honor in the world.

We officially invite and ask the Arabs and the Muslims, addressing ourselves directly to the people, and to all the states eager for peace and stability in the world, to deploy their efforts and methods to liberate al-Quds from the yoke of the Zionist occupation and to preserve its true identity and its Muslim and Christian holy sites.

Third: The Palestinian Resistance

The Palestinian people, who are waging a battle of self-defense and struggling to recover their legitimate national rights in Palestine, in the historical sense and geographical reality of those rights, exert for the most part a legitimate right, sanctified and governed by heavenly messages, international laws, and humanist values and traditions.

That right encompasses Resistance in all its forms—in the first place, armed combat—and by every means that the factions of Palestinian resistance are able to use, particularly within the context of the imbalance of power in favor of the Zionist enemy, which is equipped with the most modern weapons of devastation, destruction, and death.

Experience has constituted one irrefutable proof, leaving no place for doubt, throughout the fighting and clashes between our *ummah* and the Zionist entity, from its desecration of Palestine until our own time. It has demonstrated the importance and utility of the choice of jihadist resistance and of armed struggle in the confrontation against aggression, the liberation of the land, the restoration of rights, the achievement of the balance of terror, and the correction of the discrepancy in strategic superiority through the equations imposed by the Resistance, with its available capacities, its will, and its steadfastness in confrontation. The successive victories achieved by the Resistance in Lebanon and the cumulative feats—military and moral—on the battlefield throughout its long jihadist experience are the best illustration of that: in particular, the obligation forced on the Zionists to effect a major Israeli withdrawal in May 2000, the resounding defeat of the Zionist army during the assault of July 2006, [a battle] during which the Resistance achieved a divine, historic, and strategic victory that radically modified the equation of the conflict and inflicted the first defeat at that level on the Israeli enemy, putting an end to the myth of [its] army's invincibility.

The other proof is what the Resistance accomplished in Palestine. Its feats occurred constantly, throughout the experience of the Palestinian revolution and the choice of armed struggle that followed: the First Intifada of stones, the Second Intifada of al-Aqsa, the forced rout of the Israeli army at the time of the complete withdrawal from the Gaza Strip in 2005—unconditional, without negotiations, without an accord, and with no gain in terms of politics, security, or terrain. At that level and within these dimensions, that was the first qualitative battlefield victory. It was an indication that favored the choice of Resistance in Palestine. Given that this was the first Israeli defeat forced by the Resistance within the historical boundaries of Palestine, the indications to which they attest are of great importance at the strategic level, in the battle between us and the Zionist entity. Furthermore, the admirable tenacity of the Palestinian people in their struggle and resistance in Gaza, confronting Zionist aggression in 2008, is a lesson for the generations and a moral for the conquerors and the aggressors.

If such is the present situation of the Resistance in Lebanon and Palestine, what, then, is the present state of the choice of negotiation and compromise? What are the results, the interests, and the benefits realized by negotiations at every stage and through every accord to which they have given rise? Are these results not more Israeli arrogance, authoritarianism, and obstinacy, and more Israeli gains, self-interest, and conditions? We declare, therefore, our consistent and reliable position beside the Palestinian people and in favor of the Palestinian cause, with its historical, geographical, and political constants. We categorically declare our support, our approval, and our backing of that people and of the Palestinian resistance movements, and of their struggles in confronting the Israeli scheme.

Fourth: The Negotiations for Compromise

Our position vis-à-vis the attempt at compromise and the accords resulting from the process of the Madrid negotiations via "the Wadi ʿAraba Accord"[12] and its appendices, the "Oslo Accord" and its appendices, and before them the "Camp David Accords" and their appendices, was and will remain the same: we categorically reject the origin and principle of the option of compromise with the Zionist entity based on the recognition of

12. The Wadi ʿAraba Accord was the source of the Israel-Jordanian peace treaty.

the legitimacy of its existence and the concession to it of the territory of Palestine, Arab and Islamic, which it desecrated.

That position is a consistent, lasting, and definitive position, not subject to reversal or bargaining, even if the whole world recognizes "Israel."

Beginning from that principle and from a position of brotherhood, responsibility, and solicitude, we invite Arab leaders to conform to the choices of their peoples by reconsidering the option of negotiation and revisiting the consequences of the accords signed with the Zionist enemy, by abandoning decisively and definitively the process of illusory and unjust compromise, wrongly called the "peace process." We do so especially since those who wagered on the role of the successive American administrations, as being an honest and just partner and intermediary in that operation, have realized that these administrations have unquestionably duped them, have pressured them, and have engaged in blackmail; have displayed animosity toward their peoples, their causes, and their interests; and have totally and manifestly leaned toward their strategic ally, the Zionist entity.

As for the Zionist entity, with which—they delude themselves—they can make peace, it has demonstrated to them at every stage of the negotiations that it was not asking for or seeking peace but was using the negotiations to impose its conditions, consolidate its position, realize its own interests, and weaken the hostility and psychological barrier of their peoples against it, by obtaining an official, popular, gratuitous, and open normalization that would allow it to coexist naturally, to become incorporated in the regional system, to impose itself as a real element in the region, to be accepted, and to obtain recognition of the legitimacy of its existence, after [negotiators have] ceded to it the Palestinian land that it desecrated.

Beginning from there, we extend the invitation, anticipate and hope that, at the official and popular levels, for all Arabs and

Muslims, the question of Palestine and of al-Quds will return as a central cause, that they will unite around it, will commit themselves to liberating it from the stain of the iniquitous Zionist occupation, will fulfill what their religious, fraternal, and human duty dictates vis-à-vis their holy sites in Palestine and its oppressed people. [They must] offer all the conditions of support required to strengthen the tenacity of the Palestinian people, so that they will continue their resistance; reject and defeat all the proposals for normalization with the Zionist enemy; embrace the right of return for all Palestinian refugees to their lands and houses, from which they were expelled; categorically reject all substitute solutions proposed (naturalization, compensation, or expatriation); work immediately to break the blockade imposed on the Palestinian people, particularly the total blockade of the Gaza Strip; adopt the cause of the more than eleven thousand prisoners and detainees in Israeli prisons; and adopt practical plans and programs to free them from captivity.

CONCLUSION

This is our vision and our conception. In elaborating them, we have sought to be the mouthpiece of truth and right. These are our positions and our commitments; we have tried to be proponents of sincerity and loyalty. We believe in what is right, we proclaim it, we defend it, and we sacrifice ourselves for it even unto martyrdom. We wish thereby only the approval of our Creator and our God, Lord of the Heavens and of Earth. We hope only for the virtue of our parents, of our people, and of our *ummah*, their well-being and happiness in the world here below and in the hereafter.

O God, You know that none among us competes for power or has any desire for vanity. It is simply a matter of revitalizing the law, of slaying falsehood, of defending the oppressed among Your faithful, of instituting justice on Your land, of asking for Your approval, and of moving closer to You. That is why our martyrs died and that is why we move forward and pursue the work and the jihad. You promised us one of these two blessings: either victory or the honor of meeting you adorned in blood.

We promise You, O God, and all Your oppressed faithful, to remain men of integrity with respect to the pact, patient in the face of the promise, and steadfast—that is, to remain among those who never change.

CONCLUSION

The Hezbollah is a communitarian group[1] and a security organization based on the explicit principle of fighting an enemy that dates back centuries. Supported by popular Lebanese and Arab constituencies, it promotes the cult of a charismatic leader, defends the homogeneity of its doctrine, sanctifies its military function in the name of the fourteen hundred "martyrs" who have fallen over a quarter century, and retains its allegiance to a non-Lebanese power vested with a transcendent authority. When the battles are few, the gap grows between the daily practice of its sympathizers and its discourse. That presents a Cornelian dilemma: the Hezbollah cannot call for an Islamic regime, which would run the risk of losing it allies and some of its followers; it also cannot declare that such is not its long-term objective, since that would run the risk of acknowledging that the Islamic Republic of Iran did not inaugurate an era of "God's government on earth" and that its fundamental structure is not superior to a liberal state, one that is pluralist to varying degrees. In good times and bad, General Aoun repeats that the Hezbollah does not want to found such a state. During the Doha negotiations, Sheikh Qabalān, vice chair of

1. [That is, a group whose identity lies in a community, in this case, Shiism.—trans.]

the SISC, also provided assurances that the political leaders of his community did not intend to overthrow the established system:[2] "We also do not want the *wilāyat al-faqīh,* with all the respect we have for [it]. . . . We are not hiding anything from the Lebanese, we love Iran, but the *wilāyat al-faqīh* cannot be applied to Lebanon, and that is why we want everyone to understand us well: we are in Lebanon, condemned to get along with one another, to work as partners, to remain open to others, and to respect them."

By way of response, Nasrallah, on the eighth anniversary of the liberation of Southern Lebanon, said that he was "proud" to be associated with the "party of the *walī al-faqīh,*" but that he was ready to accept certain criticisms to guarantee the Arab identity of Lebanon, as was done in the 2009 charter. He once again denounced any option that would count on international resolutions to resolve conflicts. And, for the first time, he declared that the "Resistance" did "not need national or popular unanimity," given the changeable nature of public opinion and its vulnerability to pressure:

> When faced with occupation, people traditionally split into several categories: the largest portion initially remains neutral; another portion does not feel it affects them, and that what matters for them is to eat, drink, and go for Sunday walks; the third portion is composed of agents and mercenaries, such as Antoine Lahad's army; the fourth is made up of people whose interests coincide with those of the occupier; the fifth, generally composed of the elites, is defeatist and envisions cooperation with the occupation to reduce national losses; the sixth rejects the occupation politically and in the media but is not willing to pay the price of blood; the last portion, that of the Resistance, maintains that it is their human, moral, religious, and national duty to liberate the country from occupation, whatever the price to be paid. Such was the political situation in Lebanon in 1982,

2. That did not prevent the Shiite Intellectual Gathering headed by Raëf Rida from denouncing him for having concluded an agreement with the aim of being appointed, rather than elected, chair of the SISC.

such is the situation in Palestine, and such is, to a certain degree, the situation in Iraq.

The message is clear: the "Resistance" must preserve its independence vis-à-vis the Lebanese state, and its timetable is regional. One has only to pay heed to the voices coming from Tehran: Ali Larijani, president of the Iranian Majlis al-Shūra, includes the Land of the Cedars within the "Islamic countries" as a whole; and Ali Akbar Mehrabian, the Iranian minister of mines and industries, calls Lebanon an "Islamic and revolutionary" country.[3]

The crisis of May 2008 seemed serious enough that, on the 27th of that month, the leaders of the Bar Association of Beirut and Tripoli invited members and civic organizations to sign a "Lebanese charter for the defense of independence, the maintenance of national unity and civil peace, and the establishment of a parliamentary and democratic republican regime." Michel Suleiman's first message to the Lebanese nation clearly rejected the confessionalization of the issues. That did not prevent him from declaring, during preparations for an Islamic-Christian summit in Baabda, that religious diversity was not a flaw but an opportunity. For the new president of the country, "the Israeli enemy" and "[Islamist] terrorism" are "two sides of the same coin." He found support in all the communities, including the Shiites, when he condemned the violence occurring until early July in certain neighborhoods of Tripoli and in villages of West Bekaa. Alongside tendencies toward religious radicalism, a secularization—of action more than of discourse—remains at work in the political arena, in the justice system, and in the economy. As for the institutions, no one finds them satisfactory. "Confessional democracy exists only for the ruling bourgeoisie. It is a confessional fascism," wrote Mahdi Amil in the mid-1980s. But the Shiite-born Amil, nicknamed the "Arab Gramsci," was assassinated by his coreligionists on May 18, 1987. With the passing of time, some

3. *Kayhān al ʿarabī,* February 15, 2009, and *Iran News,* February 28, 2009.

within the dispersed ranks of the Shiites who oppose the Hezbollah (Lokman Slim, Saoud al-Mawla . . .) tell themselves that the confessional formula theorized by Michel Chiha may be better, after all, than the state according to Khomeini or a falsely "secular" state in which communitarian reflexes would come into play but without any safeguards. Ibrahim Shams al-Dīn recalls that his father went so far as to portray the Lebanese system as a necessity for the Arab and even the Muslim world, since its sole source of power is that of the people. In an interview granted to *L'Orient–Le Jour* in June 2008, he rejected the Hezbollah's claim that it was the "Party of God" and that it was backed by a plan not open to debate, namely, "to take power in Lebanon and to establish an Islamic Republic. Not in the Iranian manner, of course, but through an institutional coup d'état. Pluralism will be respected, but politically, everyone will be under the orders of the Iranian *faqīh*. He could then establish some sort of system of protections for the *dhimmis*."

Nevertheless, that confessionalism is also the weakness of Lebanon, an echo chamber of contradictory influences and the front for conflicts that originate elsewhere, "a house of many mansions" (K. Salibi) open to the four winds. Washington and Tehran were likely no more remote from the events of May 2008 than Riyadh and Damascus in efforts to instrumentalize the Salafist groups. On the eve of the June 2009 legislative elections, the March 14 camp (Future, PSP, the Lebanese Forces) more or less maintained its cohesion, acknowledging major errors in certain political choices. The March 8 camp (the Hezbollah, Amal, and their allies), with which the FPM associated itself (except in the Jezzine region), hoped for a shift in the majority that would allow it to fend off the threat to disarm the Hezbollah and open the way to Aoun's election to the presidency. Aoun, who seeks to embody the essentials of Christian public opinion and to defend a conception of "Resistance" close to the Hezbollah's views— while also acknowledging that he has no part in the strategic decision-making process—received a welcome worthy of a

friendly head of state in both Tehran (October 2008) and Damascus (December). To the surprise of most observers, the electoral victory went to the outgoing majority, headed by Saad
Hariri. The idea that there was a gap between the "legal country"
and the "real country" was thereby undermined.[4] Nevertheless,
that result did not lead to a power grab by a majority against a
minority. On the contrary, Saad Hariri, to the great displeasure of
some of his followers, extended his hand to his adversaries. It
took five months for that cabinet to come together—respecting
the principles adopted in Doha—and two members of the Hezbollah are part of it.

Because Israel's policy rests first and foremost on the force of
its weaponry, it played a role in the failure of the "road map"
signed in 2003 and of the Annapolis process throughout 2008.
The fundamental reason is that its leaders are not resigned to
granting the borders of a viable state—with Jerusalem as a dual
capital—to the Palestinian representatives who have accepted
the principle of a peace agreement. The security threat, which is
real, is an obstacle invoked to maintain the status quo in negotiations and to increase control of the area, especially around the
Old City of Jerusalem. The impossibility of Hamas and the PLO
reaching an understanding, and the repercussions of that impossibility in Lebanon among various Palestinian factions, along
with the inter-Arab divisions that prevent the application of the
joint defense treaty, have created the illusion that a policy based
solely on power relations might be the lesser evil for Israel. The
Hezbollah now possesses missiles capable of reaching targets
beyond Tel Aviv, and one editorial writer for *Yediot Aharonot*

4. In its speech following the electoral defeat, the Hezbollah continued to
distinguish between a "legal country" and a "real country," accusing the
March 14 camp of having financed—using Hariri's fortune and Saudi
subsidies—the return of Lebanese living abroad, so that they would vote for
the coalition led by Hariri. The Hezbollah was in turn accused of having
received equivalent sums of money from Iran (the figure of $1 billion was
mentioned) to finance its campaign.

did not hesitate to present the situation in terms of an exclusive alternative: "Having to choose between a Syrian Lebanon or an Iranian Lebanon, we ought to negotiate a new pact with Damascus by virtue of which Syria could annex Lebanon at a very high price, in exchange for Golan perhaps." *Haaretz* and the *Jerusalem Post* are not on the same wavelength, but, following the constitution of the Benjamin Netanyahu government, no one foresees an outcome to the conflict. Despite the failures of 1993, 1996, 2006, and 2008–2009, Israeli plans for a massive use of arms to bring down Hamas and the Hezbollah remain in force.

In the opposing camp, the Iranian nuclear program continues, despite two Security Council resolutions, accompanied by sanctions. But Reza Aghazadeh, the Iranian vice president, acknowledged, in a partial admission to the authorities at the International Atomic Energy Agency in late July 2008, that Lebanon was—once again—only a pawn in a game beyond its purview: "If negotiations were to get under way with the international community on the Iranian nuclear issue, solutions would be found for many problems, such as Iraq, Lebanon, and the price of oil." In October, the naming to Beirut of Mohammad Rida Zahidi, commander of the Pasdaran ground forces, led the Free Shiite Movement to say that "Iran therefore perceives Lebanon as a battleground for fighting the international community and Israel." A few months earlier, the Iranian general Mohammad Ali Jaafari, also an officer in the Revolutionary Guards, had let it be known, in his message of condolence for the "martyrdom" of Imad Mughniyah, that, in "the near future, we will witness the destruction of the Israel cancer cell by the Hezbollah's mighty hands." For his part, Nasrallah brandishes the threat of a regional war against Israel that could "change the face of the region." In the Hezbollah's discourse on the Palestinians, religious considerations are the chief grounds for action, but there are others as well (the nature and policy of the state of Israel): a "military jihad," with the full charge that expression carries in Arabic, is embraced as such. In the 2009 charter, the authors specify, first, that it is a battle "that our *ummah* is waging against the colonialist Zionist scheme in Palestine." Then they link together the "Muslim and Christian holy sites" before declaring that the "obligation to save, liberate, defend, and protect al-Aqsa Mosque is a religious duty and a human and moral responsibility incumbent on every free and honorable son of our Arab and Islamic *ummah* and on all free men of honor in the world." According to Ghālib Abū Zaynab, "victory" can only mean the "annihilation of Israel," placed within a messianic perspective. Nasrallah expressed that differently when he declared that the Hezbollah would choose "the place, the time, and the manner" that the final "confrontation" would unfold: "We will never recognize Israel and we are capable of annihilating it." The conclusion of the 2009 charter is explicit: "O God, You know that none among us competes for power or has any desire for vanity. It is simply a matter of revitalizing the law, of slaying falsehood, of defending the oppressed among Your faithful, of instituting justice on Your land, of asking for Your approval, and of moving closer to You. That is why our martyrs died and that is why we move forward and pursue the work and the jihad. You promised us one of these two blessings: either victory or the honor of meeting You adorned in blood."

From the perspective of Islam and Arabism, it is not possible to balance, on a single set of scales, Syria—which continues to disregard the question of Lebanese detainees and balks at the possibility of drawing clear borders[5]—and Israel. From the perspective of the Lebanese nation, that is a possibility. The Hezbollah cannot resign itself to that since, though it declares that it hews to the three terms at once (Lebanese nation, Arab nation, and *ummah* appear once again in the 2009 charter), in reality it gives priority to the religious criterion. The only reason that its

5. As these lines are being written, the cooperation treaty between Lebanon and Syria is still in force, and the Syro-Lebanese Supreme Council survives, at least formally.

plan has no immediate application is that Shiite Islam is not in the majority in Lebanon or in the Arab world. The polymorphous support from Syria and Iran is thus both an indispensable element and a handicap. There is without a doubt a national dimension in the Hezbollah's practice: this term can be understood either in the sense of a "Lebanese nation," according to European and even French conventions (different citizens decide to conclude a contract stipulating duties for living together), or in the sense of the "Arab nation," which stems rather from a legacy subject to multiple variations. Nevertheless, the term "Islamic-nationalist," which Walid Charara and Frédéric Domont use to contrast the Hezbollah to transnational Islamist movements, is unsatisfactory. Divided between these two loyalties, the leaders have always privileged the party's ideological line over national entente. The events of spring 2008 demonstrated the limits of a schema in which all the different pieces would fit together. A political strategy with the aim, in Nawaf Mūsawī's own expression, of prosecuting political adversaries on charges of treason, accusing them of serving Israeli-U.S. interests first and foremost, is convincing only to those who are already convinced.

The United States failed to establish a "democratic and pro-Western Middle East" by force of arms, and the borders emerging from the end of World War I, however relative they may be, appear more solid than strategists promoting a "Greater Middle East" had foreseen Given that state of affairs, the orientation of the new U.S. administration still lacks clarity. Barack Obama declares, on the one hand, the need for a Palestinian state alongside the Israeli state, but without specifying the means to attain it; on the other hand, he offers Iran "carrots and sticks" to choose the path of normalization rather than nuclear weapons, which would isolate the country from its neighbors and from Iranian groups opposed to the regime. By way of response, Tehran constantly repeats that it has not invaded any country in the last 250 years and rejects the chiding of Washington, whose leaders it denounces as having "imperialist" proclivities. Iran, in a position of strength at the regional level since the wars in Afghanistan and Iraq, seeks to avoid clashes with Saudi Arabia and Egypt, both of which dispute its leadership. In Iraq, the recent electoral victory of Nouri al-Maliki has shored up a strategy of marginalizing the revolutionary project of Moqtada al-Sadr—who has disappeared from the scene—and has lent legitimacy to the withdrawal plan of the U.S. forces. The predominance of Iraqi Shiites in religious institutions offers Najaf, a center of religion, a new opportunity for influence, especially since the scholarly reputation of Ayatollah Sistānī rivals that of his counterpart Khamenei.

Syria, in the aftermath of the Doha Agreement—which it supported—has undertaken an effort at rapprochement with Saudi Arabia (Kuwait Declaration, January 2009), has established security relations with the United States, and has acknowledged that it is involved in negotiating a peace agreement with Israel via Turkey, which Ibrahim Suleiman has visited. In July 2008, Bashar al-Assad participated in the Union for the Mediterranean Summit initiated by France, with representatives of the Israeli state in attendance. "Just and global peace remains our principal objective," says Bashar al-Assad, but if the Syrians' rights and demands are guaranteed, an accord will be signed with the Israelis without waiting for the Palestinian component. Behind an appearance of strength, the Syrian authorities display vulnerabilities, as indicated by the assassination of General Mohammed Suleiman—who was well versed in Lebanese questions—in August 2008. On the one hand, the Syrian regime is ruled by the Alawite minority, which is under attack from Sunni radicals; on the other, the president is facing serious rivals, including his brother-in-law Assef Shawkat, who is suspected of having attempted a coup d'état in February 2008. Like the Lebanese government and the Hezbollah's leaders, Western governments are observing with keen attention the situation in Damascus, where four proposals are in the offing: a law on parties, an electoral law, a law on local administration, and a law broadening parliamentary representation through the creation of a senate of sorts. But the Special Tribunal for Lebanon is the sword of Damocles hanging over the region; in autumn 2005—but with no further announcement since—the United Nations Investigation Commission indicated there was "converging evidence" of the involvement of Lebanese and Syrian services in Rafic Hariri's assassination.

For a long time, France was the only power to take Lebanon's existence seriously. The new situation emerging in the last decade could mean that that conviction—along with that necessity—will be shared by others. In the preface he wrote twenty-five years ago to Ghassan Tuéni's *Une guerre pour les autres* (*A War for the Others*, 1985), Dominique Chevallier defined that "'liberal' country" as follows: "A country where every group can have the freedom to thrive without suppressing the other in so doing." It will not escape the reader's attention that everything remains in the realm of potentiality, not in that of will or actuality. What is remarkable is that the Maronites, at the time of their preeminence, did not establish a Christian state. "Political Maronitism" was a reality, but it was undoubtedly limited to the hoarding of the best posts, "considered, if not so many privileges, then at least guarantees of a certain status and of the community's survival" (Ghassan Tuéni). That was because the traces left by the French Republic's *laïcité* were not only on the surface. It was also because, at the same time, Lebanese Catholic intellectuals drew from Jacques Maritain and Emmanuel Mounier to set forth the principle that the "sacral Christendom" of the Middle Ages belonged to a different time and that pluralism had to be fully accepted, and the project of a countersociety abandoned. In the end, that is why the various socialist currents have all tried their hand in Lebanon, as will be shown in a forthcoming thesis on the Lebanese Cenacle founded and run by Michel Asmar. The Shiite intellectuals of the twentieth century, within and outside Lebanon, are also affected by cross-influences, as indicated by the trajectory of Ali Sharī'atī and of Mohammad Khatami, who abandoned a race for the Iranian presidency in deference to former prime minister Mousavi, a candidate who contested Ahmadinejad's reelection in June 2009 within a context of quashed popular demonstrations.[6] In his last book, Khatami boldly declares, with slight overtones of spiritual and political evolutionism, that Islamic civilization is over, but that the Koran continues to respond to "men's questions and needs."[7] Let us leave aside the teleology and simply note that these voices contrast with those that assert the purity of the word and the authenticity of the model. These voices have always coexisted. What does that mean? Governance "in the name of God," which is presented as an alternative to regimes, many of which emerged from colonization, and as a "new" order—in contrast to the "old"—that has restored the mark of the "origin," has not taken root anywhere in a lasting or unanimous manner.

6. Some of the demonstrators, denouncing the result of the elections, also criticized the reelected president's foreign policy, declaring they were ready to sacrifice themselves for Iran but not for Gaza or Lebanon.

7. Mohammad Khatami, *Le dialogue des civilisations: L'Affaire du XXIe siècle* (Beirut: Presses de USJ, 2009), available online: www.usj.edu.lb/pusj.

This lexicon was compiled from sources originating in the Hezbollah (see sources). Therein lies its value.

'Adū (enemy)

The struggle against the "enemy" is one of the recurrent themes in the discourse of the Hezbollah and one of the aims of the ideal Islamic government. Various cases are differentiated:

The enemy par excellence is Israel, accused of having played an active role in the Lebanese War and of mounting "the Zionist occupation, which desecrated the sacred land" of Palestine and Lebanon but also the land "of the Muslims." That enemy must be combated at all cost "by weapons, by the media, by politics, by security, by the economy." Several times, Israel is called a "desecrating cancer" and a "racist Zionist entity" that resorts to "terrorism." The Western powers and the "colonizers" are also in the Hezbollah's sights, since they favored the implantation of "the Zionist enemy, considered an entity foreign to the region, introduced by global arrogance to be a cancer that spreads through the body of the Arab and Islamic *ummah* in order to break it down it, divide it, and take over its resources."[1]

---

1. *Al ma'ārif al-islāmiyya*, pp. 376–381; *Durūss fī ussūl al-'aqīda al-islāmiyya*, p. 162; *Wilāyat al-faqīh fī 'assr al-ghayba*, pp. 35–36.

The enemies are also the Umayyad "terrorists"—a qualifier also applied to the "Wahhabites," namely, "Yazīd and those who succeeded him . . . who desecrated the caliphate and who in no case represent Islam." "Genghis Khan, Hārūn al-Rashīd, [and] the treacherous caliphs" occupy the same register and are portrayed, in the absence of any chronological framework, as "corrupt, unrighteous, and . . . very often the collaborators with the East or the West, putting their arrogant policies into practice."[2] Such a representation obliterates history, a tendency to which the authors of the manuals frequently succumb to justify a struggle waged since the origin of Shiism against the "tyrants" and the "unrighteous," "usurpers" of a power that ought to have devolved on the twelve imams.

The "enemies of Islam," accused of propaganda against Islamic interests, are designated more vaguely. They are said to have attempted, over the course of the past fifteen centuries, to attack the prophet of Islam and to imitate the Koran, but without success.[3]

The Jews are portrayed as "those who have most despised Islam and the Muslims" since their appearance. Four reasons are invoked:

- Muhammad invited "men to [join] a religion that is an all-inclusive system," and he did not shape it to fit the Jews' "ambitions."
- The Jews saw the expansion of Islam and "noted that that religion refused to grant privileges in accordance with racial principles."
- The "continual deployment of Islam on the Arabian Peninsula produced the feeling [among the Jews] that they were going to lose their domination over the region

2. *Al maʿārif al-islāmiyya*, pp. 298–301; *Durūss fī ussūl al-ʿaqīda al-islāmiyya*, pp. 157–162.

3. *Al maʿārif al-islāmiyya*, p. 160; *Durūss fī ussūl al-ʿaqīda al-islāmiyya*, p. 135.

and the pagans, so they began to rise up against the
Prophet as his enemies."
- Since the "Prophet" was not one of their own, the Jews
  displayed "jealousy toward the Arabs." And the writers
  refer to the sura "The Cow": "And now that a Book
  confirming their own has come to them from God, they
  deny it"; "God's curse be upon the infidels!"[4]

The Jews of Medina thus took Muhammad to task when he
proposed that they "join Islam," and, feeding on "resentment,"
they constantly opposed Islam by every means, exerting "economic pressure on the Muslims," inciting divisions among them,
and between them and the pagans, and pressuring them to
abandon jihad. Unable to tolerate an "enemy from within,"
Muhammad therefore eliminated the three Jewish tribes (Banū
Qaynuqā', Banū Nadīr, and Banū Qurayza), whose "perfidy" is
recounted in detail until their final defeat, that is, their "submission" with the aid of "divine intervention."[5]

Imam and Ghayba (Occultation of Imam Mahdī)

For the Imami (Twelver) Shiites, the Imam represents, in the first
place, the guide of humankind. He was given the task of political
and religious leadership after the death of the prophet of Islam.
The imamate must devolve on the descendants of the family of
Muhammad, and the first Imam was Alī, his cousin and son-in-
law, followed by Alī's two sons, Hasan and Husayn. The last
Imam, the Mahdī, twelfth of the line, is considered to be "occulted" since 941. Ghayba designates the historical period extending from the moment of that "occultation" to his "reappear-
ance" at the "end of time." What is called the Major Occultation
(ghayba koubra) was preceded by the Minor Occultation
(ghayba soghra) between 874 and 941, during which the Imam

4. Koran 2:89–90.
5. Al-Sīra wa-l-Tārīkh, pp. 106–125.

was represented by *wakīls* who were in contact with him and through whom he maintained his relations with the Shiites.

The Hezbollah cadres believe that the quietist position adopted by some Shiites is unacceptable and demand an active preparation for the "advent" of the Imam: "Some people wrongly think that we must live the era of the Major Occultation of Imam Mahdī waiting for his advent, until the promised day when the awaited Imam will put an end to impiety, decadence, and corruption by seeing that Islam is applied, and that we have no role to play in preparing for and bringing about the establishment of the arbitration of Islam in every realm of our lives and particularly in the political realm, on the pretext that the responsibility for the arbitration of Islam and for the application of its laws in every realm of life lies within the jurisdiction of Imam Mahdī. . . . That negative understanding of waiting is in total contradiction with the concepts of Islam, its general laws and prescriptions, which Muslims must apply in every era."

One of the manuals insists on the work to be accomplished by the faithful in anticipation of the "advent of the Mahdī and [of] the establishment of his divine plan":

"Conform to the teachings of Islam . . . and struggle in the name of God against the enemies, the unrighteous, and the arrogant.

"Labor for the spread of Islam, to make it known and to present it to the peoples of the world as a substitute proposal and as the only path possible to lead the people from darkness to the light. Present a pure and shining image of Islam to the world through our conduct, our positions, and our jihad.

"Work for the establishment of an Islamic government . . .

"Prepare a believing, conscious, and loyal generation that assists in the advent of the Imam . . .

"Educate the *ummah*, and more especially the Shiites of the Imam, to obey him. . . ."

The faithful are called upon to obey the *walī al-faqīh* or the *walī amr*, portrayed as the Imam's replacement during his occultation. Obedience to the *walī al-faqīh* is just as necessary as that due the Imam: "If someone wants to know his level of obedience to the Imam when the Imam appears, he can observe his current level of obedience to the Imam's delegate, whom he ordered us to obey. In fact, in this period of Occultation, the norm is to obey the *walī amr,* and whoever cannot obey . . . the delegate of Imam Mahdī during the time of Occultation will not be obedient to the Imam when he appears." In that way, the doctrine of the *wilāyat al-faqīh* is legitimated: "The succession of the infallible Imam during the time of Occultation is what we call *wilāyat al-faqīh,* because it is necessary that there be a righteous Imam and *faqīh* who unites all conditions and who bears responsibility for leading that *ummah.*"[6]

Jihād

The *jihād al-nafs* (struggle against the self), the first in order of importance, is presented as the foundation of man's success, in peacetime and in wartime: "Whoever is victorious over himself is in a position to be victorious over his enemy . . . and whoever is able to change himself is able to modify his own situation." In the writings of the Hezbollah, including Qāsim's book,[7] that "struggle against the self" is systematically linked to *al-jihād al-ʿaskarī* (the act of war). Through "faith, patience, resolution, and devotion," the jihad procures boundless energy, and until the "site of blessed battle, [the jihad fighter is] joyful to meet God upon martyrdom and with the honor of the religion of God in victory." That link between the two types of jihad guarantees the establishment of Islam by means of "Muslim warriors." "No one knows the merit and greatness of jihad except the one whose eyes are opened by God and who has rid himself of his cowardice." The "act of war" unfolds in two ways: "initial" and "defensive." The aim of the initial jihad is to spread Islam, and the

6. *Al maʿārif al-islāmiyya*, pp. 344–347.
7. N. Qāsim, *Hizballah, al-minhaj, al-tajriba, al-mustaqbal*, pp. 46–69.

conquests undertaken by Muhammad are an illustration of it, according to these publications. The defensive jihad "is waged by the Muslims to defend themselves and to defend their homelands when they are attacked by the enemies of Islam, such as the wars of the Prophet against the idolaters in Badr, Uhud, and Hanin, and like the jihad of Islamic resistance against the Zionist occupation, which desecrated the land and sacred things." Both are obligatory *(fard, wājib),* and this point is underscored several times.

A parallel is established between the battles during the early days of Islam, initiated by Muhammad, and the war against Israel. The position of the Islamic Republic of Iran, after it broke off diplomatic relations with the "Great Satan" America, is also presented as a defensive jihad. Khomeini is quoted in support of that thesis: "If the Muslim countries are taken by surprise by an enemy [who constitutes a danger] for Islam and its society, then all Muslims, men and women, old and young, must defend them by any means possible, [material or human]." Also falling within the realm of jihad are "relations or agreements contracted by tyrannical and corrupt rulers, who do harm to the Muslims and who go against the interests of Islam and of the Muslims. [They] are considered null and void and are prohibited. The Muslims must oppose them by every means possible, even to the point of abolishing them, as occurred with the disastrous accord of May 17."

An analysis of Hassan Nasrallah's speeches allows us to distinguish four levels, with various inflections, in the definition of *jihād. Jihād* may involve:

- a religious act whose aim is to drive Israel—along with every "aggressor," "usurping occupier," or "exploitative colonizer"—from "Muslim lands," because its existence runs counter to "divine will";
- a political act whose aim is to liberate the Lebanese homeland;

- an ideological act whose aim is to stand up to the "West," dominated by the United States;
- a humanitarian act whose aim is to establish justice and law "in the service of the weakest, to grant them freedom and security."

Nasrallah equates the battle in Lebanon and Palestine to the defensive jihad. It is a collective duty *(fard kifāʾī)* taking various forms (gifts, weapons, the media, the spilling of blood): "This defensive jihad depends on the needs of the front; that is, if someday we need to confront the enemy to such a degree that adult men and women, laborers, and even the ill shall bear arms to fight that enemy, and if the resistance at the front depends on the participation of all, everyone, men and women, must participate, and that matter does not require the permission of the infallible Imam, or of His special delegate, or of His general delegate." Conditions must be met: "obey the guide," be "pious," "loyal" (to God, and consequently, to one's homeland or community); be "militarily at the ready"; "call upon God," to whom alone victory belongs.[8]

Jihād, being of a religious nature, is placed within an eschatological perspective. The Imams conceive "the world as only a bridge leading to eternity." One must therefore progress in stages. Efforts (courtesy, generosity, discipline) must be made on a daily basis. Prayer, "the most beneficial activity," is obligatory, and supererogatory works are encouraged. Piety, which frees "passions" from the "bonds of the world," is a necessary but not sufficient condition, as are the "prescriptions of religious law." Everything is weighed in the balance for the last day, and the punishment will be heavy for some [the "lapses," "laxity," and "intemperance" of many Muslims are denounced], light for others: "The *mujāhid* on the path of God, who abandons life's pleasures to fight the enemy, cannot, from the standpoint of

8. *Al maʿārif al-islāmiyya*, pp. 73–77 and 271–274.

divine justice, be the same as the one who remains inactive.
He places himself on a higher plane in life here below and in
the hereafter. In life he has lightness and purity of heart . . . and
in the hereafter, joy eternal. He goes to paradise in the company of the prophets, the companions, and the saints." "Martyrs" are promised an "extraordinary home near God." The
pleasures of paradise, the reward for those who deserve to go
there, are as follows (these do not apply specifically to the
mujāhid):

- moral pleasures ("to talk with God," "to be with the
  Prophet");
- physical pleasures: food, drink, sex with the *Hur al
  ʿAyn,* a dwelling in the castles of paradise, the sight of
  beautiful landscapes . . . [9]

Marjaʿ taqlīd (source of imitation)

According to the lessons delivered by the Hezbollah, everyone
who is fit and of sound mind must, from adolescence on, conform to the laws of Islamic jurisprudence *(fiqh)*. He can know
these laws by practicing *ijtihād,* that is, by deducing the laws of
jurisprudence from the Koran, the Sunna, and the Hadith (collections of Muhammad's deeds and sayings). For the majority of
Shiites, the practical rule is to follow a *marjaʿ taqlīd* (source of
imitation), a *mujtahid* (interpreter) qualified to issue fatwas (religious decisions or opinions). Conditions for being vested with
that function are provided:

- being recognized as someone capable of practicing
  ijtihād;
- being of the male sex;
- being a Twelver Shiite;
- being of legitimate birth;
- having a good memory;

9. *Durūss fī ussūl al-ʿaqīda al-islāmiyya*, pp. 176 and 182.

- being righteous;
- being alive (with a few exceptions);
- being learned;
- being informed about temporal affairs: "That ninth
  condition was noted specifically by Imam Khomeini,"
  who claimed that the *marjaʿ* cannot fail to express
  political opinions.

The writers of the Hezbollah manuals explain that all these
conditions are fulfilled by *Sayyid* Ali Khamenei: "He knows the
interests of the *ummah* and the conspiracies hatched by the imperialists, not only through his position as guardian *(walī amr)*
of the Muslims but also through his position as a source of jurisprudence. One has only to recall that there are more than sixty
written and unwritten statements about the chief imam's qualifications in the area of *fiqh,* and more than fifty written statements
on his wisdom, compiled by experts within and outside Iran.
Given that large number of statements, which no other *marjaʿ*
has had, we believe that it is sufficient to convince every believer
who seeks to please God that the imitation of Ayatollah Khamenei has been established without difficulty."[10]

Muqāwama (Resistance)

The aim of the "Resistance," explain the Hezbollah cadres, is to
vanquish the "enemy" and his "collaborators." It includes armed
struggle, as well as ideological, cultural, media, and political actions against efforts to weaken it.[11] It unfolds in three stages,
according to the manuals for militants:

The "Islamic resistance," incarnated by the Hezbollah, would
not exist without the support of Ayatollah Khomeini, who worked
to unify the *ummah* and the Muslims, wherever they might be:
"The imam maintains that the unity of the *ummah* is the means

10. *Al maʿārif al-islāmiyya,* pp. 167–171.
11. N. Qāsim, *Hizballah, al-minhaj, al-tajriba, al-mustaqbal,* pp.
93–121.

to liberate [oneself], to restore honor, dignity, liberty, and independence and to cut off the hands of the colonizers and enemies." The first cell of Hezbollah fighters was backed by the
Pasdaran, and "all came together under the banner of the imam
[Khomeini], conforming to the principle of the *wilāyat al-faqīh*."
After Ayatollah Khomeini's death, the prescriptions of his successor, Ayatollah Khamenei, must be followed in such matters.[12]
The Hezbollah maintains that fighting Israel is the duty not only
of the populations under attack but "of Muslims in every region
of the world."[13]

As for the "Arab resistance," its absence is deplored. Hassan
Nasrallah believes that the "Islamic resistance is the only thing
in this Arab world [by virtue of which] we can hold our heads
high and of which we can be proud." One of the Hezbollah's
avowed objectives is to "erase from Arab minds the illusion that
has ruled for decades [and which consists of believing in the]
legend of the invincible [Israeli] army." He condemns the Arab
states "that rushed to reconcile with the Zionist enemy" and
submitted "to the will of America." A distinction is made, however, between Arab leaders and Arab peoples; the party praises
the people's courage and encourages them to protest against the
policies of their governments.[14]

In terms of the "Lebanese resistance," the Hezbollah, in the
absence of participation by all, seeks to obtain official political
support for its actions. Believing it has achieved that support,
the party lauds "the ability of the resistance to obtain popular,
political, and official [support] despite the complications on
the political, religious, and socio-structural scene of this small
country."[15] Qāsim develops a long argument to explain the stra-

12. *Al maʿārif al-islāmiyya*, pp. 383–387.
13. Open Letter, February 16, 1985, p. 120.
14. *Al maʿārif al-islāmiyya*, pp. 394–398; *Wilāyat al-faqīh fī ʿassr al-ghayba*, pp. 34–36; Open Letter, February 16, 1985, pp. 125–126.
15. N. Qāsim, *Hizballah, al-minhaj, al-tajriba, al-mustaqbal*, pp. 394–398.

tegic and tactical reasons why the Hezbollah fighters did not associate with the other groups battling Israel in the 1990s.[16] By force of arms, the concept of "resistance" became the monopoly of the troops of the "Party of God," one sanctified by the liberation of Southern Lebanon in 2000. Since then, the question has been disputed, and the battles of spring 2008 have made manifest the terms of the problem. In Iran, the Pasdaran have existed as a party, a social organization, and a parallel army, despite a strong army and a strong state.

Mustadʿafūn (disinherited, oppressed) / Mustakbirūn (imperialists, arrogant ones, oppressors)

The struggle of the "oppressed" against the "oppressors" is part of jihad in its eschatological dimension; at the same time, however, it has a civic dimension. In the discourse of the Hezbollah, the *mustadʿafūn* may include various social and political categories:

- populations exploited by U.S. "imperialism": "to prevent the domination of the arrogant forces, particularly that of America over Lebanon";[17]
- peoples whose material means against Israel are limited: "Liberating al-Quds, which constitutes the central cause of the *ummah* . . . requires the support of all the disinherited forces and categories and their aid, so that they will rise up to realize their goals, defend and protect them from the oppressors and from those who work to crush them, to strip them bare, and to steal their personalities and identities from them. [We must] side with them in a way that involves them in the great battle against the Zionist enemy."[18]
- poor citizens whose rights are encroached upon by the state: defend "the cause of the disinherited and the

16. Ibid., pp. 114–116.
17. *Al maʿārif al-islāmiyya*, p. 396.
18. Ibid., p. 395.

oppressed" by demanding that "the government settle
the economic problem by adopting a sound and just
policy that remedies the economic crisis and assures
citizens of opportunities for work."[19]

Coordinated revolutionary action by an "international front
of the disinherited" against the states and "regimes of the colonial world" is one of the pillars of the "Open Letter" of 1985.
Ayatollah Khomeini used the notion of *mustad'afūn*—with
everything it entails in terms of mobilization—during the Islamic
revolution. He "incited [the young from the poorest classes] to
go farther and to completely monopolize the entire political field
of society, rejecting and excluding by every means those who
had no right to that revolution: the *mustakbirūn,* that is, the arrogant, the oppressors, the non-disinherited. The disinherited
had become 'pure,' the others 'impure,' because they had wan-
dered from the straight path of a sacred revolution."[20] Thirty
years later, the dichotomy between the two terms is still very
present in Iran. The press echoes the discourses of its leaders,
who declare that nations that stand up to the "arrogance" and
"oppression" currently incarnated by the United States are defending their interests and thwarting the plots of their enemies.
Hugo Chavez's Venezuela and Ahmadinejad's Iran thus constitute an "anti-U.S. front" and maintain that "global domination
and arrogance are losing and are about to disappear." The two
chiefs of state, according to interviews reported by journalists,
feel that "the revolutionary peoples in Iran and Venezuela [must
continue] together their resistance and their battle against imperialism [*istikbār*], until the final victory and the disappearance of
the threats over all peoples."[21]

19. Ibid., p. 396.
20. Akbar Molajani, *Sociologie politique de la révolution iranienne*
(Paris: L'Harmattan, 1999), p. 286.
21. *Iran News,* February 17, 2009; *Kayhān al-'arabī,* February 14, 2009.

Shahīd, pl., shuhadā' (martyr, martyrs) / shahāda (martyrdom)
Those who meet their death while performing jihad are "martyrs." That martyrdom is conceived as a sacrificial witnessing, a transfiguration of earthly suffering into eternal bliss. It is a purifying and sacred death that, according to a passage from the Koran, expresses the love for the professed God *(hubb Allāh)* by the gift of one's own life: "Do not say that those slain in the cause of God are dead. They are alive, but you are not aware of them." Or again: "Let those who would exchange the life of this world for the hereafter fight for the cause of God; whoever fights for the cause of God, whether he dies or triumphs, We shall richly reward him."[22] Martyrdom reverses the order of worldly values: what appears to be a defeat in earthly life is in reality a glorious victory for eternity.[23] The remains of the "martyrs" are not washed before being buried because they were purified in sacrifice, and no one who touches the body of a "martyr" has any obligation to repeat his ablutions.[24] That conception is part of Shiite history, which truly began with the death of Husayn, son of Alī and grandson of Muhammad, at the Battle of Karbala. His "position, expressing refusal and confrontation" *(mawqaf al-rafd wa-l muwājaha)* is glorified. The public celebration of Ashura, which commemorates the event, has taken on increasing importance over the last quarter century. For the Hezbollah, Karbala constitutes "the cry of the *ummah*'s conscience, making the thrones of tyrants tremble over the course of the centuries." Husayn's spilled blood prevails over the sword of Yazīd, which killed him.

The theme of *shahīd* is central in that, according to the cadres of the Hezbollah, the ability to give one's life for the cause

22. Koran 2:154 and 4:74.
23. *Al maᶜārif al-islāmiyya*, pp. 79–82.
24. Ibid., p. 197.

without hesitating constitutes the essential difference between its warriors and enemy soldiers. "The secret of the Resistance lies in Ashura" (May 19, 1996), declares Nasrallah, for whom Husayn's standard is always raised, transmitted from generation to generation until "the day of Resurrection," according to *al sayyid al qāʾid* [Khamenei]. Love of martyrdom is seen as a weapon, sometimes superior to all others because it cannot be muzzled or overcome: "All of us can possess the weapon of martyrdom, in order to become, in accordance with the concept of martyrdom, the strong who make History and not the weak whom History forgets, whom God rejects, and who therefore lose life here below and in the hereafter." The impulse toward martyrdom must not be blind, however, and must not constitute an end in itself, as Qāsim explains: it is at once the weapon of those who do not possess the technical means to do battle on equal footing with their "enemy" and the last resort. In that sense, that weapon of the "disinherited" is supposed to correct part of the imbalance in military forces and to valorize the heroic courage of those who sacrifice themselves over those who tally up their dead.[25] The purpose of these explanations is to counter the criticisms of Muslim scholars, who equate that type of "martyrdom" with suicide and therefore consider it unlawful from the standpoint of the Sharia. The debate continues, and the Hezbollah leaders cling to their interpretation. Furthermore, the success of the column in *al-ʿAhd* called "Biographies of the Martyrs, Memory of the Resistance" and of the testaments and eulogies retransmitted on television or over the Internet show that their sympathizers are amenable to that discourse. As for the Martyrs' Association, it does not compensate all families equally: widows and children of "martyrs of the resistance" receive housing along with a monthly allowance, and their parents receive a sum of money. But in the case of civilians who were involuntary victims, only

25. Ibid., pp. 79–82.

their widows and children receive a sum of money. That may be a way of anticipating, in the world here below, the hierarchy of the "seven Heavens."

Taqiyya (dissimulation)

According to the *Lisān al-'arab,* an Arabic-language reference dictionary, *taqiyya* refers to a situation "when people are cautious with one another, displaying harmony and agreement, while inside they feel exactly the opposite." In the Koran (16:106), that practice is linked to the ability to protect oneself when the Muslim would otherwise have to suffer because of his faith. The interpretation of that verse has been extended, especially in Shiite circles, to a context where it has sometimes seemed necessary to conceal part of one's convictions from the Sunni authorities.

The term *taqiyya* appears only rarely in the writings of the Hezbollah, but a chapter is devoted to a synonym: *kitmān.* That "dissimulation" is understood as the need to "keep a secret," based on a quotation from Imam Alī: "Your secret is your prisoner, and if you reveal it, you will be its captive." The application of that precept helps assure the "triumph" of "believers" in "their general affairs, social and religious." Secrets must be kept from "enemies" but also from "friends" who have no particular interest in knowing their content, and because, according to Imam Sādiq, "a friend" may someday become an "enemy."

Two grounds are given to justify the practice of "dissimulation." The first concerns the achievement of "victory," with no specifics as to content. The second is linked to the preservation of the "moral balance of society," since "the revelation of secrets leads to situations of anarchy." Revealing a secret is associated with ignorance, a lack of awareness, a "blind trust" in others, or a deficient piety verging on the "irritation of God": "the believer concerned with educating himself and building up his personality must hold his tongue about sacred things; keeping secrets is part of that."[26]

Wilāyat al-faqīh (authority or regency of the jurist-theologian)[27]

This concept appears late in Shiite history, in the Persia of the Safavids. Khomeini adopts it, making it the core of his theory of the Shiite clergy's power. The reasoning is as follows: as the representative *(nāʾib)* of the "occulted" Imam, and in the aim of preparing for his return, the jurist-theologian can shoulder the responsibility of Islamic authority *(al-hukūma al-islāmiyya)*. If he gives a ruling in the Imam's name, he does so with the aim of creating a righteous society governed by God. These positions were contested in 1979–1980, even among partisans of the revolutionary order, but they are included in the Iranian Constitution. From the start, the Hezbollah leaders adopted the concept without reservations, making it the cornerstone of their ideological system: "The Islamic government is not a monarchy, an empire, or an empty democracy, it is the government of God and of true justice."[28] The "Party of God" gives the following definition: "It is the authority *(wilāya)* and magistrature *(hākimiyya)* of the jurist, who unites all conditions in the era of the Imam's occultation. The *walī al-faqīh* replaces the awaited Imam in the leadership of the *ummah* and in the establishment of God's kingdom on earth," and the "*wilāyat al-faqīh* represents the leadership of Imam Mahdī on an interim basis during his occultation."[29]

Nasrallah's views, reported by Sabrina Mervin, show the Hezbollah's attachment to that concept: "The secret of our strength, our growth, our unity, our struggle, and our martyrdom is in the

26. *Tazkīat al-nafs*, pp. 113–115.

27. *Wilāyat al-faqīh fī ʿassr al-ghayba* is devoted entirely to the study of this notion. See also N. Qāsim, *Hizballah, al-minhaj, al-tajriba, al-mustaqbal*, pp. 70–80.

28. *Al maʿārif al-islāmiyya*, pp. 358–365.

29. Ibid., pp. 371–375.

wilāyat al-faqīh [of Khamenei], the backbone of the Hezbollah."
Elsewhere Nasrallah explains that "when the infallible Imam
disappears [from our sight], we must see [his] characteristics
[wisdom, courage, and so on] in another figure who possesses
them more than someone else." Qāsim theorizes that affiliation:
the *walī* combines competence and probity, he participates in
defining the main lines of the doctrine, and his judgment is infallible in determining jihad and in determining the "enemy." Qāsim
calls for a dual emancipation: with respect to time (ultimately,
non-Muslims will accept the principle of the *wilāyat al-faqīh*);
and with respect to space (compared to the *ummah*, national
borders are of little worth), even if it is sometimes necessary to
make concessions to Arab identity to answer criticisms that the
Hezbollah has submitted to the "Persians." As for the conditions
for implementation, they are the province of those who have a
knowledge of local realities.

The connection to the Iranian "supreme guide" is strengthened by the fact that the Hezbollah leaders attached themselves
to Khomeini's *marjaʿiyya*, then to that of Khameini. Like his pre-
decessor, Khameini holds the dual title of *walī al-faqīh* (1989)
and *marjaʿ* (1994). In the political realm, they explain, the opinions issued by the *walī al-faqīh* are superior to those of the *marjaʿ
taqlīd*. Therefore, a Shiite whose *marjaʿ taqlīd* has opinions contradicting those of the *walī* must follow the *walī* as his first priority: "Everyone, even a religious scholar, must obey the orders of
the guide of the Muslims, and no one must contradict him, since
he is the most capable"; "the *marjaʿ taqlīd* cannot issue fatwas
contradicting the guide of the Muslims"; "it is the opinion of the
guide of the Muslims that is followed to direct the Islamic country and [to answer] general questions relating to the Muslims."
That concept, however, has become a focal point for the opposition forces, rooted in the refusal by some Shiite clerics—within
and outside Iran—to recognize Khamenei's *marjaʿiyya*. In December 1994, in fact, Khamenei declared that, given the burden-
some task of "supreme guide" and the presence of many *marjaʿ*

more qualified than he in Iran, he would not seek to be *marjaʿ* for the Muslims inside Iran, but he accepted that responsibility for those who were outside the country. But *Sayyid* Mohammad Hussein Hashemi, former Iranian cultural attaché in Lebanon, as cited by Roschanack Shaery-Eisenlohr, believes that to follow the *marjaʿiyya* of Ayatollah Khamenei amounts to obeying the Iranian government.

In Lebanon, more and more of the Hezbollah's opponents denounce that recourse to the *wilāyat al-faqīh*. The criticisms that carry the most weight, because they are part of the same frame of reference, come from Shiites. During the Doha negotiations, Qabalān, vice chair of the SISC, declared that the *wilāyat al-faqīh* cannot be applied to Lebanon. In August 2008, Ali al-Amin, mufti of Tyre, declared that it is not possible to compare the institution of the *wilāyat al-faqīh* to that of the Vatican for the Catholics: "The Vatican has no parties outside its borders and does not provide them with explosive shells or theories or anything else. The relation to the *wilāyat al-faqīh* is therefore not spiritual; it transcends [that relation and takes on aspects that are] political, in order to assert its ascendancy."[30] To those who reproach the group for following a guide appointed by an assembly of Iranian experts—who therefore cannot be well informed about what is happening outside that country—the Hezbollah responds as follows:

—the choice of the experts . . . is not to grant the *wilāya* but to find the most competent one. For that, nationality, or national or regional allegiance, is not important. It is enough simply to have a sufficient number of experts, even if they are inside the Islamic republic.
—the experts are supposed to know the people they will judge, in order to choose the most competent among them. But the reality is that the Islamic republic is the country

30. *Al-Nahār*, August 23, 2008.

where there are the greatest number of *fuqahā* [pl. of *faqīh*] competent to fulfill that mission. The experts outside Iran may not know adequately the particularities of the candidates proposed, or they are far away, and their opinion therefore cannot be used if the number of experts in the Islamic republic is sufficient.

—the council of experts does not designate the *walī* specific to the Islamic republic, as some might think.

—the one whom the council of experts designates as the most competent becomes the *walī* for all the Muslims in the world, based on the uniqueness of the *wilāya*, of which we have already spoken, even though the Iranian Constitution did not speak of it and the experts did not mention it in their report because of known political considerations that prevent them from declaring it.

According to M. J. Michael Fischer, Khomeini maintained that the Iranian revolution was not a national but an Islamic revolution, "which respected neither the political boundaries drawn by Western colonialism in an attempt to divide the Islamic world nor the tyrannical puppet regimes imposed on long-suffering Muslims."[31]

31. Michael M. J. Fischer, *Iran from Religious Dispute to Revolution* (Cambridge, Mass.: Harvard University Press, 1980), p. 232.

Amin, Ali al-, _Sayyid_
Mufti of Tyre and of Jabal ʿAmil. He came to prominence through his refusal to consider the 2006 war a "divine victory." He opposed the sit-in initiated by the Hezbollah and the FPM in late 2006 and rejected the _wilāyat al-faqīh_. He was threatened during the battles of May 2008.

Aoun, Michel (1935)
Aoun, a Maronite from modest circumstances who grew up in the suburbs of Beirut, was in the Lebanese army. In 1973, he commanded a unit against the attack of fedayeen in Khalde. He was in touch with Bachir Gemayel during the first splintering of the Lebanese army in 1975 and, under the name Gébrayel, became a member of the Committee for Strategic Studies, whose aim was to make Bachir head of state. Military chief of staff from 1984 to 1989, he was named to lead an interim government between 1988 and 1990. He attempted to bring the militias to heel, beginning with the Lebanese Forces, and launched a "war of liberation" against the Syrian occupiers in 1989. Defeated in 1990, he lived in exile in France. He returned to Lebanon in May 2005, after the Syrian troops had left. During the June elections, his Free Patriotic Movement slates were broadly supported by the Christians. Aoun formed the Change and Reform Bloc. As

part of the opposition, he negotiated a "memorandum of understanding" with the Hezbollah, which was made public in February 2006. He promoted a regional rapprochement with Damascus and Tehran.

Arafat, Yasser (1929–2004)

Born into a family of landowners from the Jerusalem region, Arafat fought against the Israelis in 1948–1949, then pursued his education in Cairo. In 1958, he created the embryonic Fatah, which advocated armed struggle against Israel. In 1969, he assumed the leadership of the Palestine Liberation Organization, founded five years earlier at Nasser's initiative, and signed the Cairo Accords. Within the PLO, the Fatah emerged as the most powerful and well-organized group. Arafat, driven from Jordan with the fedayeen in September 1970, received in 1974 the support of the Arab League, which made him the sole representative of the Palestinian people, allowing him to be received by the United Nations General Assembly. Driven from Beirut by the Israelis in 1982, then from Tripoli by the Syrians in 1983, he installed the PLO's headquarters in Tunisia. His oral recognition of the Israeli state in 1988 was belied by his support for Saddam Hussein in 1990. But negotiations resumed after the Gulf War, and references to the disappearance of Israel were deleted from the PLO charter. In 1994, after the signing of the Oslo Accords, Arafat, Shimon Peres, and Yitzhak Rabin were jointly awarded the Nobel Peace Prize. Arafat was elected president of the Palestinian Authority in 1996, but the opposition, Hamas and the Islamic Jihad, and Netanyahu's coming to power in Israel hobbled the Oslo peace process. The failure of the Camp David Talks and the outbreak of the Second Intifada in 2000 led to a deterioration in Israeli-Palestinian relations. Sharon, Israeli prime minister as of February 2001, sought continually to isolate Arafat.

Assad, Hafez al- (1930–2000)

Assad, from an Alawite family, was a member of the Baath Party from the age of sixteen and entered the Syrian Military Academy in 1952. He participated in the coup d'état of March 8, 1963—organized by the Baath and Salah Jedid—and became minister of defense in 1966. After the Arab defeat in the Six-Day War, disputes erupted between Jedid and Assad, exacerbated by the failure of a Syrian intervention in Jordan during Black September. Two months later, Assad launched a coup within the party, then a government coup. He became president of Syria in 1971, receiving more than 99 percent of the vote, and was reelected in 1978, 1985, 1992, and 1999. The founder of a "democratic, popular, and socialist state" supported by the USSR, Assad established an authoritarian regime and repressed any tendencies toward uprising. The Muslim Brotherhood, for example, was crushed in Hama in 1982. He defended a pan-Arabist line, with, at its core, the restoration of Syria's past greatness. As a result, he opposed Saddam Hussein and maintained close—and sometimes tense—relations with Iran. The Lebanon War allowed him to establish his influence as arbitrator of the different factions, by persuasion and by force. The Treaty of Cooperation, imposed in 1991, permitted him to legalize his oversight with the consent of the United States. Involved several times in negotiations with Israel, Assad was prepared to sign a peace agreement only on condition that all of the Golan Heights be recovered.

Berri, Nabih (1938)

Nabih Berri is the son of Mustafa Berri, a trader in Sierra Leone, where Nabih was born. A lawyer concerned about the fate of the Shiite community, he assumed the leadership of Amal in 1980. In summer 1982, he agreed to participate in the National Salvation Committee founded by Bachir Gemayel and accepted the principle of negotiating with the Israeli invader. In February 1984, he called for disobedience to Amine Gemayel and took control of West Beirut. He occupied various government posts between

May 1984 and 1992. Supported by Damascus, he waged the "war of the camps" (1985–1988) against the Palestinians and the inter-Shiite war (1988–1990) against the Hezbollah. He was elected speaker of parliament in 1992 and remains in that post. Despite disagreements on matters of substance, he concluded an "objective" alliance with the Hezbollah, which gave the party broad representation of the Shiites. Since 2005, Amal has been a member of the March 8 camp, headed by the Hezbollah and supported by Frangieh's Marada, the Communist Party, the Syrian Social Nationalist Party, and soon thereafter the FPM. Berri marked his opposition to Siniora but maintained contacts with the March 14 leaders, especially Jumblatt, even in the heat of the battles of May 2008.

Chamrān, Mostafā (1932–1981)

An Iranian engineer, Chamrān earned a Ph.D. in electrical engineering from the University of California–Berkeley. He moved to Lebanon in 1971 and directed the Bourj al-Shamali Technical Institute, founded by Mūsa al-Sadr. He played a key role in the formation of Amal. In April 1980, while minister of defense in Iran, he was one of the twenty-four members on Amal's executive council. He died at the front during the Iran-Iraq War.

Fadlallah, Mohammad Hussein, *Sayyid* (1935–2010)

Born in Najaf, Fadlallah came from a family of religious scholars from Southern Lebanon. He was close to the *marjaʿ* Muhsin al-Hakīm, and became one of the éminences grises of al-Daʿwa Party, headed by Mohammad Bāqir al-Sadr. He achieved prominence for the editorials he published in the review *al-Adwāʾ al-islāmiyya*. After returning to Lebanon in 1967, he was a personal and ideological rival of Mūsa al-Sadr, even as he shared his plan for a struggle against Western domination and the reform of the state. He preached at the Bir al-ʿAbed and Haret Hreik mosques. He founded sociocultural-religious institutions, including a *hawza* called al-Maʿhad al-sharʿī al-islāmī (Islamic

Legal Institute). The Phalangists destroyed that multifaceted institution in 1976. Fadlallah retired to Bint Jbeil, but not before publishing *Al-islām wa mantiq al-quwwa (Islam and the Logic of Force)*. After the 1978 Israeli invasion, he lived in Bir al-ʿAbed, in the southern suburbs of the capital. He was then the *wakīl* of Ayatollah al-Khūʾī, a position that allowed him to found the association al-Mabarrāt. He preached in al-Ridā Mosque and reopened its *hawza*. He went to Iran several times, where he met with Khomeini (he disapproved of the cult of the ayatollah practiced by his most fervent followers) and became friends with Khamenei. In the review *al-Muntalaq,* the organ of the Lebanese Union of Muslim Students, he defended the exportation of revolution and considered Iran *dawlat al-islām* (the state of Islam), which was the title of a column devoted to Iran in that review. He supported the founding of the Hezbollah. His sermons, popular and broadly disseminated, earned him a weekly column in *al-ʿAhd,* which made him both its ideologue and a figure of legitimation. He justified jihad against Israel and was the target of several assassination attempts. In October 1984, he declared that he had no organizational ties to the Hezbollah, which gave him complete latitude after the war to act on his aspirations for the highest existing posts in the Shiite clergy: *murchid* (guide), *ustādh* (upper-level master), *ʿālim* (scholar), *huijjat al-islām,* and, after Ayatollah al-Khūʾī's death, *marjaʿ.* The title of *marjaʿ,* which the Shiites in Lebanon, Iraq, and the oil-producing monarchies of the Gulf recognized, placed him in the position of rival to Khamenei, especially since he had ceased to defend the Khomeinist interpretation of the *wilāyat al-faqīh* and the exportation of revolution to Lebanon. He developed a network of educational institutions, health organizations, social institutions, and media outlets parallel to that of the Hezbollah. His relations with that group were sometimes tense—in 1995 and 2006, for example—but the cement binding them together, namely, the struggle against Israel's existence, has continued to hold.

Frangieh, Samir (1945)

An intellectual and Maronite MP, member of the Qornet Che-hwān Union, Frangieh is the author of the "Beirut Manifesto," which appeared in *Le Monde* on June 22, 2004. It opposed Syria's instrumentalization of Lebanon and was signed, notably, by the Shiite Saoud al-Mawla. Frangieh was one of the partici-pants in the "Intifada of Independence" and, within the March 14 alliance, promoted a form of Lebanese citizenship without regard to community identity.

Frangieh, Suleiman, Jr. (1965)

A cousin of Samir Frangieh and grandson of Lebanese president Suleiman Frangieh, he is the leader of the Marada Party centered on the district of Zgharta. He served as minister several times between 1990 and 2005. A supporter of the Hezbollah and a virulent critic of the Maronite patriarchate, he represented the Christians within the March 8 alliance until the return of General Aoun, who made him one of his allies.

Geagea, Samir (1952)

From a modest Maronite background, Geagea interrupted his studies in medicine at the start of the Lebanese War to join with Bachir Gemayel against the fedayeen and the Syrians. He was one of the agents of the Christian "unification of the rifle" policy that led to the assassination of Tony Frangieh, father of Sulei-man Frangieh Jr. After the assassination of Bachir Gemayel, Geagea conducted and lost the Chouf war that the Lebanese Forces waged against Jumblatt's Druze. He imposed his author-ity by force against Hobeika and ran a Maronite proto-state ex-tending from East Beirut to Batroun. He supported the Taif Agreement and waged an inter-Christian war against the army headed by Aoun. Rejecting Syrian rule, he was the only militia leader to be convicted and imprisoned (1994–2005). When he was released from prison, he joined the March 14 alliance alongside Jumblatt and Saad Hariri. He reorganized the Lebanese Forces and invited its members to participate fully in the institutions of the Lebanese state. He is a major opponent of the Hezbollah.

Gemayel, Amine (1942)

President of Lebanon from 1982 to 1988, Amine Gemayel is from a family of Maronite notables whose fief is in Bickfaya. As an MP, he became leader of the Phalanges (Kataëbs), founded by his father, Pierre, when he succeeded his brother as head of state. He attempted to surround himself with a group of technocrats to modernize the state and reconstitute the army but was met with mistrust from the Sunnis, Shiites, and Druze, who criticized him for his partiality. In a country torn apart and occupied by multiple forces, he signed the Israel-Lebanon Treaty on May 17, 1983, which made him the Hezbollah's bête noire. He did not promulgate the agreement, however, and seeing that the United States had lost interest in Lebanon, he moved closer to the Syrians. Lacking a successor, he conferred power on General Aoun in 1988 and went into exile in 2000. He returned to Lebanon and joined the opposition to President Lahoud. His son, Pierre, MP and minister in the Siniora government, was assassinated in late 2006. Amine Gemayel has called for the disarmament of the Hezbollah.

Gemayel, Bachir (1947–1982)

Amine's younger brother, Bachir was a man of action who founded the Lebanese Forces militia in 1976. He fought the fedayeen and assumed responsibility for the massacre of Palestinian civilians. Within the context of war, his aim was not a "Christian state" but a "state for the Christians," so that they would never find themselves in the position of a minority, as is the case in the rest of the Arab world. His opponents criticized him for confessionalizing the issues. His feats of arms against the Syrians in Achrafieh and in Zahlé made him a hero to his followers. Against Frangieh and Camille Chamoun, he imposed his authority by violent means within the Maronite community. The Israelis supported him

politically and militarily, and the United States allowed itself
to be convinced that he was more than a militia leader. In the
face of the 1982 Israeli invasion, Bachir organized the National
Salvation Committee. He managed to win the votes of Muslim
MPs, thanks to his charisma and the notion of Lebanon that he
was defending. Soon after his election, he distanced himself from
his Israeli allies, but he was assassinated by a Christian hired by
the Syrians.

Harb, Rāghib (1952–1984)

Born in Southern Lebanon in the village of Jibchit, Harb was from
a Shiite family. In 1970, he went to Beirut, then to Najaf, to study
religion. In 1974, he suffered the first persecutions conducted by
the Baathist Iraqi authority. After returning to Lebanon, he committed himself to the poor of his community, founded a credit
agency for Muslims, and encouraged the construction of schools
in the southern part of the country. He took up arms against the
1978 Israeli invasion and tried to promote "Islamic revolution."
Arrested several times, he was assassinated by the Israelis on
February 16, 1984. Nicknamed "sheikh of martyrs" by the Hezbollah, he became a symbol of a new generation of sheikhs, who
are somewhat emancipated from the traditional bonds of solidarity and who "resist the Zionist occupier."

Hariri, Rafic (1944–2005)

Born in Sidon, Hariri, a Sunni, earned a degree in business at the
Beirut Arab University. A teacher and then a businessman, he made
his fortune in Saudi Arabia with the support of King Fahd, who
granted him Saudi nationality. He built an empire (banking, real
estate, manufacturing, media) in the Arab world (Al-Hoda, Sawt
al-ʿArabiya) with outlets in North America and Europe (Radio
Orient), where he maintained relations with influential political
figures, including Jacques Chirac. Over ten years, the Hariri
Foundation, created in 1982, supported more than fifteen thousand Lebanese scholarship students in Lebanon or abroad. Hariri

attended the national reconciliation conference in Lausanne in 1984 and was one of the chief architects of the Taif Agreement in 1989. He was named prime minister five times between 1992 and 2004 and launched major reconstruction projects in Lebanon, banking on the high-end tourism and services industries, which earned him as much criticism as support. His fortune allowed him both to promote an elite and to win the loyalty of an electoral clientele. His vision clashed with that of the Hezbollah, supported by President Lahoud. Hariri's relations with Syria deteriorated after Hafez al-Assad's death, and he was assassinated during the 2005 electoral campaign. Under the leadership of his sister, Bahia, then of his son, Saad, his al-Mustaqbal (Future) Party became the mainspring of the March 14 alliance.

Hobeika, Elie (1956–2002)

A member of the Lebanese Forces, Elie Hobeika headed its *jihaz al-Amn* (security arm). In that capacity, according to convergent statements—including that of his former bodyguard—he was responsible for the massacre of Palestinians in La Quarantaine camp, of hundreds of Lebanese Shiites, of the four Iranian "diplomats" who vanished in 1982, and of some of the civilians in the Sabra and Shatila camps. In 1985, in face of the (partial) Israeli withdrawal, he chose Syria as his new ally but lost the fight with Samir Geagea to head the Lebanese Forces. He became a key actor in Lebanese political life again in 1990, thanks to Syrian support. He was named minister several times but was assassinated in 2002.

Hoss, Selim al- (1929)

A graduate in economics from the American University of Beirut and a Ph.D. in business and economics from Indiana University, Hoss was named prime minister three times (1976–1980; 1987–1990; 1998–2000). He opposed the appointment of General Aoun in 1988 and attempted without success to propose an economic policy different from that of Hariri in the late 1990s. He opposed U.S. policy in the Middle East. In 2005, though officially retired from politics, he attempted to promote a third way between the March 8 and March 14 coalitions.

Hrawi, Elias al- (1926–2006)

President of the Lebanese Republic from 1989 to 1998. His election took place in Bekaa, under Syrian occupation. Damascus was also the force behind the extension of his term in 1995.

Husseini, Hussein al- (1937)

Husseini joined Mūsa al-Sadr's Movement of the Disinherited in the early 1970s. He was secretary general of Amal from 1978 to 1980 and speaker of the Lebanese parliament from 1984 to 1991.

Jumblatt, Walid (1949)

Walid, belonging to a family of Druze notables, studied at the American University of Beirut and in France and was the son of Kamal (1917–1977), founder of the Progressive Socialist Party (PSP) in 1949. After his father's assassination, Walid, who until that time had seemed no more than a dilettante, proved to be a war leader and astute politician. An important leader of a community at the heart of Lebanese identity, but one that is institutionally marginalized and demographically weak, he had a three-point ideological platform: prevent the domination of one religious body over the others; root Lebanon firmly in the Arab world and its particular causes; and promote the advent of a democracy of merit and an open culture. An opponent of "political Maronitism," even to the point of forming an alliance with those responsible for his father's assassination, he defeated the Lebanese Forces in Chouf and did not hesitate to commit massacres. He accepted the Taif Agreement and played a role in various governments. In 2001, he began a reconciliation process with the Maronites, going so far as to support the release of Geagea. From 2004 on, aided by his coreligionist Marwan Hamadeh, he spearheaded the opposition against Lahoud's Syrian path and consequently against the Hezbollah. That group even characterized him as a rabbi during certain demonstrations. He was still prominent during the crisis of May 2008. He refused to agree to the prospect of one community imposing its authority over the others, but, aware of the fragility of the Druze's demographic and geographical position, he distanced himself from the March 14 camp after the 2009 elections (while still proclaiming his fidelity to Saad Hariri) and met with General Aoun to advocate the return of Christians to Chouf.

Khamenei, Ali, *Sayyid* (1940)

Born in Mashhad, Khamenei studied in Qom under Khomeini, with whom he kept in touch during the latter's forced exile in Iraq. His role in the revolutionary process is poorly understood. He was named Khomeini's personal representative on the Supreme Defense Council. After the assassination of Mohammad Ali Rajai (1933–1981), he served as president of Iran until 1989. He then succeeded Khomeini as supreme guide of the Islamic revolution, duties he combined with the title of *marja'* in 1995.

Khomeini, Rūhollāh Musavi, *Sayyid* (1902–1989)

The son of a cleric, Khomeini studied religion in Qom beginning in 1921, under Ayatollah Hā'eri Yazdi. He quickly became a recognized *'ālim* and, in 1944, published his first writings against the secularization of Iranian society, which the shah was promoting. His renown grew, but he remained discreet during the August 1953 coup orchestrated by the CIA, which put an end to the Mossadegh ministry. Upon Ayatollah Boroujerdi's death in 1961, Khomeini acceded to the status of *marja' al-taqlīd,* along with Ayatollah Sharī'atmadāri. He was arrested four times, provoking riots that were violently repressed. In late 1964, he was expelled to Turkey, then settled in Najaf, but was driven out by Saddam Hussein in 1978. His manifesto, *Islamic Government,* dates to 1969. He built up an "anti-imperialist struggle" network around himself that encompassed Beirut, Tripoli (Libya), and Paris. His eldest son was assassinated by one of the shah's agents in 1977. A scathing article he published in early 1978 led to a series of demonstrations that culminated in the 1979 revolution and his return to Iran via France. An Islamic Republic, founded on the *wilāyat al-faqīh,* was proclaimed on April 1. Opponents were prosecuted, allies and critical clerics thrust aside (Sharīʿatmadāri, who was removed from office, and Mahmoud Tāleghāni). Khomeini advocated the exportation of a social and religious revolution, which was encouraged by events: the war against Iraq, the fight against Israel, and the Lebanon War.

Khūʾī, Abū al-Qāsim al- (1899–1992)

Born in Iranian Azerbaijan, Khūʾī arrived in Najaf at the age of thirteen. He was a student of the Shiite defenders of "religious constitutionalism" in Iraq, including Sheikh Mohammad Hussein Naʾīni and Ayatollah Khorasani. Upon the death of Muhsin al-Hakīm, he became the most important *marjaʿ.* The development of religious education centers was one of his pet causes. He was acknowledged in particular as *marjaʿ al-taqlīd* by Mūsa al-Sadr, Fadlallah, and Shams al-Dīn. The Khūʾī Foundation in London, run by two of his sons, is a sort of "extension of the *marjaʿiyya*" of Najaf (Luizard).

Lahoud, Emile (1936)

Commander of the Lebanese army from 1989 to 1998, Lahoud owed his unanimous election to the presidency of Lebanon in 1998 to the Syrian trusteeship. He was the chief institutional supporter of the Hezbollah and refused to apply UN Resolution 1559. In September 2004, the parliament extended his term, but a handful of opponents protested. Decried during the Cedar Revolution by a mob of demonstrators calling for his resignation, he remained in office until the end of his term in November 2007. The presidency was vacant until May 2008, at which time Michel Suleiman succeeded him.

Moawad, René (1925–1989)

Elected president of the Lebanese Republic after the Taif Agreement on November 5, 1989, he died on November 22, in an attack attributed to Syria and, by certain observers, to the Hezbollah. His wife, Nayla, MP of Zgharta within the March 14 coalition, is a declared adversary of the "Party of God."

Mohtashamipur, Ali Akbar, *Sayyid* (1946)

An Iranian cleric and disciple of Khomeini in Qom and Najaf, Mohtashamipur conducted activities in the Palestinian camps in Lebanon. After the Khomeinist revolution, he was a member of the central bureau of the Association of Combatant Ulema outside Iran. Ambassador to Damascus, he applied himself to spreading the values specific to the Iranian revolution throughout the Arab world. Nabih Berri described him as the man who "wrote, produced, and directed" the Hezbollah. He escaped an assassination attempt in 1984. As minister of the interior (1985–1989), he gradually came to be seen as a "reformer" close to Khatami and served as his adviser for social affairs in 1997. He heads four international institutions supporting the rights of the Palestinians and "al-Quds."

Montazeri, Hussein Ali, *Sayyid* (1922–2009)

Montazeri, an ayatollah, was expected to succeed Khomeini but was thrust aside by Khamenei, Rafsanjani, and Ahmad Khomeini. His son Mohammad Montazeri (1944–1981) was close to Muammar Gaddafi. The elder Montazeri trained in the Fatah camps in Lebanon and worked for an "Islamic Internationale."

Motahhari, Mortada (1920–1979)

Motahhari, from a religious family, was one of the theorists of the Iranian Islamic revolution. A student of Khomeini in the 1950s, he became one of his close collaborators.

Mughniyah, Imad Fayez (1962–2008)

Mughniyah was a Shiite from a Southern Lebanon family of religious scholars. According to his mother, he was singled out by Mostafā Chamrān. He trained in Arafat's commandos in the late 1970s and may have collaborated with the Palestinian leader Salah Khalaf, alias Abu Iyād. Impressed by Sheikh Fadlallah's sermons, Mughniyah is said to have become his bodyguard. According to Judith Harik, he met with the Iranian Mohsen Rafiq-doost, the future leader of the Revolutionary Guard Corps. He played a major role at the time the Hezbollah was being constituted (1982–1985). According to the Arab Information Center, he had two plastic surgeries. He was accused of being involved, under the pseudonym Jawad Noureddine, in the attacks against the Multinational Force, in the abduction of French hostages, and in the hijackings of TWA Flight 847 (1985) and a Kuwaiti airliner (1988). He was suspected of having committed attacks in Kuwait, a state deeply involved with Iraq during the war against Iran (1980–1988). Wanted by forty-two nations, Mughniyah was also suspected of participating in an anti-Jewish attack in Argentina after the assassination of Mūsawī. He was supposedly very active in building the fortifications in Southern Lebanon after 2000 and appears to have been involved in smuggling weapons to the Palestinians during the Second Intifada. Nicknamed Hajj Radwān within the Hezbollah, he is said to have been the brains behind the "Active Resistance" branch and/or the security service, along with ʿAbd al-Hādī Hamadi, and also to have been responsible for the successful operation against Israeli soldiers on July 12, 2006. According to disputed Saudi sources, he was assassinated in Damascus, where he had gone to attend a meeting with Palestinian leaders of Hamas and Syrian and Iranian information services. Allegations concerning his death focused on three suspects: Israel, the Syrian regime (which sent no representative to his funeral), and radical Sunni cells. Eighteen months later, Damascus still had not revealed the conclusions of its investigation, and Nasrallah, targeting Israel without sparing Arab "traitors," promised a response to the authors of the attack.

Mūsawī, ʿAbbās, *Sayyid* (1952–1992)

Born in the Beirut neighborhood of Shiyāh, Mūsawī was trained for combat from an early age in a Palestinian camp close to Damascus. Between the ages of eighteen and twenty-six, he studied and then taught in Najaf. He left in 1977 as a result of the Baathist repression and settled in Baalbek. A member of al-Daʿwa Party, he obtained support from his mentor, Mohammad Bāqir al-Sadr, and of Fadlallah and Mūsa al-Sadr, to found al-Imām al-Muntazar *hawza* and to assemble the clerics of Iraq forced into exile. Some of them, like him, became members of the Committee of Bekaa Ulema. Mūsawī then moved closer to Qom. When the Hezbollah was founded, he put Mohammad Yazbak in charge of the *hawza* and became involved in organizing armed actions. After prevailing over al-Tufaylī to be named the party's secretary general in May 1991, he was assassinated by the Israelis in February 1992.

Nasrallah, Hassan, *Sayyid* (1960)

Nasrallah was born in the neighborhood of Charchabūk, where Shiites, Armenians, and (Kurd) Sunnis coexisted, near La Quarantaine Palestinian refugee camp. He spent his childhood in Nabaa, went to Sin al-Fil secondary school, and attended the Usrat al-Taʾākhī Mosque headed by Fadlallah. In the mid-1970s, he fled the neighborhood of Nabaa for al-Bazourieh, his ancestral village. He entered the eleventh grade at the high school in Tyre; an admirer of Mūsa al-Sadr, he then became involved in the Amal movement. He was named organizational leader for the movement in the village of al-Bazourieh. He left for Najaf in late 1976, encouraged by Sheikh Mohammad Mansūr al-Gharawī, who gave him a letter of recommendation for his friend Mohammad Bāqir al-Sadr. Nasrallah was trained in that *hawza,* where he was welcomed by ʿAbbās Mūsawī. He managed to remain in Iraq until summer 1978. To avoid the Israeli occupation zone in

Southern Lebanon, he joined his friend Mūsawī in Baalbek. He completed his *muqaddima* training at al-Imām al-Muntazar *hawza*. Nasrallah was named a member of Amal's political bureau for the Bekaa and president of the organizational tribunal. He left Amal in June 1982 in protest against Nabih Berri's participation on the National Salvation Committee. He was known to be a "member of the Bāseq Force of the Resistance," leader of the Baalbek region, of the Bekaa as a whole, and then, it seems, of the Beirut region. He is said to have become a member of the decision-making council of the Hezbollah and head of the executive council, both in 1987. He spent a year in Qom in 1985, 1987, or 1989. His role within the Amal-Hezbollah conflicts is unknown. He succeeded Mūsawī in 1992, a choice confirmed by elections in 1993, 1995, 1998, 2001, 2004, and 2008. He was head of the United Jihad Council and made the most of the various conflicts with Israel between 1993 and 2006. His stoic attitude following the death of his eldest son, Hādī, in a skirmish with Israeli soldiers (1997) earned him the respect of a very large number of Lebanese. His virulent attacks against the Arab regimes in general, and the Egyptian regime in particular, tempered the enthusiasm he had elicited from the Arabic-speaking public. He has been the target of several assassination attempts. As Sabrina Mervin has shown, he possesses a religious authority that extends far beyond his position as Khameini's *wakīl*.

Qāsim, Na'īm (1953)

A Shiite cleric, Qāsim participated in the creation of the Lebanese Union of Muslim Students in the 1970s. Concerned about the question of education in Shiite circles, he headed the Association for Islamic Religious Education from 1974 to 1988 and maintained a supervisory role over al-Mustafa schools. His military duties, if any, are unknown. He has been deputy secretary general of the Hezbollah since 1991 and is responsible for monitoring the party's parliamentary activities. In 1999 he presided over a conference in Beirut on the hundredth anniversary of Khomeini's birth. His book, *The Hizbullah: The Story from Within* has been through four editions since 2002.

Raad, Mohammad (1955)
A member of al-Da'wa Party, then of the Hezbollah, Raad is a nonclerical Shiite. He was a member of the Hezbollah's Executive Consultative Council until 2001. An MP, head of his party's parliamentary bloc, he represented the Hezbollah at the negotiating table for "national dialogue."

Rafsanjani, Ali Hashemi (1934)
A cleric, president of the Iranian Republic from 1989 to 1997, Rafsanjani is in control of a large fortune and is considered a pragmatist in the sense that he believes Iran's interests ought to take precedence over those of the revolution.

Ruhāni, Fakhr
A Hojatoleslam (authority on Islam), Ruhāni was Iran's ambassador to Lebanon in 1979. Interviewed for the Iranian newspaper *Ettela'at*, he is said to have declared: "Lebanon today resembles Iran in 1977, and if we observe more closely, it will fall into our hands with the aid of God. Because of its [geographical] position at the heart of the region, [and as one] of the most important international centers, when Lebanon falls into the hands of the Islamic republic, the others will follow."

Sadr, Mohammad Bāqir al- (1935–1980)
Born in Al Kāzimiyah, Iraq, Sadr settled in Najaf with his family in 1945. He studied religion under al-Khū'ī and Muhsin al-Hakīm. One of his most important writings is *Iqtisādunā (Our Economy)*, which lays the foundations for an economy inspired by Islamic law. The creation of al-Da'wa Party in 1957 has often been attributed to him. Imprisoned by Saddam Hussein's regime following the Najaf uprising in February 1977, he was released two years later but was kept under house arrest. In 1980, he and

his sister, Amina Bint al Huda, having been judged too dangerous, were arrested and then executed.

Sadr, Mūsa al-, *Sayyid* (b. 1928, disappeared in 1978)

An Iranian born in Qom, Mūsa al-Sadr's history, like that of certain Shiite clerics, went hand in hand with that of Jabal ʿAmil. He settled in the land of his ancestors in 1959. He became the first chair of the Supreme Islamic Shiite Council. Against the advice of Fadlallah and other Shiite clerics, he played a major role in the creation of the council, which was established to give visibility and autonomy to a community that until then had been dependent on the Sunnis. He also created the Movement of the Disinherited (1974), whose armed branch is Amal, and a network of technical schools and charity organizations. Against leftist parties that wanted to relegate everything relating to religion to the private sphere, he defended a public but nonexclusionary dimension to Islam. Privileging debate in the religiously diverse Lebanon, he participated in conferences promoting interfaith dialogue and delivered speeches in churches, which earned him widespread criticism from his opponents. He disappeared in Libya in 1978.

Salameh, Abu Hassan (1957–1999)

A Shiite from the South involved in the Fatah in the early 1970s, Salameh was one of the founders of the Islamic Resistance, the armed branch of the Hezbollah. He was nicknamed "Platinum" because of the pins in his legs.

Sfeir, Nasrallah Boutros, Monsignor (1920)

The Maronite patriarch of Antioch and of the entire Orient since 1986, Monsignor Sfeir is a moral authority recognized well beyond his community. Some of his statements took a political turn after Syria's takeover of Lebanon. In 2011, he handed in his resignation because of his advanced age.

Shams al-Dīn, Mohammad Mahdī (1936–2001)

From a Lebanese family of the Shiite faith, Shams al-Dīn, along with Mohammad Bāqir al-Sadr, was a member of the *kulliyyat al-fiqh* (training institute in Islamic law) founded in Najaf in 1958. With Mūsa al-Sadr, he followed the teachings of ayatollahs al-Khū'ī and al-Hakīm, serving as al-Hakīm's *wakīl* in a neighboring city. He collaborated in the reform of religious studies, which incorporated the profane disciplines within the Jam'iyyat muntada al-nashr. Having returned to Lebanon in 1969, he participated in the establishment of the Supreme Islamic Shiite Council, becoming its vice chair in 1975 and the principal leader after Mūsa al-Sadr's death. He created various educational and social foundations. In 1979, he defied Fadlallah by opposing the justification for the *wilāyat al-faqīh,* which, according to him, could not be applied in Lebanon's multifaith society. He seems to have accommodated himself to the idea between 1983 and 1986 and, via fatwas, justified the fight against the Israeli occupier. The war between Amal—which he supported—and the Hezbollah unsettled him. He became an advocate of coexistence between the Lebanese communities, defended a form of separation between religious and political power, and, in what became his testament *(al-Wassāya),* called on the Lebanese Shiites to participate in the construction of a pluralistic state.

Sharaa, Farouk al- (1938)

Syrian vice-president. He was minister of foreign affairs between 1984 and 2006.

Tufaylī, Subhī al- (1948)

Born in Brital, in the Bekaa, al-Tufaylī went to Najaf in 1965, where he studied under Mohammad Bāqir al-Sadr. Beginning in 1976, he took classes from Kāzim al-Hā'irī in Qom for two years. A member of al-Da'wa Party, he was the principal leader of the nascent Hezbollah. Elected secretary general in November 1989, he left that post before the end of his term in 1991 because of a fundamental clash between his Iranian protector, Ali Akbar Mohtachami, and two strongmen of the regime, Ayatollah Khamenei and President Rafsanjani. According to members of the Hezbollah, he was held partly responsible for the tensions and conflicts with Amal. He opposed the principle of participation in the 1992 electoral process. He left the ranks of the Hezbollah with a portion of the militants in 1997, calling for the *thawrat al-jiyā*ʿ (revolution of the hungry) in the region of Baalbek-Hermel. He was officially ousted from the party in January 1998 and was forced to flee after the *hawza* to which his followers had retreated was besieged. In 2000, he reappeared and supported a slate that constituted an opposition to the Hezbollah. In 2008, at the funeral of Imad Mughniyah, he paid tribute to "the most ferocious combatant . . . despite the bitterness of recent years."

Velāyatī, Ali Akbar (1945)

Minister of foreign affairs for the Iranian Islamic Republic between 1981 and 1997, then diplomatic adviser to the "Guide of the Revolution."

Yazbak, Mohammad

Member of the Committee of Muslim Ulema. He succeeded ʿAbbās Mūsawī as head of al-Imām al-Muntazar *hazwa*. In 1995, along with Nasrallah, he was named *wakīl* by *marja*ʿ Khamenei, to whom he did not fail to declare his loyalty. Israel is suspected of having tried to kidnap him in 2006.

Note: The following list is incomplete.

Hassan Nasrallāh, secretary general
Na'īm Qāsim, deputy secretary general
Hajj Hussein Khalil, political aide to the secretary general
Hashem Safieddine, chair of the Executive Consultative Council,
Nasrallah's designated successor (and cousin)
Mohammad Yazbak, member of the Executive Consultative
Council

Nawaf Mūsawī, head of foreign relations
Mahmoud Komaty, vice president of the Political Bureau
Abū Ghālib Zainab, member of the Political Bureau
Nabil Kaouk, military chief for the Southern Lebanon sector
Hassan Ezzedine, political chief for the Southern Lebanon sector
Hussein Naboulsi, press bureau chief

Hezbollah Members of Parliament (2005–2009)

Ali Ammar
Amine Cherri
Hassan Fadlallah
Hassan Hussein Hajj
Hassan Hubballāh

Ali Mokdad
Mohammad Raad
Nawar Sahili

Ministers Who Resigned from the Siniora Government

November 11, 2006, five Shiite ministers:
Mohammad Fneish, minister of energy (Hezbollah)
Trad Hamadeh, minister of labor (Hezbollah)
Mohammad Jawad Khalifeh, minister of health
Talal Sahili, minister of agriculture
Faouzi Salloukh, minister of foreign affairs

November 13, 2006, one Greek Orthodox minister:
Yaaqoub Sarraf

Categories

Cadres
Combatants (six hundred full-time, three thousand to five thousand mobilizable, ten thousand "reservists"?)
Militants
Sympathizers (two hundred thousand?)

The party may have five thousand to six thousand people on its payroll, in addition to the full-time combatants.

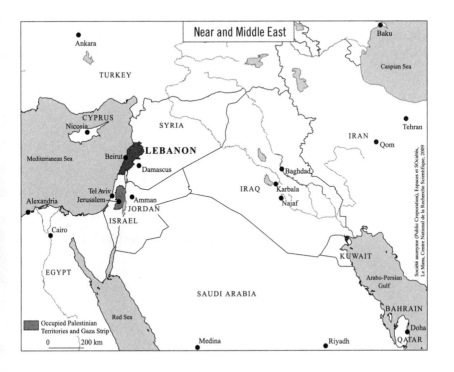

Near and Middle East

Ankara

TURKEY

CYPRUS
Nicosia

SYRIA

LEBANON
Beirut
Damascus

Mediterranean Sea

Tel Aviv
Jerusalem
Amman
JORDAN
ISRAEL

Alexandria

Cairo

EGYPT

IRAQ
Karbala
Baghdad
Najaf

IRAN
Qom
Tehran

Baku

Caspian Sea

KUWAIT

Arabo-Persian
Gulf

BAHRAIN
Doha
QATAR

SAUDI ARABIA

Red Sea

Medina

Riyadh

Occupied Palestinian
Territories and Gaza Strip

0   200 km

Société anonyme (Public Corporation), Espaces et SOciétés,
Le Mans, Centre National de la Recherche Scientifique, 2009

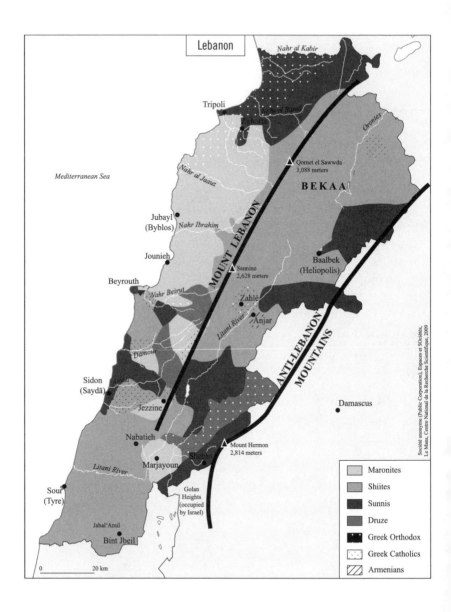

Lebanon

Nahr al Kabir

Tripoli

Zghorta

Nahr al Bared

Orontes

Qornet el Sawwda
3,088 meters

BEKAA

Mediterranean Sea

Nahr al Jaauz

Jubayl
(Byblos)

Nahr Ibrahim

Jounieh

Sannine
2,628 meters

Baalbek
(Heliopolis)

Beyrouth

Nahr Beirut

MOUNT LEBANON

Zahlé

Litani River

Anjar

Damour

ANTI-LEBANON MOUNTAINS

Sidon
(Saydā)

Jezzine

Damascus

Nabatieh

Litani River

Shebaa

Mount Hermon
2,814 meters

Marjayoun

Sour
(Tyre)

Golan
Heights
(occupied
by Israel)

Jabal ªAmil

Bint Jbeil

0   20 km

Société anonyme (Public Corporation), Espaces et SOciétés,
Le Mans, Centre National de la Recherche Scientifique, 2009

	Maronites
	Shiites
	Sunnis
	Druze
	Greek Orthodox
	Greek Catholics
	Armenians

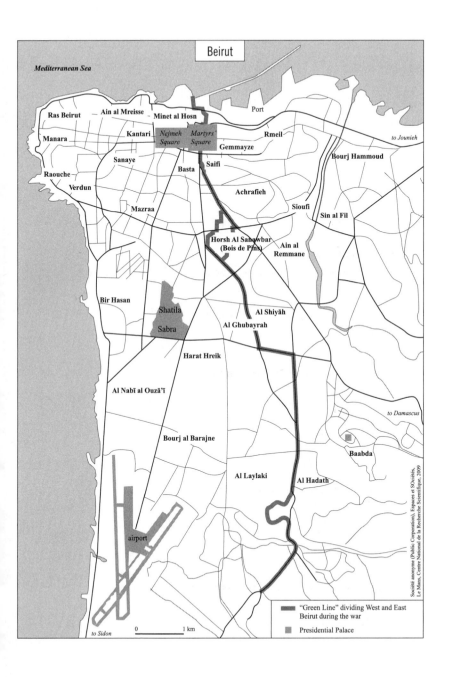

Beirut

Mediterranean Sea

Port

Ras Beirut
Ain al Mreisse
Minet al Hosn
Rmeil
to Jounieh
Manara
Kantari
Nejmeh Square
Martyrs' Square
Gemmayze
Bourj Hammoud
Sanaye
Saifi
Raouche
Basta
Achrafieh
Verdun
Sioufi
Sin al Fil
Mazraa
Horsh Al Sanowbar
(Bois de Pins)
Ain al Remmane
Bir Hasan
Shatila
Al Shiyāh
Sabra
Al Ghubayrah
Harat Hreik
Al Nabī al Ouzā'ī
Bourj al Barajne
Baabda
Al Laylaki
Al Hadath
to Damascus
airport

to Sidon

0   1 km

Société anonyme (Public Corporation), Espaces et SOciétés, Le Mans, Centre National de la Recherche Scientifique, 2009

"Green Line" dividing West and East Beirut during the war

Presidential Palace

SOURCES

TELEVISION STATION

Al-Manār: viewed directly or via the website

PRESS

Lebanese press (followed regularly 2004–2009)
Al-Nahār
L'Orient–Le Jour

Arab Press (surveyed periodically since 1992)
Al-Ahram
Al-Hayat
Al-Masri al-Yom (founded in 2003)
Al-Sharq al-Awsat
Teschrin
Le Progrès Égyptien

Iranian press (consulted in February 2009)
Al-Wifāq [Arabic]
Kayhān al-'arabī [Arabic]
Iran Daily [English]
Iran News [English]
Tehran Times [English]

TEXTBOOKS PUBLISHED BY THE ASSOCIATION FOR ISLAMIC RELIGIOUS EDUCATION [ARABIC]

Al-Islām risālatunā, 2006, nos. 9 and 12
Nahnu wa-l tārīkh, 2007, esp. no. 6

TRAINING MANUALS FOR HEZBOLLAH MILITANTS PUBLISHED [IN ARABIC] IN BEIRUT BY THE JAMʿIYYAT AL-MAʿĀRIF AL-ISLĀMIYYA AL-THAAQĀFIYYA

Al maʿārif al-islāmiyya (Islamic Notions). N.d.
Durūss fī ussūl al-ʿaqīda al-islāmiyya (Lessons on the Principles of Islamic Doctrine). 1999.
Wilāyat al-faqh fī ʿassr al-ghayba (The Wilāyat al-Faqīh during the Occultation). 2nd ed. 2000.
Tazkīat al-nafs (Purification of the Soul). 2001.
Al-Sīra wa-l-Tārīkh (The Life of Muhammad and History). 2000.

DOCUMENTARIES

Harb Lubnān (The Lebanon War). Al-Jazīra, 2001.
"Special Mission" broadcast on the "Four Vanished Iranian Diplomats." Al-ʿArabiyya, September 23, 2004.
Jean-François Boyer and Alain Gresh. "Le mystère Hezbollah" ("The Hezbollah Mystery"). France 5, July 15, 2007.
Bernard de la Villardière and Amal Hamelin des Essarts. "Qui a tué Rafic Hariri?" ("Who Killed Rafic Hariri?"). France 3, April 3, 2009.
Jean-Charles Deniau. "Le temps des otages" ("The Age of Hostages"). France 2, April 9, 2009.

TELEVISED POLITICAL SPEECHES

Hassan Nasrallah, Naʿīm Qāsim, Michel Aoun, Walid Jumblatt, Saad Hariri, Fouad Siniora, Samir Geagea, Nabih Berri, and Marwan Hamadeh

WEBSITES (LAST CONSULTED MAY 2009)

http://www.hizbollah.tv/
http://hezbollah-resistance.over-blog.com/
http://www.shamseddine.com/
http://www.bayynat.org/
http://www.al-khoei.us/
http://www.mabarrat.org.lb/
http://www.naimkassem.net
http://www.tayyar.org/tayyar/
http://www.aljazeera.net/
http://www.almanar.com.lb

ESSAYS AND COLLECTIONS

America fī fikr al-Imām al-khomeynī (America in the Thought of Imam Khomeini). Qom: Dār al-wilāya lil thaqafa wal iʿlām, 2003.

Amil, Mahdi (pseud. for Hamdan Hassan). *L'État confessionnel: Le cas libanais*. Montreuil: Éditions la Brèche, 1996.

Qāsim, Naʿīm. *Hizballah, al-minhaj, al-tajriba, al-mustaqbal*. 4th. ed. Beirut: Dār al-Hādī, 2008. English translation: *Hizbollah: The Story from Within*, translated by Dahlia Khalil. London: Saqi, 2005. French translation: *Hezbollah: La voie, l'expérience, l'avenir*, translated by Raghida Ousseiran with an original introduction by the author, pp. 8–22. Beirut: Al Bouraq, 2008.

Rahnema, Majid. *Quand la misère chasse la pauvreté*. Paris: Fayard/Arles: Actes Sud, 2003.

Rizk, Hiām, and Mohammad Hussein Bazzi. *Sayyed al-Qādat (The Leader of Leaders)*. Beirut: Dār al-Amīr, 2002.

Sadr, Mūsa, al-. *Hiwārāt sahāfiyya (Newspaper Interviews*, vol. 1: *Creating a Society of Resistance)*. Beirut: Center for Research and Study of Imam Mūsa al-Sadr, 2000.

———. *Hiwārāt sahāfiyya (Newspaper Interviews*, vol. 2: *Unity and Liberation)*. Beirut: Center for Research and Study of Imam Mūsa al-Sadr, 2007.

MEMOIRS

Chamoun, Tracy. *Au nom du père*. Paris: Jean-Claude Lattès, 1992.

Fisk, Robert. *Liban nation martyre*. Paris: A&R Éditions, 2007.

Hatem, Robert M., aka "Cobra." *Dans l'ombre d'Hobeika . . . en passant par Sabra et Shatila*. Paris: Jean Picollec, 2003.

Seurat, Marie. *Les corbeaux d'Alep*. Paris: Gallimard, 1988.

Sneifer, Regina. *J'ai déposé les armes: Une femme dans la guerre du Liban*. Paris: Éditions de l'Atelier, 2006.

BIBLIOGRAPHY

ENGLISH

Azani, Eitan. *Hezbollah: The Story of the Party of God, from Revolution to Institutionalization*. New York: Palgrave Macmillan, 2009.

Chehabi, H. E., ed. *Distant Relations: Iran and Lebanon in the Last Five Hundred Years*. London: Center for Lebanese Studies; New York: I.B. Tauris, 2006.

Fischer, M. J. Michael. *Iran from Religious Dispute to Revolution*. Cambridge, Mass.: Harvard University Press, 1980.

Ghoraïeb, Amal Saad. *Hizbullah, Politics, Religion*. London: Pluto, 2001.

Hamze, Ahmad Nizar. *In the Path of Hizbullah: Modern Intellectual and Political History of the Middle East*. New York: Syracuse University Press, 2004.

Harik, Judith Palmer. *Hezbollah: The Changing Face of Terrorism*. New York: I.B. Tauris, 2005.

Mearsheimer, John J., and Stephen M. Walt. *The Israel Lobby and U.S. Foreign Policy*. New York: Farrar Straus & Giroux, 2007.

Mervin, Sabrina. *Shi'a Worlds and Iran*. London: Saqi, 2010.

Morris, Benny. *Righteous Victims*. New York: Vintage, 2001.

Norton, Augustus Richard. *Hezbollah*. 5th ed. Princeton, N.J.: Princeton University Press, 2009.

Picard, Elizabeth. *Lebanon, a Shattered Country*. New York: Holmes & Meier, 1996.

Richard, Yann. *Shi'ite Islam: Polity, Ideology, and Creed*. Oxford: Blackwell, 1995.

Salibi, Kamal. *A House of Many Mansions: The History of Lebanon Reconsidered*. Berkeley: University of California Press, 1988.

Sankari, Jamal. *Fadlallah: The Making of a Radical Shi'ite Leader*. London: Saqi, 2005.

Shaery-Eisenlohr, Roschanack. *Shi'ite Lebanon: Transnational Religion and the Making of National Identities*. New York: Columbia University Press, 2008.

FRENCH

Amir-Moezzi, Mohammad. *Dictionnaire du Coran*. Paris: Robert Laffont, 2007.

Amir-Moezzi, Mohammad Ali, and Christian Jambet. *Qu'est-ce que le shî'isme?* Paris: Fayard, 2004.

Assaf, Raoul, and Liliane Barakat. *Atlas du Liban: Géographie, histoire, économie*. Beirut: Presses de l'Université Saint-Joseph, 2003.

Balta, Paul, and Georges Corm, eds. *L'avenir du Liban, dans le contexte régional et international*. Paris: Éditions ouvrières/Études et Documentation internationale, 1990.

Carré, Olivier. *Le nationalisme arabe*. Paris: Payot, 1996.

———. *L'utopie islamique dans l'Orient arabe*. Paris: Presses de la Fondation Nationale des Sciences Politiques, 1991.

Chaigne-Oudin, Anne-Luce. *La France et les rivalités occidentales au Levant: Syrie-Liban 1918–1939*. Paris: L'Harmattan, 2006.

Charara, Walid, and Frédéric Domont. *Le Hezbollah: Un mouvement islamo-nationaliste*. Paris: Fayard, 2004.

Corm, Georges. *Le Liban contemporain: Histoire et société*. Paris: La Découverte, 2003.

———. *Orient-Occident. La fracture imaginaire*. Paris: La Découverte, 2002.

Djalili, Mohammad-Reza. *Géopolitique de l'Iran*. Brussels: Complexe, 2005.

"Document: L'islam au Liban: Courants islamiques et manifeste du Hezbollah." *Les Cahiers de l'Orient* 2 (1986): 237–259.

Dupont, Anne-Laure. *Atlas de l'islam dans le monde: Lieux, pratiques et idéologie*. Paris: Autrement, 2005.

Encel, Frédéric. *Atlas géopolitique d'Israël: Aspects d'une démocratie en guerre*. Paris: Autrement, 2008.

Karam, Karam. *Le mouvement civil au Liban: Revendications, protestations et mobilisations associatives dans l'après-guerre*.

Paris: Karthala/Institut de Recherche et d'Études sur le Monde Arabe et Musulman, 2006.

Kepel, Gilles. *Fitna: La guerre au coeur de l'islam.* Paris: Gallimard, 2004.

———. *Jihad: Expansion et déclin de l'islamisme.* Paris: Gallimard, 2000.

Khoury, Gérard D. *Une tutelle coloniale: Le mandat français en Syrie et au Liban, Écrits politiques de Robert de Caix.* Paris: Belin, 2006.

Laurens, Henry. *Le Grand Jeu: Orient arabe et rivalités internationales.* Paris: Armand Colin, 1991.

Le Thomas, Catherine. "Agences de socialisation et dynamiques partisanes: Fonctions et usages des écoles de la mouvance Hezbollah au Liban." In *Returning to Political Parties? Partisan Party Development in the Arab World,* edited by Myriam Catusse and Karam Karam. Beirut: Lebanon Center for Policy Studies, 2010.

———. "Mobiliser la communauté: L'émergence d'un secteur éducatif chiite depuis les années 60 au Liban." Graduate thesis under the directorship of Gilles Kepel, Institut d'Études Politiques, Paris, 2009.

Luizard, Pierre-Jean. *La question irakienne.* Paris: Fayard, 2004.

Ménargues, Alain. *Les secrets de la guerre du Liban: Du coup d'État de Bachir Gémayel aux massacres des camps palestiniens.* Paris: Albin Michel, 2004.

Mervin, Sabrina, ed. *Le Hezbollah: État des lieux.* Arles: Sindbad/Actes Sud, 2008.

Molajani, Akbar. *Sociologie politique de la révolution iranienne.* Paris: L'Harmattan, 1999.

Mozaffari, Mehdi. *Pouvoir chiite, théorie et évolution.* Paris: L'Harmattan, 1998.

Naba, René. *Rafic Hariri: Un homme d'affaires Premier ministre.* Paris: L'Harmattan, 1999.

Naraghi, Ehsan. *Enseignements et changements sociaux en Iran du VIIe au XXe siècle.* Paris: Édition de la Maison des Sciences de l'Homme, 1992.

Picard, Elizabeth, ed. *La politique dans le monde arabe.* Paris: Armand Colin, 2006.

Razoux, Pierre. *Tsahal: Nouvelle histoire de l'armée israélienne.* Paris: Perrin, 2006.

Romani, Vito. "Le Hezbollah, un instrument de la politique étrangère iranienne?" *Les Cahiers de l'Orient* 87 (September 2007): 79–96.

Roy, Olivier. *Le croissant et le chaos*. Paris: Hachette Littératures, 2007.

Samaan, Jean-Loup. *Les métamorphoses du Hezbollah*. Paris: Karthala, 2007.

Sarkis, Jean. *Histoire de la guerre du Liban*. Paris: PUF, 1993.

Seguin, Jacques. *Le Liban-Sud: Espace périphérique, espace convoité*. Paris: L'Harmattan, 1989.

Tuéni, Ghassan. *Une guerre pour les autres*. Beirut: Dār An-Nahar, 2004. New edition with afterword by the author.

Verdeil, Éric, Ghaleb Faour, and Sébastien Velut, eds. *Atlas du Liban: Territoires et société*. Beirut: Institut Français du Proche-Orient, 2007.

ARABIC

Balqizīz, ʿAbd al-Ilāh. *Hezbollah min al-tahrīr ila al-radʾ (1982–2006) (Hezbollah from Liberation to Dissuasion [1982–2006])*. Beirut: Markaz dirāssāt al-wihda al-ʿarabiyya, 2006. Augmented edition of the first version, which appeared under the title *The Resistance and Liberation of Southern Lebanon*.

Charara, Waddah. *Dawlat Hezbollah: Lubnān, mujtamaʿan islāmiyyan (The State of Hezbollah: Lebanon as Islamic Society)*. 5th ed. Beirut: Dār al-Nahār, 2007.

Kawthrānī, Wajīh. *Bayna fiqh al-islāh al-shīʿī wa wilāyat al-faqīh: Al-Dawla wa-l-mouwātin (Between Reformist Shiite Law and the Authority of the Theologian-Jurist: State and Citizen)*. Beirut: Dār al-Nahār, 2007.

Qāzzī, Fāīz. *Min Hassan Nasrallah ila Michel Aoun Qirāʾā siyāssiyya lī Hezbollah (From Hassan Nasrallah to Michel Aoun: A Political Reading of the Hezbollah)*. Beirut: Riad El-Rayyes, 2009.

INDEX